ADMINISTRATIVE LAW AND HUMAN RIGHTS

The University of Law

ADMINISTRATIVE LAW AND HUMAN RIGHTS

THIRD EDITION

Nancy Duffield

Published by
The University of Law
2 Bunhill Row
London EC1Y 8HQ

British Library Cataloguing in Publication Data

A catalogue record for this book is available from the British Library

ISBN 978 1 80502 215 2

Preface

This book is part of the 'Foundations of Law' series of textbooks, designed to support postgraduates in their study of the core subjects of English law.

It is anticipated that the reader can then move on to studies for their professional examinations (eg the SQE and BSB assessments) comfortable that they have an understanding of foundational legal principles.

Each textbook aims to provide the reader with a solid knowledge and understanding of fundamental legal principles and rules. The series aims to give the reader the opportunity to identify and explore areas of critical interest whilst also identifying practice-based context.

For those readers who are students at The University of Law, the textbooks are used alongside other learning resources to best prepare students to meet outcomes of the Postgraduate Diploma in Law and related programmes.

We wish you every success as you learn about English Law and in your future career.

The legal principles and rules contained within this textbook are stated as at 1 May 2025.

Contents

Table of Cases

Table of Legislation

Primary Legislation

Statutes

International

Secondary Legislation

1 Introduction to the European Convention on Human Rights and the Protection of Human Rights in the UK

Learning outcomes

When you have completed this chapter, you should be able to:

- appreciate the nature and scope of the key provisions of the European Convention on Human Rights (ECHR);
- assess whether a right under the ECHR is absolute, limited or qualified;
- explain how the Human Rights Act 1998 gives effect to the Convention rights within the UK.

1.1 Introduction to the European Convention on Human Rights

This chapter will introduce you to the main Articles which make up the European Convention on Human Rights (ECHR). However, before we look at these, it is worth pausing to consider what we mean by human rights. Human rights are generally accepted as meaning those fundamental rights to which a person is entitled simply by virtue of being human. Unlike other legal rights, they usually cannot be removed by the state. However, it is open to debate what rights should be included in the concept of 'human rights'. In this textbook we will be looking only at those rights included within the ECHR as it is those rights which have been incorporated into UK law.

The ECHR is distinct from EU law, with its own institutions and procedures. The Convention was adopted in 1950 and was drafted by the Council of Europe, an international organisation that was formed after World War II ('the War'), in an attempt to establish a common European heritage.

In adopting the Convention, the member states of the Council recognised an obligation to 'accept the principles of the rule of law and of the enjoyment by all persons within its jurisdiction of human rights and fundamental freedoms'. Thus, signatory states must respect the human rights of all those who are within their jurisdiction, regardless of their nationality. The Convention was a response to the serious human rights violations Europe had witnessed during and before the War, and also to the spread of Communism into Central and Eastern Europe after the War. The idea was that the Convention would be a statement of the fundamental principles of liberty accepted by the countries of Western Europe and would prevent future violations of human rights.

The Convention is an international Treaty which has 46 state parties. Belarus is the only European state that has not signed it. Russia was a signatory but, as a result of the war in Ukraine, Russia ceased to be a member of the Council of Europe in March 2022 and ceased to be a contracting party to the ECHR from 16 September 2022. Disputes relating to rights under the ECHR are determined by the European Court of Human Rights (ECtHR). The ECtHR comprises of one judge from each of the signatory states.

The UK ratified the Treaty in 1951. The effect of this is that the UK is bound as a matter of international law to comply with the Convention, by ensuring that UK law gives effect to a list of rights set out in the ECHR. If the UK breaches the Convention, it is possible for other states who are parties to bring proceedings before the ECtHR in Strasbourg, in addition to individual applications to enforce Convention rights. Judgments of the ECtHR are binding on the UK as a matter of international law. The UK has a good record of complying with judgments of the ECtHR.

1.2 Procedure to bring a case before the European Court of Human Rights

As mentioned above, there are two ways in which proceedings may commence:

(a) *State applications.* If the UK is in violation of the Convention, proceedings may be brought against the UK by another signatory state.

For example, Ukraine has three outstanding applications against Russia (commenced whilst Russia was a member state) concerning the conflict between those states.

In January 2024 the Irish Government lodged an inter-State application against the UK. It claims that certain provisions in the Northern Ireland Troubles (Legacy and Reconciliation) Act 2023 are incompatible with a number of Articles in the ECHR. In particular, it alleges that the sections which provide immunity from prosecution for Troubles-related offences breach Articles 2 (right to life) and 3 (prohibition of torture and inhuman or degrading treatment) ECHR.

(b) *Individual petitions to the ECtHR.* Individuals who allege that their Convention rights have been breached as a result of UK law may start their own proceedings against the UK in Strasbourg. However, it must be shown that any domestic remedies which exist have first been exhausted. Furthermore, there is a time limit. The petition must be made within four months of the final UK decision. The final UK decision will usually be the decision of the highest UK court having jurisdiction.

In 2024, 36,800 cases were disposed of by the ECtHR. There were 1,097 judgments after full proceedings (many of these cases were joined, so the judgments covered 10,829 applications), and 25,988 applications (over 70%) were declared inadmissible or struck out. Most cases therefore do not proceed to a full hearing.

1.2.1 Two-stage process

There are two main stages in cases brought before the Court: the admissibility stage and the merits stage. A single-judge formation will declare an application inadmissible should inadmissibility be obvious from the outset; there is no right to appeal against its decisions.

Cases that are covered by well-established case law of the Court will be allocated to a three-member Committee, which will rule on admissibility and, where the case is admissible, give a final decision or judgment.

Other cases will be heard by a Chamber of seven judges. This will include the 'national judge', that is the judge for the state against which the application has been made. The Chamber will rule on admissibility and give judgment by a majority. The Chamber's judgment will become final only after three months, during which the applicant or state party may ask for the case to be referred to the Grand Chamber for fresh consideration. The Grand Chamber consists of 17 judges, including the President and Vice-President of the ECtHR and the national judge. If the request for referral is accepted by the panel of the Grand Chamber, the Grand Chamber will reconsider the case and hold a public hearing if necessary. The Grand Chamber judgment will be final.

1.2.2 Remedies

Possible remedies include the court awarding compensation or requiring the state to change its law. However, individual decisions are only binding as a matter of international law under the Convention and have no direct binding force in domestic law. The Court relies on the willingness of states to abide by the Convention and accept its judgments. Although the UK usually complies with judgments against it, in December 2020 the Council of Europe, which oversees the ECHR, passed a resolution which expressed 'profound concern' at the UK government's failure to enforce judgments by the ECtHR involving security force killings and suspected collusion cases in Northern Ireland. In these judgments, the ECtHR had found procedural violations of Article 2 (the right to life) of the ECHR due to various shortcomings in the investigations into the deaths. This concern was reiterated in June 2024.

The Committee of Ministers of the Council of Europe is responsible for ensuring that states comply with judgments of the ECtHR.

1.3 General principles under the ECHR

A number of general principles permeate the ECHR.

1.3.1 Subsidiarity

Subsidiarity is the principle which states that human rights should primarily be protected at national level and the system under the ECHR is subordinate to this.

1.3.2 Margin of appreciation

Initially developed by the ECtHR, but included in the ECHR from August 2021 under Protocol 15, the margin of appreciation doctrine reflects the fact that national authorities are in principle better placed than the ECtHR to evaluate local needs and conditions. This means that where member states may legitimately reach different conclusions on a particular issue, the ECtHR will respect the judgment of a member state as to what the public interest requires. However, the state's margin of appreciation is subject to the supervision of the ECtHR, which will review whether decisions taken by member states are compatible with the ECHR.

The extent of any margin of appreciation will vary depending on the context. So, for example, where the principle to be upheld is an important one or there is a general consensus amongst the member states as to its meaning and extent, no margin or only a narrow margin will be allowed. On the other hand, where there are diverging views, such as in respect of issues of morality, a greater margin of appreciation is allowed. Thus in *Handyside v UK* (1979) 1 EHRR 737 the ECtHR held that the UK had not breached Article 10 (freedom of expression) when its obscenity laws prohibited publication of a sex education manual for children. In *SAS v France* (2014) 36 BHRC 617 the claimant challenged a ban on wearing clothing designed to conceal the face in public on the basis that this breached the right to respect for private life (Article 8) and the right to manifest religion or belief (Article 9). The ECtHR stated that, as views on this could differ in a democratic society and as there was little agreement on this subject within member states, the state had a wide margin of appreciation. There was no violation of either Article 8 or 9 as the ban could be justified on the basis of upholding the rights and freedoms of others.

1.3.3 Living instrument

The ECHR is a 'living instrument' in the sense that it has to be generously interpreted in the light of its aim of protecting human rights, the understanding of which may change with evolving social conditions. Thus, the content of the rights may change over time as the ECtHR reinterprets the ECHR to keep it attuned to changing values. This means that, unlike courts within the UK, the ECtHR does not operate a strong system of precedent. The 'living instrument' principle is controversial and has led to criticism by those who claim that it gives too much power to unelected judges or that it subjects member states to legal obligations they did not sign up to.

1.4 The scope of the ECHR

Before we look in more detail at the Convention rights, it will be useful to consider the scope of the ECHR.

ACTIVITY 1 The scope of the ECHR

Consider the following claims that the UK Government has acted unlawfully. Under which Articles of the Convention (if any) do you think proceedings could be brought?

(You may find it helpful to use the text of the ECHR, which can be found in Sch 1 to the HRA 1998, to help you with the content of each right, but the purpose of the activity is to ensure that you appreciate the general scope of the Convention, rather than its detailed application.)

1. The police monitor A's use of the Internet and find that he is distributing pornographic materials.
2. B is killed as a result of troops using plastic bullets to control a riot.
3. An Act of Parliament introduces birching as a punishment for criminal offences. C is birched by a prison officer.
4. An Act of Parliament permits detention of suspected offenders for up to six days before they are charged and brought before the magistrates. D is detained for seven days by the police without charge.
5. Parliament abolishes public funding of legal services in criminal cases. E lacks the money to defend himself against a criminal charge.
6. A local authority passes a byelaw preventing F, an anti-nuclear protester, from camping in the vicinity of an Atomic Weapons Establishment.
7. In order to enable a new railway line to be built, Parliament passes an Act which enables houses to be demolished without compensation for the owners. J owns a house which the railway company is proposing to demolish.

COMMENT

1. Article 8 – right to respect for private life. If A is charged with an offence arising from his use of the Internet, Article 10 – freedom of expression.
2. Article 2 – right to life.
3. Article 3 – prohibition of degrading treatment (punishment by birching in the Isle of Man held to infringe the Convention in *Tyrer v UK* (1978) 2 EHRR 1).
4. Article 5 – right to liberty and security of the person (*Brogan v UK* (1989) 11 EHRR 117).
5. Article 6 – right to a fair trial (refusal of public funding to someone charged with perjury but without means to pay for representation held to infringe the Convention in *Granger v UK* (1990) 12 EHRR 469).
6. Article 10 – freedom of expression, and Article 11 – freedom of assembly and association (*Tabernacle v Secretary of State for Defence* [2009] EWCA Civ 23 – this case is discussed in **Chapter 3**).
7. Article 1, Protocol 1 – right to peaceful enjoyment of possessions.

In each case where the act of the public authority is authorised by an Act of Parliament, the victim of a breach would (in the domestic courts) only be able to obtain a declaration of incompatibility, rather than a decision that the public authority has acted unlawfully (see **para 2.1** below).

1.5 Absolute, limited and qualified rights

1.5.1 Introduction

You will have noticed in looking through the ECHR that not all Convention rights are absolute. Sometimes a public authority may be able to show that its action is within one of the limitations or qualifications permitted by the Article in question, and is therefore lawful. You will be looking at some of the limitations and qualifications in more detail later, but it is important at this stage to understand the general concepts. These are derived from the case law of the ECtHR in Strasbourg.

Convention rights are normally divided into three types:

(i) Absolute rights: These rights can never be interfered with in any circumstances whatsoever. States must uphold them at all times.

(ii) Limited rights: These rights can only be limited in clearly defined and finite situations.

(iii) Qualified rights: These rights require a balance between the rights of the individual and the wider public interest, and so may be interfered with to protect an important general interest or the rights of others.

Before you look at the Articles in detail, it is important to establish which rights are absolute, which are limited and which are qualified. **Table 1.1** below indicates whether each right is absolute, limited or qualified. The distinction between absolute and limited rights can sometimes be a difficult one to draw. In this regard you should distinguish between:

- rights which list exceptions which help to define the rights; these are absolute rights as any conduct which falls within an exception does not constitute an interference with the right in question; and
- rights which list specific and finite situations in which they can be interfered with; these are limited rights as there are set circumstances where an interference is permissible.

Note that there is scope for disagreement with some of the categorisations made in the table below. The distinction between absolute and limited rights is not made in the Convention itself, and there is no authoritative list. For example, while there is universal agreement that Article 3 is an absolute right, some sources agree with the below categorisations of Articles 2 and 6, but others regard them as limited.

Generally speaking, Articles 2–7 and 12 (absolute and limited rights) cover the most fundamental human rights and contain either no exceptions whatsoever or narrow express exceptions, and Articles 8–11 and Articles 1–3 of Protocol 1 cover qualified rights which can be overridden in the public interest.

Table 1.1 Absolute, limited and qualified rights

Convention right	Absolute	Limited	Qualified
Article 2 (right to life)	Absolute. Note that deprivation of life resulting from the use of no more force than is absolutely necessary in narrowly defined circumstances does not constitute an interference with this right		

(continued)

Table 1.1 (continued)

Convention right	**Absolute**	**Limited**	**Qualified**
Article 3 (freedom from torture, inhuman and degrading treatment)	Absolute		
Article 4 (freedom from slavery, etc)	Absolute. Note that certain activities are excluded from the scope of compulsory labour and so do not constitute an interference with this right		
Article 5 (liberty and security of the person)		Limited – contains exceptions in relation to lawful arrest and detention	
Article 6 (fair trial)	Absolute as to a fair trial	Limited in relation to the trial being in public	
Article 7 (punishment according to existing law)	Absolute. Note that Article 7 does not preclude the trial and punishment of acts that are criminal according to general principles recognised by civilised nations		
Article 8 (respect for private and family life)			Qualified
Article 9 (freedom of thought, etc)	Absolute in relation to freedom of thought, etc		Qualified in relation to manifestation of freedom in worship, teaching, practice or observation
Article 10 (freedom of expression)			Qualified
Article 11 (freedom of assembly and association)			Qualified
Article 12 (right to marry)	Absolute, but according to national law governing the exercise of the right		
Article 1 of Protocol 1 (right to peaceful enjoyment of possessions)			Qualified

1.5.2 Qualified rights

We shall now look in more detail at how the courts determine whether the interference with a qualified right can be justified.

1.5.2.1 Qualifications must be express

Only restrictions on qualified rights which are expressed in the ECHR are recognised, and these must be used for the purpose for which they have been prescribed (Article 18).

In addition, a restriction may only be relied upon if it is prescribed by law, has a legitimate aim and is necessary in a democratic society. It must not be applied in a discriminatory fashion (Article 14) (see **1.7** below). We will now look in more detail at each of these requirements.

1.5.2.2 Qualifications must be prescribed by law (or be 'in accordance with the law')

A government can rely on a Convention qualification to justify a restriction on a Convention right only if provisions of that state's law actually take advantage of the qualification. So, for example, it would not be possible for the UK Government to justify infringement of the right to respect for private life (eg by telephone tapping) on the basis that it was needed for the prevention of crime (Article 8), unless UK law clearly permitted the infringement. The law giving effect to the qualification may be written or unwritten, but the qualification must be embodied in law.

Moreover, the law must be accessible (in published form) and sufficiently precise to enable the citizen to regulate their conduct. So in *Malone v UK* (1985) 7 EHRR 14, the ECtHR held that English law on telephone tapping was not clear enough at that time to provide a sufficient legal basis for a restriction on the right to respect for private life.

In the case of multiple sclerosis sufferer Debbie Purdy, the absence of a crime-specific policy relating to assisted suicide, identifying the facts and circumstances that the DPP would take into account when deciding whether to prosecute an individual for assisting another person to commit suicide, meant that the statutory offence of assisted suicide was not *in accordance with the law* for the purposes of Article 8(2) and amounted to a violation of her right to lead a private life (*R (on the application of Purdy) v DPP* [2009] UKHL 45). The existing law was insufficiently clear about the factors the DPP would take into account, and therefore a person could not accurately predict if they were likely to be prosecuted with assisting another's suicide. The DPP subsequently issued such guidance (see **2.2.1.2** below).

1.5.2.3 Legitimate aims

Qualifications must be justified by reference to the aims specified for each right. The principle is that the interests of society may justify restrictions on the rights of individuals.

The following are frequently specified in the Convention as legitimate state aims:

(a) the interests of national security, public safety or the economic wellbeing of the country (eg Article 8);

(b) the prevention of disorder or crime (eg Articles 8 and 10);

(c) the protection of health or morals (eg Articles 8 and 10);

(d) the protection of the rights or freedoms of others (eg Article 8). The scope of this legitimate aim is not entirely clear. Whilst it undoubtedly covers the rights of others under the ECHR, it is wider than this. In *Chassagnou v France* (1999) 29 EHRR 615 the ECtHR stated that, where the right was not one within the ECHR, it would only be covered if it amounted to an 'indisputable imperative'. This appears to have been quite generously interpreted in subsequent case law. For example, in *R (ProLife Alliance) v British Broadcasting Corporation* [2004] 1 AC 185 the BBC refused to transmit a party political broadcast which showed graphic images of aborted foetuses. The House of Lords held that the 'rights of others' included the right for a person not to be affronted by offensive material transmitted into their home. In *Lambeth LBC v Grant* [2021] EWHC 1962 (QB), when making a possession order against occupiers of a camp on Clapham Common in London, the court stated that the rights of others included the rights of the public to use and enjoy the Common;

(e) the prevention or disclosure of information received in confidence (eg Article 10);

(f) maintaining the authority and impartiality of the judiciary (eg Article 10).

1.5.2.4 Necessary in a democratic society

Qualifications are usually required to be 'necessary in a democratic society' (eg Articles 8 and 10). This means the following:

(a) There must be a 'pressing social need' (rather than an absolute necessity for any restriction imposed).

(b) The interference with the Convention right must be proportionate. This means that in order to justify the restriction, public authorities may have to show that they have chosen methods of achieving legitimate aims which do not go further than is necessary. Thus, for example, any restriction imposed upon freedom of expression based on concerns for public order must be shown to be a proportionate response to the fears. You will consider the 'proportionality test' in more detail in **Chapter 3**.

The qualities of a 'democratic society' include tolerance of minority opinions and lifestyles. So the fact that a majority in a state opposes homosexuality does not excuse a law which criminalises homosexual conduct in private contrary to Article 8 (*R v Dudgeon* (1983) 5 EHRR 573).

1.5.2.5 Example of qualifications at work

To illustrate how the qualifications at **1.5.2.2**, **1.5.2.3** and **1.5.2.4** work in practice, please consider the following example:

Example

Under the Waste Management Act 2021 (fictitious), the Waste Disposal Commission is established to decide where incinerators to dispose of household waste shall be built in England and Wales. Rehana has objected to the building of an incinerator 200 metres from her home, on the ground that emissions will harm her and other people living nearby.

Rehana may be able to argue that her Article 8 right is being breached. However, this is a qualified right. The qualification has a legal basis here – the Waste Management Act 2021. The legitimate aim(s) being pursued by the Act are likely to be the 'economic well-being of the country'. However, the qualification must also be 'necessary in a democratic society'. The relevant test here is the proportionality test, which is covered in more detail in ***Chapter 3*** *below. In other words, is the interference with Rehana's rights proportionate to the objective being achieved, or would any lesser interference be possible? In this case, it seems unlikely that there is no other site suitable for the incinerator, away from residential areas.*

1.6 Protection from discrimination

Article 14 requires that all of the rights and freedoms set out in the ECHR must be protected and applied without discrimination on any ground such as sex, race, colour, language, religion, political or other opinion, national or social origin, association with a national minority, property, birth or other status.

The protection against discrimination in the ECHR is not 'free-standing'. To rely on this right, a victim must show that the discrimination has affected their enjoyment of one or more of the other rights in the Convention. This means that the issue 'must be within the ambit of another right', but the applicant does not need to show that the state has breached that right (*Inze v Austria* (1988) 10 EHRR 394).

Article 14 covers both direct and indirect discrimination.

1.7 Derogations

Under Article 15 of the ECHR, a state may derogate from part of the Convention 'in time of war or other public emergency threatening the life of the nation'. This means that for the period of the derogation the State is not bound to apply the specified provisions. There are, however, conditions which limit the power to derogate so that any derogation must only be to the extent that is strictly necessary, and no derogation is possible in respect of Articles 3 (torture, etc), 4(1) (slavery), or 7 (retrospective criminal offences), or from Article 2 (right to life) except in respect of deaths resulting from lawful acts of war. The principle is clearly that some violations of human rights are so wrong that no state should countenance them, even in wartime.

Section 14 of the Human Rights Act 1998 creates a statutory procedure for enacting a derogation as part of UK law, and s 1 states that Convention rights are to be read subject to any such derogation. As a result, a UK court will not be able to enforce Convention rights where a derogation is in operation.

The UK has issued derogations from Article 5 of the Convention (personal liberty) in respect of the prevention of terrorism legislation in Northern Ireland (now expired) and the Anti-terrorism Crime and Security Act 2001. The delegated legislation implementing the latter derogation was quashed by the House of Lords in *A v Secretary of State for the Home Department* [2004] UKHL 56, and the Government subsequently removed the derogation on the enactment of the Prevention of Terrorism Act 2005.

1.8 The Human Rights Act 1998

The ECHR is an international convention which was ratified by the UK in 1951 (see **1.1**). This allowed individuals to take a case to the ECtHR where they alleged that their human rights had been breached by the UK. However, individuals were unable to give effect to their rights under the ECHR within the UK until the passing of the Human Rights Act (HRA) 1998. The number of cases taken against the UK to the ECtHR has declined substantially since the HRA 1998 was passed. In 2024 only one judgment was made against the UK by the ECtHR.

1.8.1 An overview of the Act

The main sections of the HRA 1998 are as follows:

- Section 1 – incorporates and gives effect to the Convention rights. These are Articles 2–12 and 14 ECHR, Articles 1–3 of the First Protocol and Article 1 of the Thirteenth Protocol. They are set out in Sch 1 to the HRA 1998.

- Section 2 – domestic courts must 'take into account' judgments of the ECtHR but are not bound to follow them.
- Section 3 – 'So far as it is possible to do so, primary and subordinate legislation must be read and given effect in a way which is compatible with the Convention rights.' This applies to past and future legislation. Section 3 has proved controversial, with some arguing that the courts have used s 3 more widely than intended by Parliament. For example, in *Ghaidan v Godin-Mendoza* [2004] UKHL 30, the House of Lords interpreted the words 'as his or her wife or husband' to include same-sex couples.
- Section 4 – provides that the High Court and higher courts may declare an Act of Parliament to be incompatible with Convention rights. Such a declaration does not affect the validity, continuing operation or enforcement of the provision in question, and does not bind the parties to the proceedings (s 4(6)). However, it does put political pressure on the Government to change the law.
- Section 6 – it is unlawful for a public authority (including a 'court') to act in a way which is incompatible with Convention rights (unless giving effect to an incompatible statute).
- Section 7 – a person who claims that a public authority acted contrary to s 6 may 'bring proceedings against the authority' or 'rely on the Convention right ... in any legal proceedings'. The person must be a 'victim of the unlawful act'. Any proceedings must be brought within a year of the date of the alleged breach of Convention rights. However, this time limit is subject to any shorter time limits which may be imposed for specific types of proceedings. Thus, if the claim is brought by way of judicial review, the relevant judicial review time limits will apply (see **6.4.2**).
- Section 8 – a court in civil proceedings may award damages where a public authority unlawfully infringes a Convention right, if it is necessary 'to afford just satisfaction' to the injured party.
- Section 10 – creates a 'fast-track' procedure for changing legislation. Where a UK court or the ECtHR has found UK legislation to be in breach of Convention rights, the Government may, if there are 'compelling reasons' to do so, make a 'remedial order' changing UK law. This is delegated legislation which has to be approved by Parliament under the 'affirmative procedure'. Remedial orders cannot be used to change the common law. Should the Government choose not to use this 'fast-track' procedure, it can instead submit a bill to Parliament to amend or repeal the offending legislation.
- Section 19 – a Minister introducing future legislation must make a written statement stating that the bill is compatible with Convention rights (a 'statement of compatibility') or that, although they are unable to make a statement of compatibility, the Government wishes to proceed with the bill.

The most important sections of the HRA 1998 for bringing a claim for breach of human rights are ss 6–8. We will now consider some aspects of these sections in more detail.

1.8.2 Acts of public authorities

As well as making the ECHR a yardstick against which to measure UK legislation, the HRA 1998 also makes Convention rights a standard with which the actions of public authorities must comply. Section 6(1) of the HRA 1998 provides that it is unlawful for a public authority to act in a way which is incompatible with Convention rights. However, this does not apply if, as a result of an Act of Parliament, the authority could not have acted differently, or the authority is giving effect to, or enforcing, provisions of an Act which are incompatible with the Convention (s 6(2)).

Therefore, s 6 gives a freestanding cause of action for breach of Convention rights and is also relevant for judicial review cases, as in effect it adds a ground of challenge in judicial review of administrative acts – breach of a Convention right.

The Court of Appeal, in the case of *R (on the application of Beer) v Hampshire Farmers Market Ltd* [2003] EWCA Civ 1056, held that the terms 'public body' and 'public authority' are synonymous. In other words, if a decision-maker is a public body under the traditional principles of judicial review (see **Chapter 6**) then it will also be a 'public authority' for the purposes of a decision which breaches a Convention right. This, of course, is extremely helpful to the claimant who wishes to raise traditional grounds for review alongside an allegation of breach of a Convention right.

1.8.3 Enforcement against private individuals

Notice that the 1998 Act only makes it unlawful for *public authorities* to infringe Convention rights. It does not expressly make it unlawful for private individuals to infringe the rights of other individuals. Does this mean that cases between individuals are unaffected by the ECHR? For example, can the right to respect for private life given by Article 8 be used only against public authorities? What about cases where the Press intrudes on the private life of celebrities? **Chapter 4** will enable you to consider these issues further. However, you should note that the court is a public authority within the meaning of s 6 of the HRA 1998. It therefore has a duty to apply the Convention. The effect is referred to as 'horizontality', as it means that Convention rights can affect relations between private citizens (or companies) and not merely relations between state and citizen ('vertical effect').

1.8.4 Section 6 and delegated legislation

Although courts are bound to apply Acts of Parliament which are incompatible with Convention rights, judicial review may be available under s 6 of the HRA 1998 to set aside incompatible delegated legislation. For example, in *A v Secretary of State for the Home Department* [2004] UKHL 56, the House of Lords quashed delegated legislation made under s 14 of the 1998 Act (see **1.7** above).

1.8.5 Standing

Section 7 of the HRA 1998 states that a person can bring proceedings for breach of a Convention right only if they are a 'victim' of the breach. A 'person' will include individuals and non-governmental organisations such as companies, political parties or trade unions. Such an individual or organisation must be directly and personally affected. Pressure groups will not be victims under s 7 and therefore cannot bring claims for breach of Convention rights (*R (Adath Yisroel Burial Society) v HM Coroner for Inner North London* [2018] EWHC 969 (Admin)).

However, the case of *Verein KlimaSeniorinnen Schweiz and Others v Switzerland* (App No 53600/20) [2024] ECHR 53600/20 states that, exceptionally, pressure groups may have standing in cases relating to the alleged failure of a signatory state to take adequate measures to protect people against the adverse effects of climate change on human lives and health. In order to have standing to bring a case, the group must be: (a) lawfully established in the relevant jurisdiction; (b) with the purpose of defending the human rights of its members or other affected individuals against the threats arising from climate change; and (c) able to demonstrate that it can be regarded as genuinely qualified and representative to act on behalf of such people. Relevant factors in deciding this include the purpose for which the group was established, whether it is non-profit making, the nature and extent of its activities, its membership and representativeness, its transparency of governance and whether the grant of such standing is in the interests of the proper administration of justice. Nonetheless, the ECtHR has confirmed in the case of *Cannavacciuolo v Italy* (App No 51767/14) that recognition of the standing of pressure groups is limited to the context of climate change. Thus, pressure groups were found not to have standing in this case which related to environmental pollution.

In certain situations, cases may be brought by close relatives of the victim as 'indirect victims', for example where it is alleged that the state is in breach of Article 2 or 3 and the victim is dead or has disappeared in the custody of the state (*Van Colle v UK* [2012] ECHR 7678/09).

The victim should bring proceedings in 'the appropriate court'. So, for example, if the claim involves employment rights, it would be commenced in the Employment Tribunal. A victim can also rely on their Convention rights in 'any legal proceedings' so can, for example, raise breach of Convention rights as a defence.

1.8.6 Damages for breach of Convention rights

Under s 8 of the HRA 1998, a court can award damages for breach of Convention rights where it is 'necessary to afford just satisfaction', taking into account principles laid down by the ECtHR. In many cases there will be no need to do so, as there will be a common law cause of action (eg misuse of private information) under which damages can be awarded. Moreover, in judicial review proceedings, the courts will often regard a quashing order and/or one or more of the other available remedies as just satisfaction.

Summary

- The ECHR is an international treaty which has been ratified by the UK and is binding on the UK in international law.
- The ECHR protects many fundamental human rights such as the right to life and freedom of expression. The rights within the ECHR can be classified as absolute, limited or qualified.
- Individuals can bring a claim for breach of their human rights to the ECtHR provided that they have exhausted all domestic remedies and apply within four months of the final decision.
- Human rights have been given effect within the UK by the Human Rights Act 1998.
- Section 6 of the HRA 1998 allows individuals to bring claims for breach of human rights against public authorities. This can be done by way of a freestanding application or as part of a judicial review claim.
- To bring a claim for breach of human rights, an individual must be a victim of the breach of those rights.

Figure 1.1 Bringing proceedings for breach of Convention rights

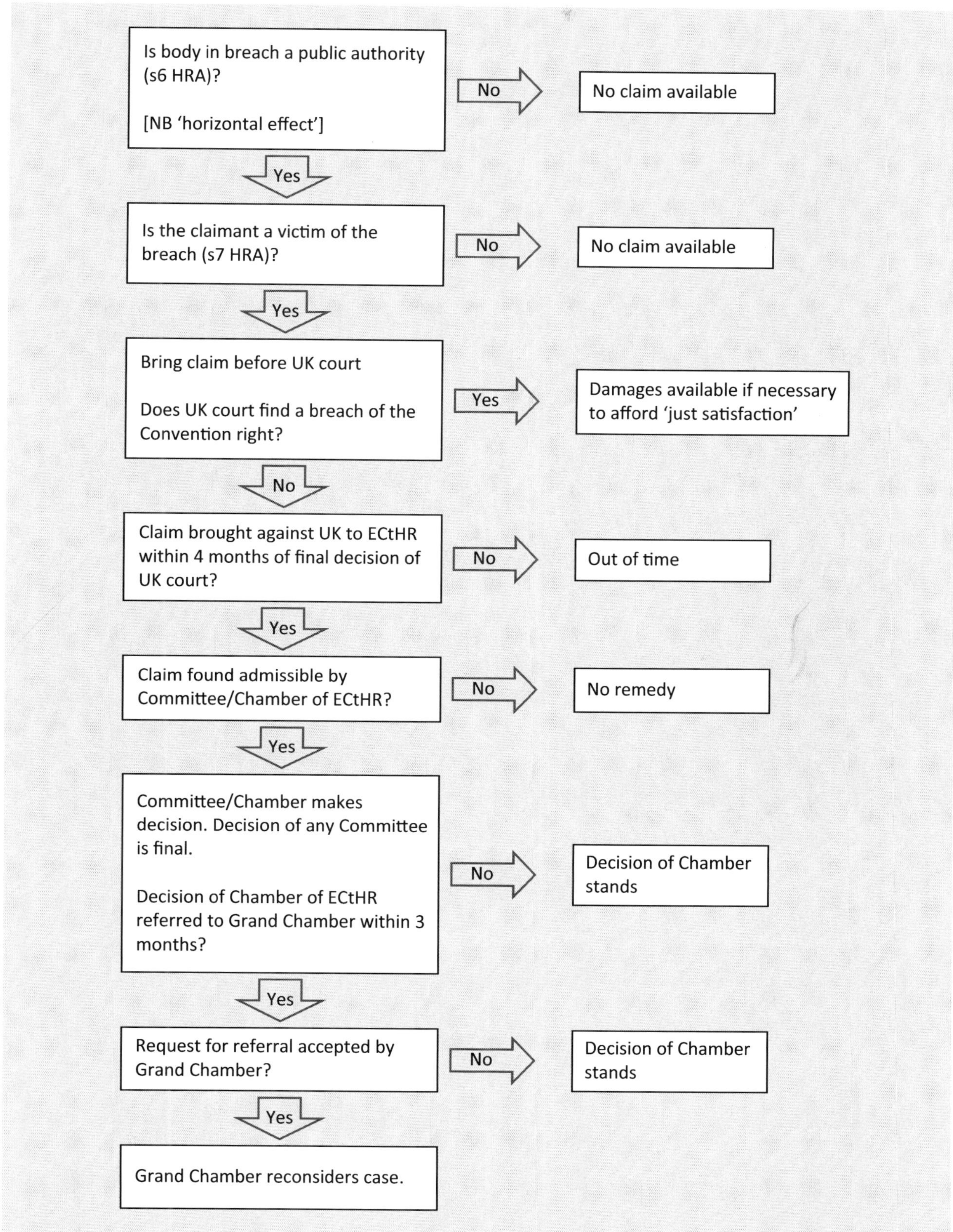

Figure 1.2 Convention rights and the HRA 1998 – summary

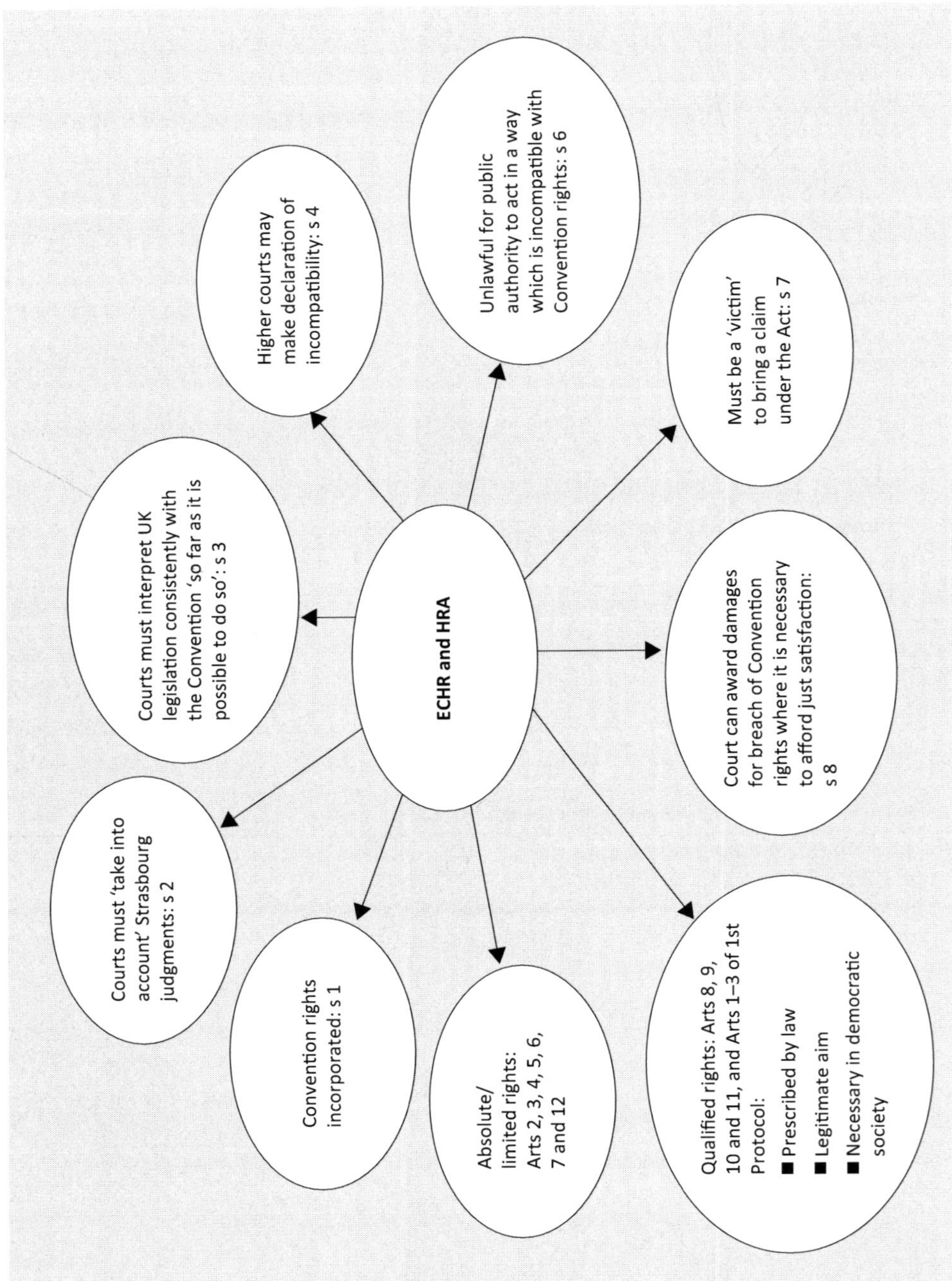

2 Absolute and Limited Rights

Learning outcomes

When you have completed this chapter, you should be able to:

- explain the protections provided by the absolute rights under the European Convention on Human Rights;
- understand the scope of Article 2 and analyse the positive and procedural obligations it places on states;
- explain Article 3 and assess its application in particular areas of law, such as asylum and deportation cases;
- explain the protections provided by Article 5 and analyse whether there has been a 'deprivation of liberty' in particular circumstances;
- identify and analyse the main rights provided by Article 6.

2.1 Introduction

We will now look in greater detail at the absolute and limited rights within the European Convention on Human Rights (ECHR) and cases associated with them. It is important for you to understand the scope of these rights and how they have been interpreted by the courts.

2.2 Article 2 – right to life

Article 2 is an absolute right, but with exceptions that define its scope. It:

(a) prohibits the state from taking life; and

(b) places on the state a positive duty to protect life. This necessitates that the state puts in place effective criminal law provisions to deter the commission of offences against the person, backed up by law enforcement machinery to prevent and punish breaches of such provisions. In certain well-defined circumstances, there may be a positive obligation on the authorities to take preventive operational measures to protect an individual whose life is at risk from the criminal acts of another individual (*Osman v United Kingdom* [1999] 1 FLR 193). However, in *Tkhelidze v Georgia* (Application no 33056/17) [2021] ECHR 614, the European Court of Human Rights (ECtHR) accepted that the police must make difficult operational choices. This means that such a positive obligation will only arise where the authorities knew or ought to have known of the existence of a real and immediate risk to the life of an identified individual from the criminal acts of a third party and they then failed to take measures within the scope of their powers which, judged reasonably, might have been expected to avoid that risk. This will depend on the facts. In this case, a woman had been murdered by her partner after escalating episodes of domestic abuse, which had been reported to the police but not acted upon. The ECtHR found that there had been a breach of Article 2.

Article 2 does not prohibit the use of the death penalty, but Article 1 of the 13th Protocol (which came into force in the UK in 2004) does.

No derogation from Article 2 is possible, except in respect of deaths resulting from lawful acts of war.

Article 2(2) permits the use of force that results in the deprivation of life, but only if certain conditions are met. The first condition is that the use of force must be no more than absolutely necessary.

The second condition is that the use of force must be in pursuit of one or more of three objectives:

- the force is used in defence of any person from unlawful violence;
- the force is used to effect a lawful arrest or to prevent the escape of a person lawfully detained;
- the force is used in action lawfully taken for the purpose of lawfully quelling a riot or insurrection.

The leading case in this area is *McCann v United Kingdom* (1996) 21 EHRR 97 (the 'Death on the Rock' case), which involved a challenge by the relatives of three Provisional IRA members who were shot dead by SAS soldiers in Gibraltar in 1988. The relatives won by a slim majority (10:9) on the basis that the force used was more than absolutely necessary. Whilst the actions of the SAS soldiers who had killed the terrorists did not violate Article 2, the control and planning of the operation lacked sufficient regard for the protection of the lives of the suspects, so Article 2 had been violated.

2.2.1 Scope of Article 2

Case law has helped to define the scope of Article 2. This has determined that the duty to protect life applies to any activity, whether public or not, where there is a 'real and imminent' risk to life. The obligation to take appropriate steps to protect life is particularly important where activities may pose a risk to life due to their inherently hazardous nature, such as the operation of waste collection sites or nuclear testing.

2.2.1.1 Embryos/foetuses

The ECtHR has stated that, as there is no consensus amongst signatory states as to when life begins, the issue as to when the protection of Article 2 commences is within their margin of appreciation. Article 2 has been held not to protect embryos by preventing their destruction when one party withdraws their consent to implantation (*Evans v UK* [2007] ECHR 6339/05). In this case, the ECtHR dismissed an appeal by the applicant under Article 2 and accepted the decision of the domestic courts that the embryos had no independent right to life under Article 2. The Court said this decision was within the margin of appreciation allowed to member states. In the case of *Re F (In Utero) (Wardship)* [1988] 2 FLR 307 it had already been established that a foetus has no such right to life, so the right could clearly not apply to an embryo.

2.2.1.2 The right to die

There is also case law on whether the right to life encompasses the right to die in the context of litigation regarding whether laws banning assisted suicide breach Article 2. In *Pretty v UK* (2002) 35 EHRR 1, Diane Pretty suffered from motor neurone disease. Both the Divisional Court and the House of Lords held that the Director of Public Prosecutions (DPP) had no power to give an undertaking that her husband would not be prosecuted if he assisted her to commit suicide. The case went to the ECtHR, which held that the right to die could not be read into the right to life protected by Article 2.

This does not mean, on the other hand, that laws permitting assisted suicide would breach Article 2 provided such laws include effective safeguards to prevent abuse and thus respect for the right to life (*Mortier v Belgium* (App No 78017/17) (2022)). In the *Pretty* case, the ECtHR also held that Mrs Pretty's rights under Article 8(1) (the right to private and family life) were engaged, as Article 8(1) encompasses the right to decide how and when to die in order to prevent a distressing and undignified end to one's life. Nonetheless, she failed in her claim because the interference with her right (the ban in UK law on assisted suicide) was justified by Article 8(2). Although the legal ban remains in place, as discussed at **1.5.2.2** above, the Director of Public Prosecutions has issued guidelines indicating that a person acting out of compassion to help a terminally ill patient with a 'clear, settled and informed wish to die' is unlikely to be prosecuted. Nonetheless, assisted suicide remains a controversial issue as the next activity shows.

ACTIVITY 1 Article 2 and Article 8

In *R (on the application of Nicklinson)* v *Ministry of Justice* [2014] UKSC 38, Tony Nicklinson had suffered a massive stroke, leaving him completely paralysed except that he was able to move his head and eyes. He wanted someone to kill him by injecting him with a lethal drug or, failing that, to kill himself by using a machine loaded with a lethal drug that he could digitally activate via an eye blink computer.

Although s 1 of the Suicide Act 1961 decriminalised suicide itself, s 2 of that Act provides that encouraging or assisting a suicide remains a crime. Mr Nicklinson applied to the High Court for, amongst other things, a declaration that the current law on assisted suicide was incompatible with his right to a private life under Article 8. The High Court rejected his application. After his death, his wife pursued an appeal.

The Supreme Court held unanimously that Article 8(1) was engaged as s 2 prevented someone who was not able to end their life from doing so. It also held unanimously that the question whether the current law was incompatible with Article 8 fell within the UK's margin of appreciation, and was therefore a question for the UK to decide. The issue therefore arose whether the ban on assisted suicide could be justified under Article 8(2).

However, the Supreme Court was divided over whether it should issue a declaration of incompatibility. The right to life guaranteed by Article 2 obliges states to establish a procedure capable of ensuring that a decision to end one's life does indeed reflect the free wish of the individual concerned, so some restrictions on assisted suicide are required, but the Supreme Court justices disagreed over the appropriateness of the existing law.

Which of the following views do you prefer?

(i) A declaration of incompatibility should not be made. Whether the current law was compatible with Article 8 involved a consideration of issues which Parliament was inherently better qualified than the courts to assess, and so the courts should respect Parliament's assessment.

(ii) It was not yet appropriate to decide whether to make a declaration of incompatibility. Assisted suicide is a sensitive and controversial issue on which great significance should be attached to the judgment of the democratically elected legislature. This did not, however, justify the court ruling out the possibility that it could make a declaration of incompatibility. Nonetheless, it would be inappropriate for a court to decide this before giving Parliament the opportunity to consider the position in the light of its judgment.

(iii) A declaration of incompatibility should be issued. Article 8 confers a right on an individual to decide by what means and at what point their life will end, provided that they are capable of freely reaching a decision. In making no exception for exceptional cases where the wish to die reflects a freely made desire rather than being the result of undue pressure, the current ban on assisting suicide was disproportionate and incompatible with Article 8.

COMMENT

There is no right or wrong answer to this question. The three views summarised represent the diverging views put forward by the nine Supreme Court justices hearing the case. Four of them supported the first view – that a declaration of incompatibility should not be made;

three the second – that it was not appropriate to decide the issue until Parliament had considered the court's view; and two the third – that a declaration should be made. Although no single view commanded a majority of the nine justices, the appeal was dismissed as only two of them considered that a declaration of incompatibility should be made at that time, although three others left open the possibility for a future case. The Assisted Dying Bill, a private member's bill promoted by Lord Falconer, was given a second reading soon after the decision but failed to pass into law.

In *R (on the application of Conway) v Secretary of State for Justice* [2018] EWCA Civ 1431, the appellant was terminally ill with motor neurone disease and applied for a declaration of incompatibility of s 2(1) of the Suicide Act 1961 under s 4 of the HRA 1998, arguing that the blanket ban on assisted suicide in s 2(1) was a disproportionate interference with his Article 8 rights. Although the Court of Appeal accepted that Article 8 was engaged, it nonetheless held that the blanket ban on assisted suicide in s 2(1) was a necessary and proportionate interference with the appellant's Article 8 rights.

2.2.1.3 Environmental pollution

In the case of *Cannavacciuolo v Italy* (App No 51767/14), 41 local residents complained about the disposal of waste in unauthorised sites and the illegal burying and burning of hazardous waste which had been occurring for many years. They argued that the Italian authorities had not taken adequate measures to protect their lives.

The ECtHR noted that this case involved a particularly complex and widespread form of pollution which occurred primarily on private land. It did not concern dangerous activities, such as industrial activities, carried out against the backdrop of an existing regulatory framework but instead concerned activities carried out by organised criminal groups, businesses and individuals. However, there was ample evidence that the national authorities had known about the existence of these dangerous activities for many years. Given the seriousness of the circumstances, the Italian state had not done enough to protect the applicants' lives. The state had therefore violated Article 2.

2.2.2 The procedural duty under Article 2

Article 2 provides expressly that everyone's right to life shall be protected by law. By implication, it also places a procedural obligation on the state to investigate when individuals have been killed as a result of force. This was made clear in *McCann v UK* (1995) 21 EHRR 97 (the 'Death on the Rock' case discussed at **2.2** above).

There is therefore an important practical consideration here: namely, that breach of Article 2 can give a legal remedy even where a criminal prosecution would not succeed.

One of the most controversial cases regarding the duty to investigate followed the death of Jean Charles de Menezes. On 22 July 2005 (shortly after the attacks of 7 July 2005 when suicide bombers had murdered 52 people in London), Mr de Menezes was wrongly identified as a suspected suicide bomber. He was followed to an underground station and shot dead by armed officers while on board a stationary train. In 2007, the Office of the Commissioner of the Police of the Metropolis was found guilty of breaches of the Health and Safety at Work Act of 1974 in connection with Mr de Menezes's death, but no individual police officers were prosecuted. A cousin of Mr de Menezes (Patricia da Silva) brought judicial review proceedings against the DPP for failing to prosecute any of the police officers involved. The cousin failed in her claim in the UK and then brought her case before the ECtHR.

In *Da Silva v United Kingdom* (2016) 63 EHRR 589, the ECtHR stated that for an 'effective investigation':

- It was necessary for the persons responsible for carrying out the investigation to be independent from those implicated in the events.
- It must be adequate, that is it must be capable of leading to the establishment of the facts so determining whether the force used was or was not justified in the circumstances and of identifying and – if appropriate – punishing those responsible.
- The nature and degree of scrutiny necessary would depend on the circumstances but would need to be stringent where death was at the hands of a state agent.
- The investigation must be accessible to the family, although they may not be entitled to police reports or investigative materials containing sensitive material which may prejudice other private individuals or investigations.
- There must be a sufficient element of public scrutiny, the degree of which may vary from case to case.
- It must be carried out promptly.

The decision not to prosecute any individual officer in this case was not due to any failings in the investigation or the state's tolerance of or collusion in unlawful acts. Rather, it was due to the fact that, following a thorough investigation, a prosecutor considered all the facts of the case and concluded that there was insufficient evidence against any individual officer to meet the threshold evidential test in respect of any criminal offence. On that basis the ECtHR held that the DPP's decision did not breach Article 2.

In *Re Dillon (Northern Ireland Troubles (Legacy and Reconciliation) Act 2023)* [2024] NIKB 11, the Northern Ireland High Court ruled that provisions in the Northern Ireland Troubles (Legacy and Reconciliation) 2023 Act ('the Act') which grant immunity from prosecution breached both Article 2 and Article 3 of the ECHR. This was on the basis that such an amnesty did not represent either the only way out of a violent dictatorship (not the situation in Northern Ireland even during the Troubles) or interminable conflict (as the relevant conflict in Northern Ireland had ended over 20 years before). The Act provided that the Independent Commission for Reconciliation and Information Recovery (which was set up under the Act) must grant immunity to an applicant if certain conditions were met and did not provide for any exceptions for grave breaches of fundamental rights including allegations of torture. The previous Conservative government appealed this ruling, but its appeal on this point was dismissed by the Northern Ireland Court of Appeal in September 2024. The current Labour government has stated its intention to 'repeal and replace' the Act.

In December 2024, the government published the draft Northern Ireland Troubles (Legacy and Reconciliation) Act 2023 (Remedial) Order 2024 to remedy some of the incompatibilities with the ECHR. However, it has also decided to appeal the decision of the Northern Ireland Court of Appeal. The Supreme Court has granted permission for this appeal and it is due to be heard before the end of June 2025.

2.3 Article 3 – prohibition on torture, inhuman or degrading treatment or punishment

Article 3 of the ECHR provides very simply that 'No one shall be subjected to torture or to inhuman or degrading treatment or punishment'. It is an absolute right and there are no limitations or exceptions to this. Any treatment of an individual that falls within the scope of Article 3 violates the Convention. The importance of Article 3 is also reflected in the fact that it is one of those articles from which the state is not permitted to derogate under Article 15.

2.3.1 Scope of Article 3

The leading case on what amounts to torture and inhuman treatment is *Ireland v United Kingdom* [1978] ECHR 5310/71. This case concerned the ill treatment of suspected Irish Republican Army terrorists in Northern Ireland in 1971. As part of the interrogation techniques adopted by the police and security services, the suspects were made to stand against a wall in an unnatural position for long periods of time and were also placed in hoods and deprived of sleep and food. The ECtHR defined 'torture' as being 'deliberate inhuman treatment causing very serious and cruel suffering', whilst it defined 'inhuman treatment' as treatment or punishment likely to cause 'actual bodily injury or intense physical and mental suffering'. The ECtHR found that the conduct in this case constituted inhuman or degrading treatment, albeit it was not severe enough to be torture.

The European Court of Human Rights in *Pretty v UK* (see **2.2.1.2** above) defined degrading treatment as 'treatment which humiliates or debases an individual showing a lack of respect for, or diminishing, his or her human dignity or arouses feelings of fear, anguish or inferiority capable of breaking an individual's moral and physical resistance'. Mrs Pretty was frightened and distressed by the suffering and indignity that she would have to endure as the motor neurone disease progressed and wished to control how and when she died to be spared such suffering and indignity. The Court held that Article 3 applied to some positive form of treatment or intentionally inflicted acts by the state. The state's alleged failure to prevent Mrs Pretty from suffering in the later stages of her disease by not granting immunity to her husband could not amount to inhuman or degrading treatment.

A number of cases relating to corporal punishment in schools came before the ECtHR in the late 1970s and 1980. In *Tyrer v United Kingdom* [1978] ECHR 5856/72, a court in the Isle of Man sentenced the applicant to three strokes of the birch for the offence of assault occasioning actual bodily harm against another pupil at his school. A policeman administered the birch to the applicant's naked buttocks while he was being held down by two other policemen. The ECtHR held that the punishment did not amount to torture or inhuman treatment within the meaning of Article 3, as it did not meet the test set out in the *UK v Ireland* case. The ECtHR did, however, find that Tyrer was subjected to degrading punishment under Article 3. As a result of such cases, Parliament enacted legislation to outlaw corporal punishment in both state and - later - private schools.

The ECtHR has also held that the state has an obligation to ensure that non-state actors such as parents or guardians do not punish children to a level at which Article 3 will be engaged. In *A v United Kingdom* [1998] ECHR 25599/94, between the ages of 6 and 9, A had been frequently beaten with a garden cane by his stepfather. These beatings had left significant bruising. The stepfather was subsequently charged with assault occasioning actual bodily harm. At trial, he raised the defence available under English law that the beatings represented reasonable chastisement, which he was entitled to inflict. The stepfather was acquitted and A applied to the ECtHR, arguing that his treatment constituted a violation of his rights under Article 3.

The Court found that the injuries inflicted on A were sufficient to engage Article 3, and that the state had failed to put in place laws that would satisfactorily protect the rights of children such as A. Parliament subsequently amended the law in this area.

2.3.2 The procedural duty under Article 3

Article 3 imposes a procedural duty on the state, in much the same way as for Article 2, where an individual makes a credible assertion that they have suffered treatment which breaches Article 3 at the hands of state authorities. As for Article 2, the investigation must be independent; capable of leading to the identification and, if appropriate, punishment of those responsible; thorough; and carried out promptly. Additionally, the victim should be able to participate effectively in the investigation (*Mocanu v Romania* (2015) 60 EHRR 19).

In *D v Commissioner of Police for the Metropolis* [2018] UKSC 11 the claimant claimed that the failure by the police to investigate her allegations of rape amounted to a breach of Article 3, which had meant that the perpetrator (the 'Black Cab Rapist') had continued to attack women for many years before being arrested. The Supreme Court held that there could be a breach of Article 3 where, as here, the harm was inflicted by a non-state agent. The police investigation was seriously flawed and breached the investigatory duty under Article 3.

2.3.3 Asylum cases

The United Kingdom has a long history of granting political asylum. Those seeking asylum in the UK are citizens of other countries seeking refuge here on the basis that they fear persecution in their home country.

In recent years, a number of those seeking political asylum in the United Kingdom have alleged that the treatment they have received at the hands of UK authorities has violated their right under Article 3 not to be subjected to inhuman and degrading treatment.

Unlike UK citizens and others who are entitled to live in the UK, asylum seekers are not given access to the extensive system of welfare benefits which exists in the UK. The courts have had to determine whether denying these asylum seekers the basics of life, such as food and shelter, is in breach of Article 3.

In *R (Limbuela) v Secretary of State for the Home Department* [2005] UKHL 66, three asylum seekers were refused support on the ground that they had not claimed asylum as soon as reasonably practicable after their arrival in the UK. They were prohibited by law from taking employment and so were reliant on charity to provide them food. They were either sleeping on the streets or would imminently be doing so. They applied for judicial review of the Home Secretary's decision to refuse them support on the basis that this breached their rights under Article 3.

The court stated that Article 3 would be breached if an asylum seeker with no means or alternative support is 'by the deliberate action of the state, denied shelter, food or the most basic necessities of life'. Thus if there was persuasive evidence that an asylum seeker was seriously suffering because (i) they had to sleep on the street, unless this was for a short period, (ii) they were seriously hungry, or (iii) they were unable to satisfy the most basic requirements of hygiene, then Article 3 was likely to be breached. Factors to take into account in deciding whether a particular asylum seeker was subjected to inhuman or degrading treatment included gender; age and health; any sources of support available; and the length of time spent or likely to be spent without support.

The obligation under Article 3 was absolute and it made no difference that the suffering was caused as a result of legitimate government policy.

2.3.4 Deportation, removal and extradition cases

A controversial area in which Article 3 has been applied involves cases where those who are not British citizens are required to leave the UK. These cases usually involve people who are being deported under the Immigration Act 1971. This Act allows the Government to deport those who are lawfully in the UK but are not UK citizens if either they have been convicted of a serious offence or their presence in the UK is not conducive to the public good. This latter reason would cover those who are viewed as a risk to national security.

Other situations in which individuals may be required to leave the UK are removal and extradition cases. Removal is where those who are not in the UK lawfully are removed. Extradition cases involve anyone living in the UK being sent to another country in order to be tried for a criminal offence allegedly committed in that country. Extradition is regulated by the Extradition Act 2003 which sets out the law relating to extradition to countries with which the UK has extradition arrangements. The UK has an extradition treaty with many countries.

The ECtHR has held that it would be a violation of Article 2 and/or Article 3 of the Convention if an individual were to be deported to, removed to or extradited to a country where there was a real risk that they might be killed, tortured or treated in any other way that would violate one or both of these Articles.

The Court outlined this principle in *Soering v United Kingdom* (1989) 11 EHRR 439. In this case, the United States had applied to the UK for the extradition of Soering, who was alleged to have committed two murders while in the US.

The Court found that the proposed extradition of Soering to the United States would breach his rights under Article 3. This was because, were Soering to be convicted of murder and sentenced to death, the time he would spend on death row while awaiting execution would cause him to suffer intense psychological suffering that would fall within the scope of Article 3.

The Soering case was decided before Article 1 of the 13th Protocol came into force (see **2.2** above). This Article bans the imposition of the death penalty. As a result, it would now also violate Article 2 for an individual to be deported, removed or extradited to a state if there are substantial grounds to believe that there is a real risk of that individual facing the death penalty.

What is the position if the deportation of an individual to another country will not result in their death but may lead to them suffering other forms of ill treatment?

This was considered by the ECtHR in *Chahal v United Kingdom* (1997) 23 EHRR 413. In 1990, the Secretary of State decided to deport Chahal, an Indian citizen lawfully resident in the UK, in the interests of national security. In 1984, on a visit to India, he had been detained and tortured by the Punjabi police due to his participation in a campaign for a Sikh homeland.

The Court found that Article 3 contained an absolute prohibition on the use of torture or inhuman or degrading treatment, regardless of the circumstances of the case. There was substantial evidence of serious human rights abuses by the Indian authorities, and promises that they had given as to Chahal's safety were unreliable. The Court concluded that, where there was a real risk that the receiving country would treat an individual in such a way as to breach his Article 3 rights, any deportation would be unlawful.

R (on the application of AAA (Syria)) v Secretary of State for the Home Department [2023] UKSC 42 concerned a challenge to the Secretary of State's policy of relocating asylum seekers to Rwanda for determination of their asylum claims, on the basis that Rwanda was not a safe third country. The Supreme Court stated that Article 3 would be breached, not only where there was a real risk of ill-treatment in Rwanda itself, but also if an inadequate system of asylum in Rwanda meant that there was a real risk of asylum seekers being returned, directly or indirectly, to their country of origin and there was a real risk that their Article 3 rights would be breached in that country. It decided that Rwanda was not a safe country due to the inadequacy of its asylum system, and therefore relocation to Rwanda would constitute a breach of Article 3. In response to the Supreme Court's decision, the Government passed the Safety of Rwanda (Asylum and Immigration) Act 2024. This Act declared Rwanda to be a safe place and disapplied ss 2 and 3 of the HRA 1998 in relation to the Act. Subsequently, the Labour Government elected in July 2024 cancelled the Rwanda scheme. The Border Security, Asylum and Immigration Bill 2024–25, currently before Parliament, will repeal the Safety of Rwanda (Asylum and Immigration) Act 2024.

The Illegal Migration Act 2023 requires the Home Secretary to remove, save in very limited circumstances, all those who have arrived irregularly and not directly from a country where their life and liberty is threatened. The court in the case of *In the Matter of an Application by JR295 for Judicial Review* [2024] NIKB 35 made a declaration under s 4 of the HRA 1998 that these provisions were incompatible with Article 3. It stated that this duty would require removal of persons in circumstances where they had advanced valid human rights claims which had not been assessed. Thus there would be no examination of whether or not those individuals were at real risk of being subjected to treatment contrary to Article 3. The Border Security, Asylum and Immigration Bill 2024–25, currently before Parliament, will repeal these provisions.

2.4 Article 4 – freedom from slavery

2.4.1 Introduction

Article 4 of the ECHR prohibits slavery and forced labour. Article 4(1) provides that 'No one shall be held in slavery or servitude', and Article 4(2) provides that 'No one shall be required to perform forced or compulsory labour'.

Article 4(3) states that certain forms of work do not constitute forced or compulsory labour. These are:

- work ordinarily done by convicted prisoners as part of their sentence;
- compulsory military service in those European countries that still have this;
- work required in an emergency or calamity threatening the life or wellbeing of the community; and
- any work or service that forms part of normal civic obligations.

Although slavery was abolished in most parts of the world in the 19th century, Article 4 is a response to what happened during World War II, between 1939 and 1945. During the War, Nazi Germany used millions of people from across the continent of Europe to carry out forced labour in support of the Nazi war machine.

We shall now consider the meaning of some of the terms used in Article 4.

2.4.2 Slavery

The internationally accepted definition of slavery was set out in Article 1 of the 1926 Slavery Convention. This defined slavery as 'the status or condition of a person over whom any or all of the powers attaching to the right of ownership are exercised'. The ECtHR has accepted this definition.

2.4.3 Servitude

Someone in a position of servitude is not owned by another, and so is not a slave. The ECtHR has found that servitude includes an obligation on the part of the person who is the 'serf' to live on the property of another, and an inability for that person to change that condition.

2.4.4 Forced or compulsory labour

The meaning of the term 'forced or compulsory labour' was considered by the ECtHR in *Van der Mussele v Belgium* (1984) 6 EHRR 163. Belgian law required trainee lawyers – as part of their qualification process – to carry out legal work for poor clients without receiving any payment. The trainees argued that this constituted a violation of Article 4(2), but the Court disagreed. The Court said that the requirement to do this work had to be seen in its proper context, which was that the trainees were gaining valuable experience, they were in the process of qualifying into a profession, and doing this work did not prevent them from also doing paid work for other clients.

The Court said that forced labour was work or service that an individual was forced to do against their will. Although there is no easy test to work out when this will be met, the Court said that a range of circumstances needed to be considered. These included the type of work involved, the 'penalty' or burden to be imposed if the work was not carried out, and the level of hardship or oppression to which the individual was subjected.

The Supreme Court considered the interpretation of forced labour in *Reilly v Secretary of State for Work and Pensions* [2013] UKSC 68. This case involved a challenge to the requirement that a person in receipt of the state benefit called Jobseeker's Allowance had to carry out unpaid work experience as a condition of continuing to receive this benefit. The Supreme Court found that this requirement did not breach Article 4. The Court said that an essential element of forced labour was that the individual had to be exploited, and that requirement was not met here.

2.4.5 Modern slavery and human trafficking

Slavery still affects millions of people worldwide. Human trafficking involves the recruitment or movement of people for exploitation by the use of threat, force, fraud or the abuse of vulnerability. Trafficking often takes place across international borders but can take place within a country. People can be trafficked for various reasons, for example to carry out labour or for domestic servitude or sexual exploitation. In *Rantsev v Cyprus* (2010) 51 EHRR 1 the ECtHR made it clear that human trafficking fell within Article 4. States were under a positive obligation to enact and enforce laws to prohibit and punish trafficking.

Where it is demonstrated that the state authorities were aware, or ought to have been aware, of circumstances giving rise to a credible suspicion that an identified individual had been, or was at real and immediate risk of being, trafficked or exploited, Article 4 may require a Member State to take operational measures to protect victims, or potential victims, of trafficking. Article 4 also imposes a procedural obligation to investigate situations of potential trafficking, both cross-border and within the state's own borders.

2.5 Article 5 – right to liberty and security

2.5.1 Introduction

The overall purpose of Article 5 of the ECHR has been described as ensuring that no one is deprived of their liberty in an 'arbitrary fashion'. In particular, it lays down procedural standards that must be followed before a person is deprived of their liberty.

Article 5(1) begins, 'Everyone has the right to liberty and security of person. No one shall be deprived of his liberty save in the following cases and in accordance with a procedure prescribed by law.'

From this, you can see that Article 5 is a limited article – it creates a right to liberty, but that right is subject to several specific limitations set out in the rest of the Article. Also, even if one of those limited situations exists, the deprivation of an individual's liberty must still be carried out through due process of law. An example of this would be if the police were to detain an individual whom they reasonably suspect to have committed a crime, but fail to carry out the arrest in the correct manner by not telling the individual that they are under arrest or the reason for the arrest.

Article 5(1)(a)–(f) lists six ways in which an individual's right to liberty may lawfully be interfered with by the state. The most significant ways in which the state may lawfully restrict the liberty of an individual are arrest and detention by the police, imprisonment after conviction of a criminal offence, detention of the mentally ill in hospitals, and detention of foreigners in the context of asylum and deportation cases (see **2.5.3** below).

2.5.2 The meaning of 'deprivation of liberty'

When a person is locked up in prison, they have clearly been deprived of their liberty, so Article 5 will be engaged. However, there are situations that are less clear-cut, so it is essential to consider what the phrase 'deprivation of liberty' means to ascertain when Article 5 is engaged.

There may be situations when an individual has their right of free movement restricted but is otherwise free to carry on with their life. An example of this is an Anti-Social Behaviour Order that prohibits an individual from entering a specific area, or a Football Banning Order that prohibits an individual from attending football matches. These restrictions on movement do not engage Article 5 because they do not deprive an individual of their liberty.

Although the above examples do not engage Article 5, the ECtHR has said that the term 'deprivation of liberty' has a wider meaning than simply detaining someone in a cell. The Court has held that what constitutes a deprivation of liberty is a matter of judgment based upon all the circumstances.

2.5.2.1 The *Guzzardi* case

The leading case in this area is *Guzzardi v Italy* (1981) 3 EHRR 333. In 1975, an Italian court ordered that Guzzardi, a suspected Mafia leader, should be placed under special supervision for three years with an obligation to reside on a small Italian island. The island measured some 50 square kilometres but the area for Guzzardi's compulsory residence was limited to some 2.5 square kilometres.

A majority of the ECtHR held that these limitations amounted to a deprivation of liberty. In its judgment, the Court said that: 'The difference between deprivation of and restriction upon liberty is one of degree or intensity, and not one of nature or substance.'

What the Court meant by this was that, in any given situation, it was necessary to look at the level of the restrictions placed on an applicant, rather than their specific nature. The Court held that deprivation of liberty may take many forms, going beyond what it referred to as 'classic detention in prison'.

In Guzzardi's case, the Court found that, whilst the area around which Guzzardi could move far exceeded the dimensions of a cell and was not bounded by any physical barrier, it covered a tiny fraction of an island to which access was difficult and about nine-tenths of which was occupied by a prison. Also, Guzzardi was housed in a tiny village, living in the company of other persons subjected to the same measure. He was not permitted to visit the main settlement on the island, and his social contacts were limited to his near family, his fellow 'residents' and the supervisory staff. In addition, Guzzardi was not able to leave his dwelling between 10pm and 7am without giving prior notification to the authorities. He had to report to the authorities twice a day and inform them of the name and number of his correspondent whenever he wished to use the telephone. In conclusion, the Court said:

> It is admittedly not possible to speak of 'deprivation of liberty' on the strength of any one of these factors taken individually, but cumulatively and in combination they certainly raise an issue of categorisation from the viewpoint of Article 5. In certain respects the treatment complained of resembles detention in an 'open prison' or committal to a disciplinary unit.

2.5.2.2 The UK context

The definition of the term 'deprivation of liberty' was considered by the House of Lords in *Secretary of State for the Home Department v JJ* [2007] UKHL 45. In this case, the Secretary of State used statutory powers to make what were called control orders over six people of Iranian or Iraqi nationality. The orders were made because the Secretary of State had reasonable grounds for suspecting them of involvement in terrorist-related activity and he considered the orders to be necessary to protect members of the public from a risk of terrorism.

The orders required each controlled person at all times to wear an electronic tagging device, to remain within their specified residence, a one-bedroom flat, except between 10am and 4pm, and to permit police searches of the premises at any time. Visitors to the premises were permitted only where prior Home Office permission had been given. During the six hours when the controlled persons were permitted to leave their residences, they were confined to restricted urban areas, which deliberately did not extend, except in one case, to any area where they had previously lived. Each area contained a mosque, health care facilities, shops and entertainment and sporting facilities. Each controlled person was prohibited from meeting anyone by pre-arrangement without prior Home Office approval.

Adopting the approach taken by the ECtHR in the *Guzzardi* case, the House of Lords held that the right to individual liberty in Article 5 connoted the physical liberty of the person, and, in cases of dispute, it was for the court to assess into which category a particular case fell. In order to do this, the court needed to consider the situation of the particular individual and, taking account of a whole range of criteria including the type, duration, effects and manner of implementation of the measures in question, to assess their impact on them in the context of the life they might otherwise have been living. Applying those factors, a majority of the House of Lords held that the right to liberty of the six individuals had been violated.

The cases of *Guzzardi* and *JJ* make it clear that a person may be deprived of their liberty under Article 5 without being detained in prison. However, in such cases, there would need to be a significant element of physical confinement, together with significant restrictions on the life that can be lived when not so confined.

2.5.2.3 Kettling

In recent years, the ECtHR has had to determine whether the 'kettling' of protesters falls within the scope of Article 5. Kettling is the practice of containing a group of people in a particular area for a limited period of time in the interests of public order.

ACTIVITY 2 Kettling and Article 5

In *Austin v UK* (2012) 55 EHRR 14, four people had been contained within a police cordon for six to seven hours during an anti-capitalism demonstration in central London. One had been taking part in the demonstration, but the others were simply passers-by. Police intelligence indicated that the demonstration presented a serious threat to public order, and a risk of damage to property and serious injury or death.

Do you think that this 'kettling' would amount to a deprivation of liberty?

COMMENT

You may have thought that kettling under these circumstances would not amount to a deprivation of liberty. This was the view of the majority of the Court, which stressed that Article 5 was not concerned with mere restrictions on liberty of movement. The difference between a deprivation of liberty and a restriction upon it was one of degree, and therefore the type, duration, effects and manner of implementation of the measure used had to be considered. The Court found that whilst the coercive nature, duration and effect of the containment on the applicants suggested a deprivation of liberty, the context was significant. The police had had no alternative but to establish the cordon to isolate and contain a large crowd and to avert a real risk of injury or damage. The applicants did not argue that they had been deprived of their liberty as soon as the cordon was imposed, and the Court was unable to identify a point at which a restriction on their freedom of movement became a deprivation of their liberty. The police had made attempts at dispersal and had kept the situation under review, but the dangerous conditions that had necessitated the imposition of the cordon existed until early evening. Containment was the least intrusive measure the police could use under the circumstances. Therefore, those within the cordon could not be said to have been deprived of their liberty within the meaning of Article 5.

On the other hand, you may have though that kettling under these circumstances would amount to a deprivation of liberty. The applicants were confined within a relatively small area and their freedom of movement was greatly reduced. They were only able to stand up or sit on the ground and had no access to toilet facilities, food or water. The cordon was maintained through the presence of hundreds of riot police officers, and the applicants were entirely dependent on the police officers' decisions as to when they could leave. The confinement was applied indiscriminately to everyone in the area, regardless of whether they were taking part in the demonstration. Thus the containment was not the least intrusive measure the police could use.

2.5.3 When may the state lawfully deprive an individual of their liberty?

Article 5(1)(a)–(f) lists six situations in which an individual may lawfully be deprived of their liberty without a violation of the basic right contained in Article 5. In summary, these limitations are:

(a) when an individual is sent to prison after being convicted of a criminal offence;

(b) when an individual is arrested or detained in order to ensure that the individual complies with a court order;

(c) when an individual is arrested on reasonable suspicion of having committed a criminal offence, to prevent them from committing an offence or to prevent them from fleeing after having committed an offence. In *O'Hara v UK* (2002) 34 EHRR 32, the ECtHR stated that 'reasonable suspicion' requires the existence of some facts or information which would satisfy an objective observer that the person concerned may have committed the offence, though what may be regarded as reasonable will depend on all the circumstances of the case;

(d) when a minor is detained for the purposes of educational supervision;

(e) when someone is detained to prevent the spreading of an infectious disease or someone who is mentally ill is detained for their own protection or the protection of others; and

(f) the detention of individuals in connection with asylum, deportation or extradition.

Even if one of the limitations exists, any deprivation of liberty will only be within the requirements of Article 5 if it takes place in accordance with a procedure prescribed by law.

This means that, if the state deprives an individual of their liberty, that detention must not be carried out in an arbitrary manner – proper legal procedures must exist and must be followed if a deprivation of liberty is to be lawful. In *Saadi v United Kingdom* (2008) 47 EHRR 17, the ECtHR stated that a number of requirements need to be met in order to prevent a deprivation of liberty being arbitrary.

(1) The detention has to be carried out in good faith. This means that it has to be closely connected to one of the purposes listed in Article 5(1)(a)–(f).

(2) The detention must be necessary. This means that it can only be justified when less severe measures have been considered and rejected.

(3) The length of the detention should not exceed that reasonably required for the purpose pursued.

(4) Proper records of the reason for the detention must be kept.

(5) The detention must be lawful within the terms of the national law of the state concerned.

For example, Article 5(1)(a) permits the lawful detention of a person after conviction by a competent court. Detention under this sub-paragraph will only be lawful if the term of imprisonment imposed is proportionate to the crime committed, and there is a clear link between the offence, the crime committed and the purpose for which the convicted person is detained in prison.

2.6 Article 6 – right to a fair trial

2.6.1 Introduction

Article 6 has three sections: Article 6(1), Article 6(2) and Article 6(3).

Article 6(1) provides:

> In the determination of his civil rights and obligations or of any criminal charge against him, everyone is entitled to a fair and public hearing within a reasonable

> time by an independent and impartial tribunal established by law. Judgment shall be pronounced publicly but the press and public may be excluded from all or part of the trial in the interest of morals, public order or national security in a democratic society, where the interests of juveniles or the protection of the private life of the parties so require, or to the extent strictly necessary in the opinion of the court in special circumstances where publicity would prejudice the interests of justice.

Article 6(1) applies both to civil and criminal cases. We shall examine each type of case in turn.

2.6.2 Civil rights and obligations

Article 6 does not provide a definition of what is meant by the term 'civil rights and obligations'. Rather, it is a term to which the ECtHR has given its own particular meaning, and that meaning goes beyond whether the national law of a particular state views a matter as being civil in nature.

As a starting point, the Court has said that Article 6 will only be invoked where a case concerns an individual attempting to assert a substantive legal right that is recognised in national law. Typical cases that are clearly civil in nature are when an individual seeks to enforce their private law rights in contract, tort or property. To take an example, the right to a fair trial under Article 6 would apply in a trial involving an alleged breach of contract by the supplier of goods, or a trial where an individual claims damages for personal injuries sustained in a road traffic accident caused by the negligence of another driver.

The Court has also recognised that employment law cases and the decisions of disciplinary bodies that have the effect of preventing an individual pursuing their chosen profession also fall with in Article 6.

Article 6 can also apply to the administrative decisions taken by local authorities and other public authorities, such as the determination of an application for a licence to carry out a particular activity or decisions on the grant or refusal of planning permission. If a public authority fails to provide an applicant in such cases with a fair hearing, the applicant will have recourse to judicial review proceedings to challenge the decision made.

2.6.3 Criminal charges

The definition of what amounts to a 'criminal charge' is again something that the ECtHR has determined. The leading case on this point is *Engel v The Netherlands* (1979–80) 1 EHRR 647, where the ECtHR needed to determine whether penalties imposed on conscripted soldiers for breaching military discipline amounted to criminal charges within the meaning of Article 6. The ECtHR found that the disciplinary measures did fall within the definition of criminal charges. The ECtHR set out a number of criteria that had to be applied by a court when deciding whether a legal process constitutes the determination of a criminal charge.

The starting point for a court is to determine whether the national law of a state classifies a matter as being 'criminal' as opposed to disciplinary or administrative. If it is so classified, Article 6 will apply.

If, however, the matter is not viewed by national law as being criminal in nature, a court must then determine whether the proceedings against an individual are similar to a criminal trial. For example, do the proceedings require a finding of guilt or innocence to be made? The court should also consider what the purpose behind the proceedings is. If the purpose is to impose some form of punishment on an individual, it is likely that the proceedings will be seen as involving the determination of a criminal charge.

Following the principles outlined in *Engel*, the ECtHR has found that cases involving prison discipline and administrative offences concerning road traffic or environmental matters constitute the determination of a criminal charge.

2.6.4 Article 6(2) and 6(3)

The provisions set out in Article 6(1) apply in both civil and criminal cases. Article 6(2) and 6(3), however, apply only to criminal matters.

Article 6(2) provides that everyone charged with a criminal offence shall be presumed innocent until proven guilty according to law. The presumption of innocence is also a longstanding part of English criminal law.

Article 6(3) sets out a series of minimum rights that apply to those charged with a criminal offence. These rights are:

- to be told promptly and fully the detail of the case against them;
- to have sufficient time and facilities to prepare their defence;
- to defend themselves either personally or with the assistance of a lawyer, who should be provided by the state where necessary;
- to call witnesses in their defence and to cross-examine witnesses who have given evidence against them; and
- to have an interpreter provided free where necessary.

These are covered in more detail at **2.6.7**

2.6.5 Article 6(1) and criminal cases

Article 6(1) sets out the elements that need to be met when the civil rights and obligations of an individual, or criminal charges against an individual, are being determined. This paragraph will concentrate on how these elements apply in a criminal context.

The elements are that:

- an individual should have access to the court;
- that court should be independent and impartial;
- the trial should be in public and the decision of the court pronounced publicly;
- the trial should take place within a reasonable time; and
- the trial itself should be conducted in a fair way.

We shall consider these elements in turn.

2.6.5.1 Access to the court

The right of access to the court is unlikely to cause problems in a criminal case as the defendant will be on the receiving end of proceedings brought against them by the state.

2.6.5.2 Independent and impartial tribunal

It is a fundamental requirement of a criminal case that the court is independent of the state and does not exhibit bias towards the prosecution.

In the case of *R (on the application of Anderson) v Secretary of State for the Home Department* [2002] UKHL 46, Anderson was convicted of murder and received a mandatory sentence of life imprisonment. He was, however, eligible for release on licence after he had served a minimum term of imprisonment, known as a tariff. Although the trial judge could recommend how long the tariff should be, the ultimate decision belonged with the Home Secretary, a member of the executive. The Home Secretary gave Anderson a tariff longer than that recommended by the trial judge. The House of Lords found that this breached Anderson's rights under Article 6(1). The imposition of a sentence, including the fixing of the tariff, is part of the trial and therefore should be imposed by an independent and impartial tribunal. As a member of the executive, with a political motive for wanting to be seen as tough on crime, the Home Secretary was not an independent and impartial tribunal.

2.6.5.3 Public trial

There is an expectation that a criminal trial will take place in public. The idea that the state should be able to routinely conduct secret trials behind closed doors is anathema to the ECHR. Trials that are open to the press and public deter courts from acting inappropriately and help to maintain public confidence in the criminal justice system.

Article 6(1) does, however, permit the press and public to be excluded from all or part of a trial in a limited number of situations. These situations are:

- where the exclusion is required in the interests of morality, public order or national security;
- where the exclusion is required in the interests of juveniles or the protection of the private life of the parties; or
- where there are special circumstances that, in the opinion of the court, would prejudice the interests of justice.

2.6.5.4 Trial within a reasonable time

Article 6(1) requires criminal trials to be held within a reasonable time. This may be particularly important for a defendant who has been refused bail by the court, and who is remanded in custody until their trial date. In the United Kingdom, rules that are known as custody time limits ensure that defendants who are remanded in custody have their trials heard within a reasonable time. These rules say, for example, that defendants awaiting Crown Court trial should not be held in custody for longer than six months prior to their trial. After this time, the defendant can apply for bail. The prosecution can apply to extend the custody time limit in certain circumstances, for example if a witness is ill.

2.6.5.5 Effective participation

A defendant should be able to participate effectively in their trial. At its most basic, this means that the trial should take place in the defendant's presence. It also means that the defendant should be able to follow and understand the proceedings. This can be a particular issue where the defendant is a child.

In *T v United Kingdom* (2000) 30 EHRR 121, two 11-year-old boys were charged with the horrific murder of a toddler. The case attracted enormous media attention and was heard in the adult Crown Court, following the rules and procedure of that court. Normally, children and juveniles are tried before the youth court, which operates on a more informal basis. Although some steps were taken to enable the boys to understand the proceedings - such as the advocates removing their wigs and gowns - the ECtHR found that these measures were insufficient to ensure their effective participation in the trial.

2.6.5.6 Exclusion of evidence

Another crucial area to consider when looking at the fairness of a criminal trial is how the court deals with prosecution evidence that has been obtained in an illegal or improper manner. The ECtHR has made it clear that detailed rules of criminal procedure and rules on the admissibility of evidence are matters for the national law of states who are signatories to the Convention.

Article 6(1) does not require a court to exclude evidence that has been obtained illegally or improperly. The Court has accepted that national laws may allow for the use of such evidence, and the Court will only involve itself where the overall circumstances of a case make a trial unfair within the meaning of Article 6.

In the UK, s 78 of the Police and Criminal Evidence Act 1984 (PACE) provides a trial court with a discretionary power to exclude any prosecution evidence. Section 78(1) provides:

> In any proceedings the court may refuse to allow evidence on which the prosecution proposes to rely to be given if it appears to the court that, having regard to all the circumstances, including the circumstances in which the evidence was obtained, the admission of the evidence would have such an adverse effect on the fairness of the proceedings that the court ought not to admit it.

The ECtHR considered the use of s 78 in the case *Khan v United Kingdom* [2000] ECHR 35394/97. Khan was convicted of drugs offences, largely on the basis of admissions he had made that were recorded on a bugging device that had been placed at premises Khan was visiting. The trial judge declined to exclude this evidence under s 78. Khan argued that this violated his right to a fair trial under Article 6 and also his right to privacy under Article 8.

The ECtHR found that the installation of the bugging device had violated Khan's right to privacy, as the law in England concerning the use by the police of a covert listening device was not sufficiently clear, and the installation of the bug was therefore unlawful. Despite this, the Court held that there had been no violation of Khan's right to a fair trial. The Court said that the key question for the purposes of Article 6 was whether the trial as a whole was fair. Khan had ample opportunity to challenge both the authenticity and the use of the recording, and had the domestic courts been of the view that the admission of the evidence would have given rise to substantive unfairness, they would have had a discretion to exclude it under s 78 of PACE.

The approach that UK courts now take to evidence that the police have obtained improperly or unlawfully is to allow the prosecution to use this evidence if it is relevant to an issue in the case. The courts will only exclude this evidence if there is something unreliable about it.

There are, however, some circumstances in which the courts must exclude prosecution evidence. The courts will refuse to allow the use of evidence in criminal proceedings if that evidence has been obtained through torture or inhuman treatment. To allow such evidence to be used at trial would be in breach of Article 3 of the Convention. Also, under s 76 of PACE, courts must exclude evidence of any confession given by a defendant in criminal proceedings if that evidence has been obtained either through oppressive behaviour by the police, or if there are any other circumstances likely to make it unreliable.

2.6.6 Article 6(2) – the presumption of innocence

A requirement of a fair trial at common law is that a defendant charged with an offence is presumed to be innocent until such time as they are convicted. If the state chooses to bring criminal proceedings against one of its citizens, it is for the state to prove the guilt of that citizen, rather than the citizen needing to prove their innocence. The citizen is not required to give evidence at their trial, to call witnesses in support of their case or to provide evidence to the prosecution that might serve to incriminate them.

Article 6(2) repeats this rule. It states that 'Everyone charged with a criminal offence shall be presumed innocent until proved guilty according to law'.

2.6.6.1 Strict liability offences

The criminal law of the United Kingdom, like many other countries, contains a number of offences of strict liability. A strict liability offence is an offence of which a defendant is guilty if the prosecution can prove the existence of certain facts. It is not necessary for the prosecution to also show that the defendant had any form of guilty mind.

The ECtHR considered whether such offences breach the requirements of Article 6(2) in *Salabiaku v France* (1991) 13 EHRR 379. In this case, the defendant was charged with an offence of smuggling prohibited goods. Under French law, there was a presumption of guilt if anyone was found in possession of prohibited goods. The ECtHR found that this provision did not violate Article 6(2). The Court said that such laws are permissible provided that they are reasonable.

2.6.6.2 Right to silence

Article 6(2) does not state explicitly that a defendant has a right to remain silent when questioned about their involvement in an offence. This right can, however, be read into the presumption of innocence in Article 6(2), as this requires the prosecution to prove its case against the defendant.

2.6.6.3 Inferences from silence

Of far greater significance is whether provisions in the criminal law that allow courts to draw negative conclusions – or adverse inferences as they are usually called – from a defendant's refusal to answer questions are compatible with the presumption of innocence in Article 6(2).

The Criminal Justice and Public Order Act 1994 contains provisions that permit a court to draw adverse inferences if a defendant does not answer questions from the police, but at their trial put forward a defence that they could have raised when questioned at the police station. The defendant must have been given an opportunity to consult a solicitor prior to being questioned before such adverse inferences can be drawn. The inference that the court may draw is that the defendant made up or fabricated their defence after leaving the police station.

Similar provisions allow a court to draw an adverse inference from a defendant's failure to account for an object or substance in their possession if asked to do so by the police, or if the defendant fails to account for the fact that they are arrested at the place where an offence has been committed shortly after the offence has occurred. The inference that the court may draw in these cases is that the defendant remained silent because they had no innocent explanation to give.

In *Murray v United Kingdom* (1996) 22 EHRR 29, Murray was charged with the offence of aiding and abetting the false imprisonment of a police informer, after being arrested in a property where Irish terrorists had been holding captive a police informer. Murray refused to answer any questions put to him at the police station, and he was convicted at trial after the judge drew adverse inferences from that silence.

The ECtHR found that this did not violate his rights under Article 6 as, in the circumstances, his presence at the property clearly required an explanation and, in the absence of such an explanation, it was reasonable for adverse inferences to be drawn. However, although the Court said that there was no rule to prevent adverse inferences being drawn, it would be in breach of Article 6 were a defendant to be convicted on the basis of their silence alone.

2.6.7 Additional rights of the defendant in criminal proceedings

Article 6(3) of the ECHR provides some additional rights to anyone charged with a criminal offence. Although set out separately, these rights are really part of the overall right to a fair trial in Article 6(1).

We shall consider each right in turn.

2.6.7.1 The right to be informed

Anyone charged with a criminal offence has the right to be told the nature and cause of the accusation against them. This information must be given promptly and in detail, so that the defendant can prepare any defence they may wish to raise. The information must be given in a language that the defendant understands. This requirement means that the police must tell an individual the detail of any offence for which that individual has been arrested and charged. It also obliges the prosecuting authorities to supply details of their case to the defendant, so that they know what evidence will be used against them at trial. In *Secretary of State for the Home Department v AF* [2009] UKHL 28, the House of Lords held that it was a breach of Article 6 to rely on closed material in a terror suspect hearing to justify the decision to make a control order. The controlled person had to be given sufficient information about the case against them to enable them to give effective instructions to the special advocate representing them.

2.6.7.2 The right to have adequate time and facilities to prepare the defence

A defendant must also be given adequate time and facilities for the preparation of their defence. A defendant may, for example, require time to contact witnesses who may assist their defence or to obtain documents relevant to their defence.

2.6.7.3 The right to defend themselves or have legal representation

A further right that the defendant has is to defend themselves in person or with legal assistance. If a defendant is unable to pay for that assistance, it should be provided free of charge when the interests of justice so require.

2.6.7.4 The right to call and cross-examine witnesses

In a criminal trial, evidence will be called. This may be in the form of documents or other exhibits, but usually the evidence comes from witnesses who give oral evidence. A defendant has the right to have examined witnesses against them and to obtain the attendance and examination of witnesses on their own behalf.

There are circumstances when a defendant may be unable to cross-examine a witness if, for example, that witness has died or is overseas. In such cases, the written statement of the absent witness may be read out to the court. This will not breach Article 6, although the judge will direct the jury to treat such evidence with caution as it cannot be tested by the defendant. Occasionally, the identity of a witness may be withheld by the prosecution. This might, for example, occur in a case involving matters of national security. The giving of evidence in this way will not breach Article 6, but again the trial judge must give appropriate directions to the jury.

2.6.7.5 The right to have the free assistance of an interpreter if required

The final right set out in Article 6(3) requires the court to ensure that an interpreter is available if a defendant is unable to understand the language of the court.

2.7 Articles 5 and 6 and domestic legislation

Having looked at Articles 5 and 6 of the ECHR, which relate to freedom of the person and the right to a fair trial, we now want you to consider UK law and the extent to which it interacts with these rights.

Remember that Article 5 is limited and contains certain express exceptions. For example, Article 5(1)(c) permits an individual to be deprived of their liberty where they are being lawfully arrested on reasonable suspicion of committing a criminal offence, or where it is necessary to prevent them committing an offence or fleeing after having done so.

In relation to arrest and detention, Article 5 requires:

(a) breach, or reasonable suspicion of breach, of some known law (Article 5(1)(a) and (c));

(b) the giving of reasons for arrest and charge (Article 5(2));

(c) the detainee to be brought promptly before a court and have any trial within a reasonable time (Article 5(3)). In *Brogan v UK* (1989) 11 EHRR 117, the four applicants had been arrested and detained for between four days and six hours and six days and 16½ hours without charge or being brought before a court. The ECtHR stated that detention for these periods without being brought before a judge breached Article 5(3);

(d) the availability of judicial review of the legality of detention (Article 5(4));

(e) the right to compensation for breach of Article 5 (Article 5(5)).

2.7.1 Police and Criminal Evidence Act 1984

2.7.1.1 Arrest

An example of UK legislation which falls under Article 5(1)(c) is the Police and Criminal Evidence Act 1984 (PACE). Section 24 of PACE (as amended by the Serious Organised Crime and Police Act 2005) provides that an arrest may be made in relation to 'any offence'. These powers are exercisable where a police officer has 'reasonable grounds' to believe that an arrest is necessary for one of the reasons specified in s 24(5). Section 28 of PACE requires the police to tell the arrested person that they are under arrest and the reasons for the arrest as soon as practicable. These provisions therefore reflect the requirements of Article 5(1)(c) and 5(2) respectively.

2.7.1.2 Rights of arrested person

An arrested person has various rights while they are detained. These include the right to have someone informed (PACE, s 56) and the right of access to legal advice (PACE, s 58). Both rights can be delayed for up to 36 hours in limited circumstances, for example where arrest is for an indictable offence and the police have reasonable grounds for believing that exercise of the right will lead to interference with evidence.

2.7.1.3 Detention

PACE also gives the police certain powers to detain an arrested person after arrest. The arrested person must normally be taken to the police station as soon as practicable where they will be brought before the custody officer. The custody officer may authorise detention of the arrested person if there is insufficient evidence to charge them, and detention is necessary either to secure or preserve evidence relating to the offence for which the person has been arrested, or to obtain such evidence by questioning (s 37). An arrestee can, therefore, be detained for samples to be taken or while premises are searched, although the most common ground for detention is to question them.

The initial period of detention is 24 hours (PACE, s 41). Extended detention can be authorised by a police officer of at least the rank of superintendent where they have reasonable grounds to believe that:

(a) the offence the person has been arrested for is an indictable offence, ie a serious crime triable by jury;

(b) the detention of that person without charge is necessary to secure or preserve evidence relating to an offence for which they are under arrest or to obtain such evidence by questioning them; and

(c) the investigation is being conducted diligently and expeditiously.

The officer may then authorise detention for up to 36 hours (PACE, s 42). If the police wish to detain the arrested person for more than 36 hours, they must apply to the magistrates' court for a warrant of further detention. The magistrates may grant a warrant of up to 36 hours' further detention. The police can then apply for further warrants from the magistrates, but the overall period of detention must not exceed 96 hours in total (PACE, ss 43–44).

2.7.1.4 Use of force

Section 117 of PACE provides that when exercising any of their powers under PACE, the police may use reasonable force where this is necessary.

The following two-part activity should help you to understand the significance of the powers contained in PACE and the extent to which they preserve an individual's rights under the Convention.

ACTIVITY 3 PACE

PART 1

Albert is arrested on suspicion of theft of computers. He is taken to Weyford police station and placed in a cell for three days without being charged.

Consider the lawfulness of the police action in this case. What legal remedies are available in respect of any unlawful acts done by them?

COMMENT

The police appear to have breached Albert's Article 5 rights.

PACE allows certain limitations on Albert's Article 5 rights, but these do not extend to keeping him locked up for three days without authorisation by the court. No mention is made of whether Albert was brought before a custody officer or the basis on which detention was authorised. In this case, Albert seems merely to have been thrown in a cell and forgotten. This would be unlawful.

Albert could therefore bring an action against the police under the HRA 1998. He is a 'victim' for the purposes of s 7 of that Act, but the court will award damages for breach of Article 5 only where it is just and appropriate to do so. In these circumstances, it would be easier for Albert to bring an ordinary civil claim for damages against the police based on the tort of false imprisonment.

PART 2

Now assume that on the fourth day of keeping Albert locked in a cell, the police interview him and tell him, 'If you confess to stealing the computers, you can go home.' Albert, who is by now suffering from severe anxiety, admits to stealing the computers. He is immediately charged with theft.

If the police prosecute Albert for theft, do you think that the courts should use their power to exclude the confession evidence at Albert's subsequent trial?

COMMENT

Article 6 of the ECHR is relevant because it guarantees a fair trial. However, in *Khan v UK* [2000] ECHR 35394/97, the ECtHR held that breach of rights protected under the Convention did not necessarily mean that evidence obtained as a result of the breach should be excluded under Article 6.

Under s 76 of PACE, however, a criminal court must exclude evidence in the form of a confession by the accused if it has been obtained by oppression, or as a result of something said or done which is likely to render it unreliable. The length of detention and suggestion that Albert can go home if he confesses appear to be things 'said or done' which are likely to make Albert's confession unreliable. In addition, under s 78, the court has a discretion to exclude any evidence in order to ensure a fair trial.

2.8 Retrospective crimes

Article 7 of the ECHR provides that a person cannot be charged with a criminal offence for conduct that was not a crime when they committed it. This means that the state must clearly define what constitutes a criminal offence so that people know when they are breaking the law. It is also a violation of Article 7 for the courts to impose a heavier penalty than was applicable at the time the offence was committed.

In *SW v United Kingdom; CR v United Kingdom* (1996) 21 EHRR 363, the applicants had been convicted of raping their wives. They complained that they had been made retrospectively criminally liable for rape within marriage, since at the time they committed their offences, an exception in the criminal law for intercourse in marriage still existed. Accordingly, they claimed that their actions were not criminal at the time they had been committed, and so there was a violation of Article 7. The ECtHR rejected the argument, as Article 7 did not preclude the gradual clarification of the principles of criminal liability on a case-by-case basis provided the development is consistent with the essence of the offence and could reasonably be foreseen.

Article 7(2) of the ECHR contains an exception, which is that people can still be prosecuted retrospectively for conduct that was 'criminal according to the general principles of law recognised by civilised nations', even if the conduct was not criminal at the time it was carried out. This was included to ensure that, after World War II, Article 7(1) did not prevent individuals from being prosecuted for war crimes that did not constitute criminal offences in Nazi Germany and other relevant states at the time of their commission.

2.9 Article 12 – the right to marry

Article 12 protects the right of men and women of marriageable age to marry and to start a family.

2.9.1 Scope

The ECtHR ruled in 2002 that the right extends to transsexual people (*Goodwin v United Kingdom* (2002) 35 EHRR 18). The ECtHR has, however, confirmed that, despite a number of states now recognising same-sex marriage, Article 12 does not currently require the state to do so (*Oliari v Italy* (2017) 65 EHRR 26).

2.9.2 Restrictions to this right

The right to marry is subject to national laws on marriage, including those that make marriage illegal between certain types of people (for example, close relatives).

Although the Government is able to restrict the right to marry, any restrictions must not be arbitrary and must not interfere with the essential principle of the right. Thus, the ECtHR held in *B v United Kingdom* (2006) 42 EHRR 11 that, in prohibiting the marriage of a father-in-law to a daughter-in-law, the Marriage Act 1949 violated Article 12. The Marriage Act was accordingly amended.

2.10 Article 3 of Protocol 1 – the right to free elections

Article 3 of Protocol 1 requires states to hold free elections at reasonable intervals by way of secret ballot.

The right to free elections is absolute, so it cannot be restricted in any way. However, governments have a wide margin of appreciation and can decide what kind of electoral system to adopt – such as 'first past the post', as in UK general elections, or proportional representation.

Prisoners serving a custodial sentence in the UK do not have the right to vote. The ECtHR ruled in *Hirst v UK (No 2)* (2006) 42 EHRR 41 that a blanket ban on all serving prisoners was not compatible with Article 3 of Protocol 1. Eventually, the UK Government agreed to allow prisoners who are released on temporary licence or on home detention curfew to vote (this did not require a change in legislation). The Council of Europe in December 2018 accepted that this was sufficient to comply with the ECtHR's judgment.

2.11 Article 1 of Protocol 13 – abolition of the death penalty

This provides that the death penalty shall be abolished. This includes crimes committed during a war or when the threat of war is imminent. The UK ratified this Protocol in 2003 and it came into force in 2004.

Summary

- The right to life under Article 2 is absolute but the use of force which results in death is permitted in certain circumstances where the force used is no more than is absolutely necessary.
- The prohibition on torture, inhuman or degrading treatment or punishment under Article 3 is absolute. The terms 'torture', 'inhuman treatment' and 'degrading treatment' have been defined in case law.
- The prohibition on slavery and forced labour is absolute and what is meant by these terms has been clarified by the ECtHR.
- Articles 2–4 impose positive obligations on the state to pass and enforce laws to prevent their breach and imply a procedural duty on the state to investigate alleged breaches.
- The right to liberty under Article 5 is a limited right and can be restricted in certain circumstances, for example the lawful arrest of someone reasonably suspected of having committed a criminal offence.
- Article 6 provides the right to a fair trial. This applies to both civil rights and criminal charges, but there are greater protections provided to those charged with a criminal offence.

Figure 2.1 Breach of absolute/limited rights

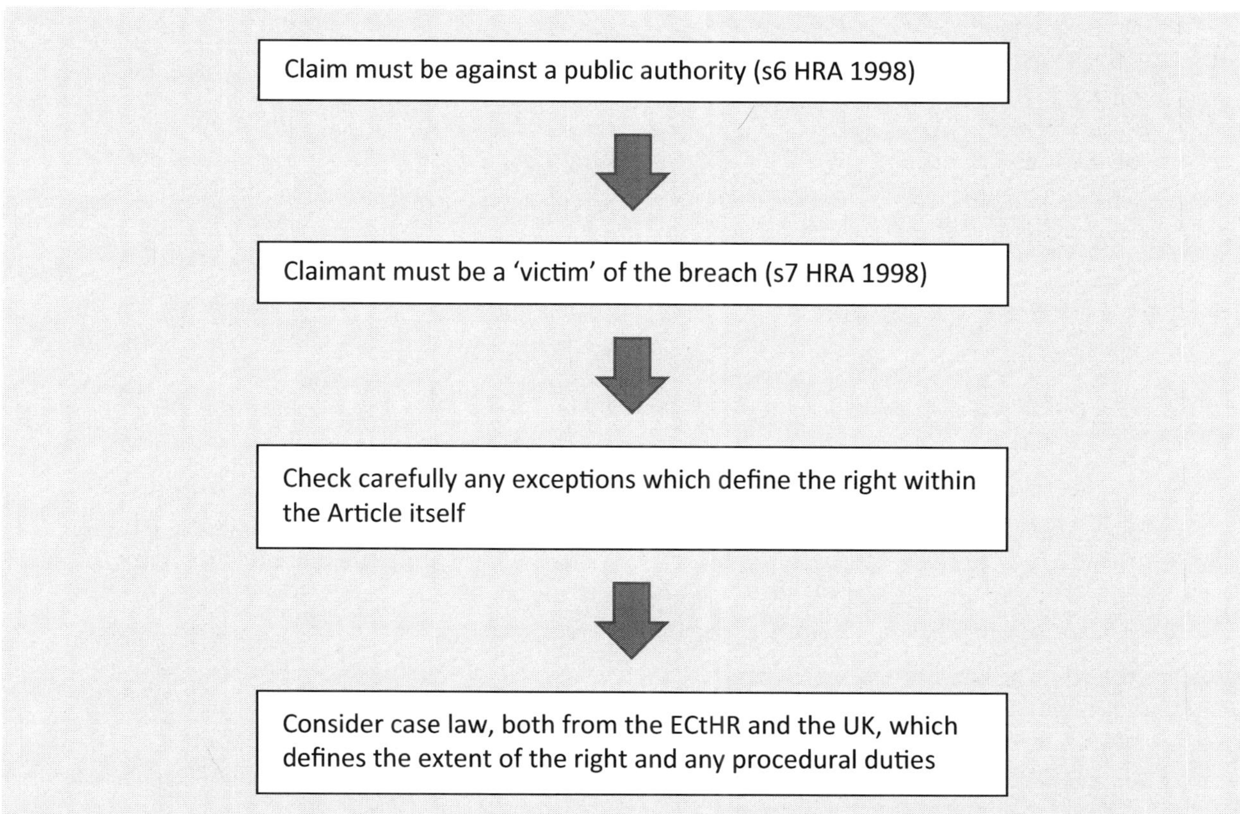

3 Qualified Rights

Learning outcomes

When you have completed this chapter, you should be able to:

- explain the proportionality test and analyse its application to different qualified rights;
- understand the scope of Article 8, the right to respect for private and family life, and analyse its application in different contexts;
- identify the two limbs of Article 9, freedom of thought, conscience and religion, and explain the restrictions on that right;
- appreciate the scope of Article 10, freedom of expression, and how it is interlinked with Article 11, which provides for freedom of assembly and association.

3.1 Introduction

We are now going to move on to consider some of the qualified rights under the European Convention on Human Rights (ECHR) in more detail. As we have already seen, these qualified rights have much wider, explicit limitations written into them (see **1.5.2**). A government can only lawfully interfere with a qualified right if the interference is prescribed by law, has a legitimate aim and is necessary in a democratic society. You will now consider the 'proportionality test' in more detail, which is the test the courts apply when deciding whether interference with a qualified right is 'necessary in a democratic society'.

3.2 The proportionality test

The 'proportionality test' is used by the courts when breach of a qualified Convention right is being relied on. The doctrine of proportionality ensures that there is a fair balance between pursuing a legitimate aim and the protection of Convention rights. The test was originally set out in the case of *R (on the application of Daly) v Secretary of State for the Home Department* [2001] UKHL 26. It was then built on in *Huang v Secretary of State for the Home Department* [2007] UKHL 11. The two tests were combined in the case of *Bank Mellat v HM Treasury (No 2)* [2013] UKSC 39. In the *Bank Mellat* case, the Supreme Court set out the following four-part test:

(i) whether the objective of the measure complained of is sufficiently important to justify the limitation of a fundamental right;

(ii) whether the measure is rationally connected to the objective;

(iii) whether a less intrusive measure could have been used; and

(iv) whether, having regard to these matters and to the severity of the consequences, a fair balance has been struck between the rights of the individual and the interests of the community.

The case of *R (on the application of Swami Suryananda) v Welsh Ministers* [2007] EWCA Civ 893 shows how this test works in practice. Following the increased incidence of bovine tuberculosis amongst cattle, the Welsh Government adopted a policy of slaughtering all cattle testing positive to reduce the spread of the disease. A Hindu community's temple bullock tested positive. Its slaughter would have been a particularly sacrilegious act to the community, so they sought to have it excepted from the policy of automatic slaughter, suggesting instead a regime of isolation and testing. The ministers entered into a dialogue with the community and took account of expert evidence before making the decision to slaughter the bullock.

The community applied for judicial review of the decision but, after success at first instance, lost in the Court of Appeal, which approached the case in the following way.

The Court asked if the slaughter of the bullock engaged the rights of the Hindu community under Article 9. The Court accepted that this was the case because the slaughter of the bullock was a violation of the community's religious beliefs.

The Court of Appeal then applied the test set out in Article 9(2).

First, the slaughter of the bullock had to be prescribed by law. This requirement was satisfied because the ministers were using powers given to them in the Animal Health Act 1981.

Secondly, the slaughter of the bullock had to be in pursuit of a legitimate aim. One of the legitimate aims contained in Article 9(2) is the protection of health. As the slaughter of the bullock was intended to prevent the spread of bovine tuberculosis, this requirement was met. The Court also said that another legitimate aim - the economic well-being of the country - was also relevant as the spread of bovine tuberculosis was having a devastating effect upon the rural economy in Wales.

Finally, the Court of Appeal considered whether the decision to slaughter the bullock was proportionate. The Court said that it was. Stopping the spread of bovine tuberculosis in Wales was an objective that was sufficiently important to limit the rights of the Hindu community. As the temple bullock had tested positive for this disease, its slaughter was a rational way to stop the spread of the disease. The Welsh ministers had considered alternatives, such as quarantining the animal, but had obtained expert evidence to suggest that this would not prevent the spread of this highly contagious disease. The Court found ultimately that an appropriate balance had been struck between the rights of the Hindu community and the rights of the wider Welsh community - whilst the slaughter of the bullock was a significant interference with the community's religious beliefs, it was justified given the catastrophic consequences the disease could have if it were not controlled.

3.3 Article 8 - right to respect for private and family life

3.3.1 Introduction

Article 8 provides:

1. Everyone has the right to respect for his private and family life, his home and his correspondence.
2. There shall be no interference by a public authority with the exercise of this right except such as is in accordance with the law and is necessary in a democratic society in the interests of national security, public safety or the economic well-being of the

country, for the prevention of disorder or crime, for the protection of health or morals, or for the protection of the rights and freedoms of others.'

Article 8 guarantees respect for four things: a person's private life, family life, home, and correspondence.

3.3.2 Private life

A lot of issues have been held to come within the scope of a person's private life, including:

(a) bodily integrity (eg being forced to have medical treatment);

(b) personal autonomy (the right to make decisions about how you live your life);

(c) sexuality;

(d) personal information (its holding, use or disclosure).

In *Peck v United Kingdom* (2003) 36 EHRR 41. Mr Peck (P) was standing in the street, attempting suicide by cutting his wrists. He was captured on CCTV, and, although the CCTV images did not show the attempted suicide, they clearly identified P brandishing a knife in a public place. The police attended the scene. P was not charged with any criminal offence, but the CCTV images were later used in a campaign by the authorities to reflect the effectiveness of CCTV in combatting crime. There was no attempt to mask P's identity. P complained to the relevant media commissions about the disclosure and unsuccessfully sought judicial review.

The ECtHR found that the disclosure by the local council of the relevant footage constituted serious interference with P's right to respect for his private life. Although disclosure pursued the legitimate aim of prevention of disorder or crime, it was disproportionate as no attempt was made to conceal P's identity or obtain his consent. The Court acknowledged that P was in a public street when he was filmed, but it stated that 'he was not there for the purpose of participating in any public event and he was not a public figure'.

3.3.2.1 Fingerprints and DNA

In the case of *S and Marper v the United Kingdom* (2009) 48 EHRR 50, the ECtHR held that the retention of fingerprints and DNA, as permitted by certain of the UK's statutory provisions, clearly both invoked Article 8 and breached the applicants' rights under that article. The relevant statutory provisions were contained in PACE as amended by the Criminal Justice and Police Act 2001. They provided for the retention of fingerprints and DNA samples obtained as a result of being investigated, including where the person is subsequently acquitted of the offence being investigated or the proceedings against them are discontinued (prior to the amendment to PACE, such samples had to be destroyed following either the acquittal of the accused or the decision being taken to discontinue proceedings). The ECtHR concluded that the retention 'constitutes a disproportionate interference with the applicants' right to respect for private life and cannot be regarded as necessary in a democratic society'.

This is a significant decision, because it is in contrast to the previous decision made when the case came before the House of Lords. The House of Lords held by majority (Baroness Hale dissenting) that Article 8(1) was not engaged and held unanimously that the retention was justified under Article 8(2).

The Supreme Court in *R (on the application of GC) v The Commissioner of the Police of the Metropolis* [2011] UKSC 21 considered the retention of fingerprints and DNA. The Supreme Court followed the finding of the ECtHR in *Marper* and ruled that a blanket policy of retaining biometric data was not compatible with Article 8. However, no action was taken by the Court, which acknowledged that legislation was before Parliament that would deal with the issue.

This legislation became the Protection of Freedoms Act 2012 (the first proposed law to be opened to public comments via the Internet), which includes provisions requiring the deletion of some DNA profiles from the DNA database.

3.3.2.2 Photographs and other images

In *Wood v Metropolitan Police Commissioner* [2009] EWCA Civ 414, the Court of Appeal held that the decision by police officers to retain photographs of an arms trade protestor involved in a peaceful protest breached his right to privacy under Article 8. The Court said that this case could be distinguished from *Marper* (see **3.3.2.1**) on the facts, because there is a qualitative difference between photographic images and fingerprints and DNA, not least in relation to the types of uses to which they might be put. In *Wood* the court decided that although the police were justified in taking the photographs to pursue the legitimate aims of the prevention of disorder or crime and the protection of the rights and freedoms of others, their retention was not proportionate. Lord Collins said: 'Nevertheless, it is plain that the last word has yet to be said on the implications for civil liberties of the taking and retention of images in the modern surveillance society.'

Lord Collins' comment has been borne out in *Bridges v Chief Constable South Wales* [2020] EWCA Civ 1058 which involved a challenge to the use of facial recognition technology ('AFR') by the police in a trial. The claimant, a civil liberties campaigner, asserted that he had been subjected to the use of AFR on two occasions and that this breached his rights under Article 8. The Court of Appeal found that the use of AFR was not in accordance with the law as the relevant policy and Codes of Practice did not sufficiently set out the terms upon which discretionary powers could be exercised by the police.

In *Glukhin v Russia* (2024) 78 EHRR 6, the ECtHR found that use of facial recognition technology on the underground to identify a participant in a peaceful protest was in breach of Article 8. The taking and use of such images was very intrusive and required a high level of justification to be lawful.

3.3.2.3 Vaccination

In *Allette v Scarsdale Grange Nursing Home Ltd* [2022] 1 WLUK 233, a care assistant claimed that she was unfairly dismissed from her job when she refused to have a vaccination against Covid-19. The Employment Tribunal stated that her employer's instruction that all staff must be vaccinated unless they had a reasonable excuse not to be engaged Article 8. The instruction had the legitimate aim of protecting the health and safety of residents, staff and visitors. It was also proportionate on the basis that the claimant's refusal to have the vaccine was unreasonable and the risk posed in the circumstances if she remained unvaccinated.

3.3.3 Family life

Family life covers one's relationship with one's close family and includes a couple who are not married but who live in a stable relationship. *Fedotova v Russia* [2021] ECHR 40792/10 involved a same-sex couple who claimed that lack of formal recognition of their relationship breached Article 8. The Court confirmed that to comply with their positive obligations under Article 8 of the ECHR, member States are required to provide a legal framework allowing same-sex couples to be granted adequate recognition and protection of their relationship. The margin of appreciation was narrow due to the importance of the issue and the fact that there was a clear trend amongst member States towards legal recognition. However, there was a more extensive margin of appreciation when determining the exact nature of the legal regime to be made available to same-sex couples, which does not necessarily have to take the form of marriage..

3.3.4 Home

This means the right to respect for one's home and where one currently lives.

3.3.5 Correspondence

This covers private communications and includes phone calls, letters, emails and internet usage.

In recent years, the ECtHR has been called upon to grapple with the correct balance to be drawn between privacy of individuals' online communications and the need for the state to protect national security and prevent crime. In *Big Brother Watch v UK* (2022) 74 EHRR 17, the ECtHR stated that bulk interception of electronic communications by the intelligence services did not of itself breach Article 8, provided that sufficient safeguards were provided at each stage of the process. The UK's processes under the Regulation of Investigatory Powers Act 2000 did not contain sufficient safeguards to prevent abuse and therefore violated Article 8. The Regulation of Investigatory Powers Act 2000 has since been replaced by the Investigatory Powers Act 2016.

Podchasov v Russia (App No 33696/19) concerned the social media and messaging app Telegram. Under Russian law, Telegram was required to store all communications data for one year and the contents of all communications for six months. In addition, it was required to disclose this data to law enforcement authorities or security services, when requested, together with information necessary to decrypt any encrypted messages. Telegram refused on the basis that the messages were protected by end-to-end encryption and messages from individuals could not be decrypted. Decryption would affect all users. The ECtHR found that there were insufficient safeguards in the storage and disclosure regime to protect against arbitrariness and the risk of abuse. In particular, although the Court accepted that the state may have legitimate aims for decrypting some messages, as this would involve weakening the encryption measures for all users, it was not proportionate to the aims pursued. Thus Article 8 was breached.

3.3.6 Environmental rights

Whilst the ECHR does not provide directly for environmental rights, the ECtHR has given these indirectly where the environment has a direct effect on Article 8 rights, such as to the right to a person's home. Thus, in *López Ostra v Spain* [1994] ECHR 16798/90, the ECtHR found a breach of Article 8 due to smells, noise and polluting fumes emanating from a waste treatment plant a few metres from the applicant's home. In the breakthrough case of *Verein KlimaSeniorinnen Schweiz and Others v Switzerland* (App No 53600/20) [2024] ECHR 53600/20 ('VKS'), the applicants argued that the Swiss authorities were not taking adequate measures to mitigate the effects of climate change in violation of Convention rights. The ECtHR held that there had been a violation of Article 8 as it encompassed a right for individuals to effective protection by State authorities from serious adverse effects of climate change on their life, health, well-being, and quality of life. While the ECtHR recognised that national authorities enjoy wide discretion regarding the choice of means to pursue objectives, the Swiss authorities had breached their obligations as they had failed to establish a domestic regulatory framework for limiting greenhouse gas emissions and had previously missed emission reduction targets.

Within the UK, the case of *R (on the application of Friends of the Earth and others) v Secretary of State for Environment, Food and Rural Affairs* [2024] EWHC 2707 (Admin) involved a challenge to the legality of the government's National Adaptation Programme on the basis that, amongst other things, it breached the applicant's Article 8 rights. One of the applicants lived in an area subject to coastal erosion, another in a care home. Both argued that the government's plans failed to include sufficient measures to protect them from the effects of climate change. The court, when referring to the VKS case, drew a distinction between measures for mitigating climate change (which was the issue in VKS) and measures for adapting to climate change, which the current case involved. It stated that in VKS it was likely that the ECtHR afforded states only a narrow margin of appreciation in the context of mitigation since:

(a) this was covered by international agreements, and

(b) any default by one state would impact other states.

By contrast, neither of these features applied to adaptation measures, and the state should therefore be afforded a wide margin of appreciation in this area. Consequently, the government was not in breach of the applicants' Article 8 rights.

3.3.7 A qualified right

As we have already discussed, Article 8 is a qualified right, and therefore interference with it can be justified provided such interference is in accordance with the law, in pursuit of a legitimate aim and necessary in a democratic society.

ACTIVITY 1 Article 8

Please read Article 8(1) and 8(2) (see **3.3.1**). Which of the legitimate aims specified in Article 8(2) of the Convention would be relevant in the following cases?

1. A court lifts an injunction and allows publication of a newspaper article about the police investigation into the financial affairs of a prominent politician suspected of fraud.
2. The police use their powers under the PACE 1984 to stop someone on the street and search his pockets.
3. The police raid a brothel and arrest the occupants.
4. The Government decides to build an incinerator for disposing of household waste on the outskirts of a housing estate.

COMMENT

1. The protection of the rights and freedoms of others (in this case, the newspaper's Article 10 rights).
2. The interests of national security or public safety, or the prevention of disorder or crime.
3. The protection of health or morals.
4. The economic well-being of the country.

3.3.8 Article 8 and deportation, removal and extradition

You have seen earlier in **Chapter 2** that the provisions of the ECHR have had a significant impact in cases where the Government seeks to deport, remove or extradite an individual from the United Kingdom. Deportation, extradition and removal cases may also engage Article 8, particularly the right to respect for family life.

3.3.8.1 Consequences to health

Some cases concern the conditions an individual will face in the country to which they are being sent. In *R (Razgar) v Secretary of State for the Home Department* [2004] UKHL 27, Razgar was a failed asylum seeker who was due to be removed back to Germany – from where he had come to the UK – or Iraq, his country of origin. Razgar was receiving psychiatric treatment for depression and post-traumatic stress disorder arising from his alleged ill treatment in Iraq, and his fear of ill treatment in Germany. He argued that the foreseeable consequences for his mental health were he to be removed from the UK would engage his rights under Article 8, and that his removal could not be justified under Article 8(2).

Although Razgar's particular claim was dismissed, the House of Lords held that Article 8 could be engaged where the main issue was not the severance of the family and social ties that the applicant had enjoyed in the expelling country, but was rather the consequence for their mental or physical health of removal to the receiving country. Their Lordships did, however, say that the threshold for establishing this was high, and it would require an applicant to show that the violation of their rights would be flagrant. This would need to be something very much more extreme than showing that healthcare standards in the receiving country were not as good as those in the expelling country.

3.3.8.2 Family ties

The much more usual situation in which those required to leave the UK raise arguments under Article 8 is when an individual argues that their deportation, removal or extradition will disproportionately damage family ties and relationships that they have established while in the UK.

This was considered by the European Court of Human Rights in *Uner v The Netherlands* (2007) 45 EHRR 14. Uner was born in Turkey but had moved to the Netherlands with his mother and two brothers in 1981 when he was 12 years old. In 1988 he obtained a permanent residence permit. In 1991, Uner entered into a relationship with a Dutch national. They started living together shortly afterwards and had a son in 1992. They lived together for some 16 months before Uner moved out. In 1994, Uner was convicted of manslaughter and assault. He had two previous convictions in the Netherlands for violent offences. He was sentenced to seven years' imprisonment.

Uner continued to see his partner while he was in prison and a second child was born to the couple in 1996. In 1997, Uner's permanent residence permit was withdrawn and a 10-year exclusion order imposed on him in view of his conviction and sentence. This meant that he could not live in the Netherlands for a 10-year period.

The Dutch authorities considered that the general interest in ensuring public safety outweighed Uner's interest in being able to continue his family life in the Netherlands. Uner argued that the authorities had violated his rights under Article 8 by failing to strike a fair balance between those competing interests.

The ECtHR held that the deportation, removal or extradition of an individual could engage the right to respect for their family life under Article 8(1), and, if it did, there were several factors that the court needed to apply to determine if that deportation, removal or extradition was proportionate. These were:

(1) the length of time the individual has been in the country;

(2) the seriousness of the offences that the individual has committed. In *Unuane v UK* (2021) 72 EHRR 24 the ECtHR made it clear that the seriousness of the crime included both the length of the sentence and the nature and circumstances of the crime or crimes and their impact on society. Thus crimes of violence and drugs-related offences were at the most serious end of the spectrum. However, the fact that the offence committed was at the more serious end of the spectrum was not determinative of the case. It was just one factor which needed to be weighed in the balance with the others in *Uner*. When considering the length of the sentence, the Court of Appeal in *Gadinala v Secretary of State for the Home Department* [2024] EWCA Civ 1410 stated that the court should take into account factors such as credit for a guilty plea and a discount to reflect the criminal's age. These may have reduced the length of the sentence but would not reduce the seriousness of the offence;

(3) the time elapsed since the offence was committed and the individual's conduct during that period;

(4) details of the particular family circumstances of the individual, such as their nationalities or the length of any relationship and whether the partner knew of the offence when they entered the relationship;

(5) the ages of and interests of the children;

(6) the seriousness of the difficulties that the family may experience in the receiving country; and

(7) the nature of the ties that the individual has with both the expelling and the receiving country.

In Uner's case, the Court found that there had been no violation of Article 8. Whilst Uner had strong ties to the Netherlands, he had only lived with his partner and first-born son for a short period. He had then put an end to the cohabitation and had never lived with the second child. Whilst Uner had arrived in the Netherlands at a young age, he still had social and cultural ties with Turkey. The offences of manslaughter and assault committed by Uner were of a very serious nature. Taking his previous convictions into account, Uner had criminal propensities. Also, Uner's children were still very young and thus of an adaptable age. The Court said that given the nature and seriousness of Uner's offences, the Netherlands had struck a fair balance between its own interests and those of Uner.

The UK case of *Norris v Government of USA (No 2)* [2010] UKSC 9 concerned extradition of a British national on charges of obstruction of justice. The Supreme Court emphasised that only where some quite exceptionally compelling feature, or combination of features, is present will interference with family life consequent upon extradition be disproportionate to the objective that extradition serves. The public interest in giving effect to a request for extradition will always be a powerful consideration to which great weight must be attached.

In *H(H) v Deputy Prosecutor of the Italian Republic, Genoa* [2012] UKSC 25 (a case also involving extradition) the Court stated that a lengthy delay since the crimes were committed may reduce the weight to be attached to the public interest and increase the impact upon family life. However, it agreed with *Norris* that the public interest in extradition will outweigh the Article 8 rights of the family unless the consequences of the interference on family life would be exceptionally severe.

3.3.9 Scope of Article 8

The case of *R (on the application of Countryside Alliance and Others) v Attorney General and Another* [2007] UKHL 52 illustrates the limits on the scope of Article 8. This concerned the prohibition by the Hunting Act 2004 of the hunting with dogs of certain wild mammals. The Countryside Alliance and other individuals argued that the ban infringed a number of their rights under the Human Rights Act (HRA) 1998, including Article 8. They argued that Article 8 was invoked because they were prevented by the 2004 Act from using or allowing others to use their land for hunting purposes, and the decline in hunting activities was likely to jeopardise their homes and livelihood.

The House of Lords held that Article 8 was not engaged because even if the feared consequences of the ban arose, they would not be caused by a lack of respect for the appellants' private or family lives or for their homes. The appellants' submissions were based on an over-wide definition of the scope of Article 8. Lord Bingham stated that:

> Fox-hunting is a very public activity, carried on in daylight with considerable colour and noise, often attracting the attention of onlookers attracted by the spectacle. No analogy can be drawn with the very personal and private concerns at issue in ... *Pretty*, ... nor with the disclosure in *Peck* of closed circuit television pictures of the complainant preparing to commit suicide. It is not of course to be expected that there will be a decided case based on facts indistinguishable from those of the case in issue, but none of the decided cases is at all close. With their references to notions of privacy, personal autonomy and choice and the private sphere reserved to the individual, they are in my opinion so remote from the present case as to give no guidance helpful to the claimants.

It was held in *Author of a Blog v Times Newspapers Ltd* [2009] EWHC 1358 (QB) that the information on an Internet blog does not have the necessary quality of confidence, nor does it qualify as information in respect of which the blogger has a reasonable expectation of privacy under Article 8, essentially because blogging is a public activity.

3.4 Article 9 – freedom of thought, conscience and religion

3.4.1 Introduction

Article 9 provides:

1. Everyone has the right to freedom of thought, conscience and religion; this right includes freedom to change his religion or belief and freedom, either alone or in community with others and in public or private, to manifest his religion or belief, in worship, teaching, practice and observance.
2. Freedom to manifest one's religion or beliefs shall be subject only to such limitations as are prescribed by law and are necessary in a democratic society in the interests of public safety, for the protection of public order, health or morals, or for the protection of the rights and freedoms of others.

So far as freedom of thought, conscience and religion are concerned, Article 9 is an absolute right. As can be seen, Article 9 does not cover religious belief alone but is wider than this. In *Kokkinakis v Greece* (1994) 17 EHRR 397 the court made clear that freedom of thought, conscience and religion is one of the foundations of a democratic society and stated that, 'It is, in its religious dimension, one of the most vital elements that go to make up the identity of believers and of their conception of life, but it is also a precious asset for atheists, agnostics, sceptics and the unconcerned.'

However, the right to manifest a religion or belief is qualified and may therefore be subject to restrictions which are prescribed by law, in pursuit of a legitimate aim and proportionate. In *Williamson v Education Secretary* [2005] UKHL 15 parents sent their children to independent private schools which had a policy of corporal punishment, to which the parents consented. They regarded the use of 'loving corporal correction' in the upbringing of children as an essential element of their Christian faith. Corporal punishment in schools was banned by legislation. The claimants, parents and teachers at the schools asserted that this legislation breached their rights under Article 9. The House of Lords stated that the school policy of using corporal punishment was a manifestation of the parents' beliefs which could be interfered with provided that such interference was prescribed by law, in pursuit of a legitimate aim and proportionate. Here, the interference was clearly prescribed by law and the legitimate aim was to protect the rights of others – the rights of the children to be protected from the deliberate infliction of physical violence upon them. The legislation was not disproportionate as Parliament was entitled to decide that it was in the best interests of children as a whole for there to be a universal ban on corporal punishment in schools.

3.4.2 Restrictions

An issue that has arisen in recent years is the extent to which individuals may be prevented from manifesting their religious beliefs either through not being permitted to wear particular items of clothing or by being required to carry out certain tasks. This has arisen in the context of what an individual may not wear or may be required to do at work, and the restrictions that a school may impose on items of clothing worn by its pupils.

3.4.2.1 The workplace

The leading case on restrictions that may lawfully be imposed in the workplace is *Eweida and others v United Kingdom* (2013) 57 EHRR 8. In this case, four separate applicants argued that their respective employers had either imposed restrictions on dress or dismissed them in violation of their rights under Article 9. They had been unsuccessful before the domestic UK courts.

(a) Eweida had been employed by British Airways. She wanted to wear a cross as a sign of her commitment to the Christian faith. Between September 2006 and February 2007, she was not allowed to remain in her post whilst visibly wearing the cross.

(b) Chaplin was a Christian who had worn a cross since 1971. She had been employed as a nurse by an NHS trust. Her employer's uniform policy prohibited the wearing of necklaces to reduce the risk of injury when handling patients. When she refused to remove the cross and chain she was wearing, she was moved to a non-nursing post, which shortly thereafter ceased to exist.

(c) Lavelle had been employed by a local authority as a registrar of births, deaths and marriages. She was a Christian and believed that same-sex civil partnerships were contrary to God's law. She refused to be designated as a registrar of civil partnerships, which resulted in disciplinary proceedings and the loss of her job.

(d) MacFarlane, a Christian, had been employed by Relate – a marriage guidance organisation – which had a policy of requiring staff to provide services equally to heterosexual and homosexual couples. He refused to commit himself to providing psychosexual counselling to same-sex couples, which resulted in disciplinary proceedings being brought against him.

The ECtHR considered each application in turn:

(a) Eweida – the Court found that a fair balance had not been struck. On one side of the argument was Eweida's desire to manifest her religious belief. On the other was the employer's wish to project a certain corporate image. Whilst the Court accepted that this aim was legitimate, it said that the domestic courts had accorded it too much weight. Eweida's cross was discreet and could not have detracted from her professional appearance, and there was no evidence that the wearing of other, previously authorised, items of religious clothing by other employees had had any negative impact on British Airways' brand or image. The Court found that the domestic authorities had failed sufficiently to protect Eweida's right to manifest her religion, in breach of their positive obligation under Article 9.

(b) Chaplin – the Court found that the reason for asking Chaplin to remove her cross – namely the protection of health and safety on a hospital ward – was much more important than the reason given to Eweida. The Court also said that hospital managers were better placed to make decisions about clinical safety than a court. The measures were therefore not disproportionate. It followed that the relevant interference with her freedom to manifest her religion was necessary in a democratic society and that there had been no breach of Article 9.

(c) Lavelle – the Court accepted that, given the strength of Lavelle's religious conviction, she considered that she had no choice but to face disciplinary action and ultimately lose her job, rather than be designated a civil partnership registrar. On the other hand, the local authority's policy aimed to secure the rights of others, which were also protected under the Convention. The Court said that national authorities should be given a wide margin of appreciation when it came to striking a balance between competing Convention rights. Therefore, the local authority that brought the disciplinary proceedings and the domestic courts that had rejected Lavelle's claim had not violated Article 9.

(d) MacFarlane – the Court accepted that the loss of his job was a severe sanction with grave consequences for MacFarlane. However, the most important factor was that the employer's action was intended to secure the implementation of its policy of providing a service without discrimination. The state authorities should be given a wide margin of appreciation in deciding where to strike the balance between MacFarlane's right to manifest his religious belief and the employer's interest in securing the rights of others. The refusal by the domestic courts to uphold MacFarlane's complaints therefore did not give rise to a breach of Article 9.

3.4.2.2 Schools

In *R (on the application of Begum) v Headteacher, Governors of Denbigh High School* [2006] UKHL 15, a schoolgirl called Shabina Begum had been excluded from her school for failure to comply with her school's dress code. Begum was Muslim and wished to wear a jilbab to school, rather than a shalwar kameez as required by the school's uniform policy. A jilbab is a more concealing form of dress than a shalwar kameez. She argued that her expulsion was a violation of her rights under Article 9, because the shalwar kameez did not comply with the requirements of her religion.

The House of Lords found that there had been no violation of Shabina Begum's right to manifest her religious beliefs under Article 9. The Lords said that what constituted interference depended on all the circumstances of the case, including the extent to which an individual could reasonably expect to be at liberty to manifest their beliefs in practice.

In this case, Begum's family had chosen for her a school outside their own catchment area. There was no evidence to show that there was any difficulty in her attending one of the three schools in her catchment area that permitted the wearing of the jilbab. Also, Shabina Begum had worn the shalwar kameez during her first two years at the school without objection. In addition, the school had taken pains to devise a uniform policy that respected Muslim beliefs but did so in an inclusive, unthreatening and uncompetitive way. The school had enjoyed a period of harmony and success to which the uniform policy was thought to contribute, and the rules were acceptable to mainstream Muslim opinion. The school feared that if they allowed Shabina Begun to wear the jilbab, other girls who did not wish to do so would be pressured into wearing it and it might promote divisiveness between different groups.

For all these reasons, the House of Lords found that the school had acted in a proportionate manner, and there had been no unlawful interference with Shabina Begum's rights.

3.5 Article 10 – freedom of expression

3.5.1 Introduction

Article 10 provides:

1. Everyone has the right to freedom of expression. This right shall include freedom to hold opinions and to receive and impart information and ideas without interference by public authority and regardless of frontiers. This Article shall not prevent States from requiring the licensing of broadcasting, television or cinema enterprises.
2. The exercise of these freedoms, since it carries with it duties and responsibilities, may be subject to such formalities, conditions, restrictions or penalties as are prescribed by law and are necessary in a democratic society, in the interests of national security, territorial integrity or public safety, for the prevention of disorder or crime, for the protection of health or morals, for the protection of the reputation or rights of others, for preventing the disclosure of information received in confidence, or for maintaining the authority and impartiality of the judiciary.

There are several forms that freedom of expression may take. It may, for example, be artistic in nature, such as the publication of a book that has graphic sexual content, or it may be a newspaper printing a story about the private life of a celebrity. However, the most important form of freedom of expression is the expression of views that are political in nature. For the state to attempt to suppress the expression of political views to which it objects would be a restriction on a fundamental right. It is no coincidence that one of the hallmarks of a dictatorial or oppressive state is the crushing of any political dissent.

3.5.2 Restrictions

Article 10 is a qualified right and may therefore be subject to restrictions that are prescribed by law, are in pursuit of a legitimate aim and are proportionate to that aim. You will now attempt an activity which illustrates how the qualifications to Article 10 operate.

ACTIVITY 2 Article 10 as a qualified right

Read Article 10 of the Convention, paying particular attention to the qualifications. Check your understanding of how they operate by answering the following questions:

1. Assume that a UK statute gives the Government power to censor (prohibit publication of) any printed material if it considers it necessary to protect morals. Would this be compatible with Article 10?
2. Which of the legitimate aims specified in Article 10(2) of the Convention would be relevant in the following cases?
   (a) A court grants an injunction preventing publication of an article in a newspaper, on the grounds that it would prejudice the fair trial of a court case.
   (b) The Home Secretary uses a statutory power to ban the broadcasting of direct speech by representatives of terrorist organisations, on the grounds that it will increase support for, and lend legitimacy to, those organisations.
   (c) A publisher is convicted of publishing an obscene article. The article was in a book designed to give advice on sexual matters to schoolchildren.
   (d) A court grants an injunction preventing publication of the memoirs of a member of the Security Services, containing confidential government information.
   (e) A court grants an injunction to prevent publication of material in the Press relating to the private life of a politician.

COMMENT

1. The protection of morals can be used under Article 10 as a basis for limiting freedom of expression. But remember that the limitation must have a 'legal basis'. It must, for example, be sufficiently precise for the citizen to be able to regulate their conduct (see **1.5.2.2**). This statute is unlikely to meet the requirement and would be incompatible with the Convention.
2. (a) The maintenance of the authority and impartiality of the judiciary (*Sunday Times v UK* (1979) 2 EHRR 245).
   (b) The interests of national security or public safety.
   (c) The protection of morals (*Handyside v UK* (1979) 1 EHRR 737).
   (d) The interests of national security, or preventing the disclosure of information received in confidence. An example of this is *Observer and The Guardian v United Kingdom* (1992) 14 EHRR 153. In this case, various newspapers complained that the granting of interim injunctions restraining them from publishing extracts from a book called 'Spycatcher' contravened their right to freedom of expression. The book was written by a former member of the security services, and it contained allegations of unlawful behaviour by the British security service. The Court was satisfied that the interim injunctions were lawful and in pursuit of the legitimate aim of national security. In addition, the injunctions were proportionate as they were only obtained on an interim basis, pending a final hearing to determine whether publication of the book should be allowed.
   (e) The protection of the reputation or rights of others (in this case the right to respect for private life).

3.5.3 Ban on political advertising

A further issue concerning political free speech and Article 10 is the ban on the broadcasting of political advertising in the UK, as set out in the Communications Act 2003. The compatibility of this ban with the rights set out in Article 10 was considered by the ECtHR in *Animal Defenders v United Kingdom* (2013) 57 EHRR 21.

Animal Defenders campaigned against the use of animals in commerce, science and leisure. It had wished to broadcast a television advertisement, but the UK's relevant broadcasting authority refused to clear it for broadcast as its objectives were political as defined in the 2003 Act. The ECtHR, by a slim majority, rejected Animal Defenders' argument that this prohibition breached its Article 10 rights. It was agreed that the prohibition was an interference with Animal Defenders' Article 10 rights, but that it pursued the legitimate aim of preserving the impartiality of broadcasting and therefore protected the democratic process. The issue was the measure's proportionality.

The ECtHR stated that, as the issue involved a restriction on a debate of public interest, namely the protection of animals, the margin of appreciation to be afforded to the UK was narrow. However, it found that the ban on broadcast political advertising had been the culmination of an extensive consideration by Parliament, having been reported on and commented on by specialist bodies, and having been enacted with support from all political parties. Further, a range of alternative media were available to Animal Defenders to disseminate its views. The ECtHR also found that the ban was a proportionate means of ensuring that the facts about the perceived exploitation of animals were not distorted. The Court's conclusion was that, for all these reasons, the ban was proportionate and did not violate Article 10.

3.5.4 Hate speech

Political free speech is given a high degree of protection by the courts. Free speech that is offensive, shocking or disturbing is also protected by Article 10 and should not be restricted by the state. But what is the position with speech that goes beyond this and, for example, expresses racial or religious intolerance? In *Jersild v Denmark* (1995) 19 EHRR 1, a Danish journalist conducted a television interview with some young people, known as 'green jackets', who made racist remarks in the course of the interview. The ECtHR ruled that the expression of outright racist views would not be protected by Article 10 because such views went beyond what was offensive, shocking or disturbing.

In the United Kingdom, the Public Order Act 1986 created several criminal offences in connection with racial, religious and sexual hatred. However, criticism of religions is permitted to a certain extent, because there are wider ethical and moral considerations that might lead someone to criticise particular religious beliefs.

A particular provision of the Public Order Act 1986 has given rise to concern due to its implications for freedom of expression. This is s 5, which provides that it is a criminal offence for someone to use threatening or abusive words or behaviour, or to display any writing, sign or other visible representation that is threatening or abusive, within the hearing or sight of a person likely to be caused harassment, alarm or distress by such actions. A defendant does have a defence if they can show that their conduct was reasonable.

Arguments involving whether a conviction for an offence under s 5 may be in violation of the right to freedom of expression have come before domestic courts on several occasions. In *Percy v DPP* [2001] EWHC 1125 (Admin), Percy – who was a protester against American military policy – appealed against her conviction for an offence under s 5. Percy had defaced an American flag, putting a stripe across the stars and writing the words 'Stop Star Wars' across the stripes. Then, while outside an American airbase, she stepped in front of a vehicle containing American service personnel, put the flag on the road and trod upon it. At her trial, the judge found that the restrictions on Percy's freedom of expression resulting from her conviction were necessary and proportionate.

The Divisional Court found, however, that her conviction had not been compatible with her right to freedom of expression. The fact that Percy could have demonstrated her message by means other than defacing the flag was a factor to be taken into account but only one of a number of factors. The Court said that other relevant considerations in similar cases included:

- whether the behaviour had gone beyond legitimate protest;

- whether the behaviour had been part of an open expression on an issue of public interest but had been disproportionate and unreasonable;
- whether the individual could have expressed their views in another way;
- the knowledge of the individual of the likely effect of their conduct upon those who witnessed it; and
- whether the use of any object – in this instance a flag – had no relevance to the conveying of the message of protest and had been used as a gratuitous and calculated insult.

The case of *Norwood v United Kingdom (Admissibility)* (Application no 23131/03) (2005) 40 EHRR SE11 is a good illustration of the ECtHR's approach to hate speech. Norwood was convicted for an offence of causing alarm or distress under s 5. Norwood was a regional organiser of the British National Party who had visibly displayed a poster on the window of his flat bearing the words 'Islam out of Britain', with graphic references to the attacks on the World Trade Centre on 11 September 2001.

After being convicted in the UK, Norwood applied to the ECtHR, but his application was rejected because the views he sought to express were aimed at undermining others and were therefore incompatible with the values that underpinned the ECHR, such as tolerance, respect and non-discrimination.

In more recent cases, the ECtHR has emphasised that only the gravest forms of hate speech will not be protected by Article 10. Thus in *Lilienthal v Iceland* (App No 29297/18), the applicant wrote an article criticising a proposal to strengthen education and counselling in schools for those who identified as LGBT. The article included use of homophobic language. The ECtHR found that, although the comments were highly prejudicial, it was not clear that they aimed at inciting violence and hatred or destroying the rights and freedoms protected by the Convention. Thus, they came within the protection of Article 10. This case should be compared with *Lenis v Greece* (App No 47833/20) where the disputed article included incitement to violence and dehumanising hate speech against a group of people identified on the basis of their sexual orientation. In deciding that this article was not protected by Article 10, the ECtHR also took into account the applicant's position as a senior official of the Church who could influence many people and of the fact that the views expressed in the article were disseminated to a wide audience through the Internet.

3.5.5 Freedom of expression in England and Wales

The traditional approach to civil liberties in the UK proceeded on the basis that individuals had the right to do anything unless it was prohibited by law (residual liberty). Thus, there was freedom of expression except to the extent that Parliament or the common law restricted it. The ECHR, on the other hand, creates a positive right to freedom of expression. This means that following the incorporation of the Convention by the HRA 1998, there has had to be a change in the UK approach to one which acknowledges the positive nature of the right.

3.5.6 Restraints on freedom of expression in England and Wales

There are many restrictions on freedom of expression in both civil and criminal law. Some examples follow, but the list is not exhaustive:

(i) *Defamation.* The most important restriction on freedom of expression which applies in civil law is the tort of defamation. Defamation is a false statement exposing someone to hatred, ridicule or contempt, or tending to lower that person in the estimation of right-thinking members of society generally.

(ii) *Misuse of private information.* This is a tort that the courts have been developing to comply with their duty to give effect to Convention rights under s 6 of the HRA 1998. In this case the relevant Convention right is Article 8. Information will be private if, in the circumstances, an individual would have 'a reasonable expectation of privacy'.

(iii) *Official secrets.* The Official Secrets Act 1989 sets out a variety of offences involving disclosure of information relating to security or intelligence work, defence matters, international relations, investigation of crime and other investigative powers, and other information resulting from unauthorised disclosures or which has been entrusted in confidence. The Act principally applies to members of the security and intelligence service, Crown servants, government contractors and others who may in certain circumstances be notified that the Act applies to them. In some situations the mere fact of disclosure is an offence, whereas in others it is an offence if the disclosure is a 'damaging' one. The Act provides a defence of lawful disclosure, but no defence of disclosure for 'the public good' or 'in the public interest'.

(iv) *Threatening, insulting or abusive words or behaviour.* Sections 4, 4A and 5 of the Public Order Act 1986 contain a range of offences involving threatening, insulting or abusive words or behaviour, involving in some way fear or provocation of violence (s 4), or causing harassment, alarm or distress (ss 4A and 5). These offences are relevant in limiting the right to peaceful assembly under Article 11 of the ECHR.

(v) *Incitement to racial and religious hatred.* The Public Order Act 1986 is also the current home of various offences concerned with incitements to racial hatred.

(vi) *Obscenity.* The Obscene Publications Act 1959 is concerned with the publication of articles, whether for gain or otherwise. An article is obscene if its effect, or the effect of one of its items, is, taken as a whole, such as tends to deprave and corrupt persons who are likely in all the circumstances to read, see or hear the matter which it contains. There are a number of defences in this very technical and complicated area of the law

(vii) *Terrorism Act 2006.* The Terrorism Act 2006 makes it a criminal offence to encourage terrorism by directly or indirectly inciting or encouraging others to commit acts of terrorism. This includes an offence of 'glorification' of terror – to 'praise or celebrate' terrorism in a way that may encourage others to commit a terrorist act.

(viii) *Contempt of court.* The law relating to contempt of court seeks to prevent publication of material which may prejudice a fair trial. This is an important area of the law, and you will look at it in more detail in **Chapter 4**.

3.6 Article 11 – freedom of assembly and association

3.6.1 Introduction

Article 11 provides:

1. Everyone has the right to freedom of peaceful assembly and to freedom of association with others, including the right to form and to join trade unions for the protection of his interests.
2. No restrictions shall be placed on the exercise of these rights other than such as are prescribed by law and are necessary in a democratic society in the interests of national security or public safety, for the prevention of disorder or crime, for the protection of health or morals or for the protection of the rights and freedoms of others. This Article shall not prevent the imposition of lawful restrictions on the exercise of these rights by members of the armed forces, of the police or of the administration of the State.

Article 11 of the ECHR gives a right of peaceful assembly, and the separate right of freedom of association. The effective exercise of these freedoms is of crucial importance for free expression and for protection of groups of a social, cultural, political and economic nature.

3.6.2 Freedom of assembly

Conduct will fall within scope of Article 11 provided that it is a 'peaceful assembly'. This covers private meetings and meetings on public highways, as well as static meetings and public processions. The assembly must be peaceful – Article 11 does not afford protection to violent behaviour.

In *Tabernacle v Secretary of State for Defence* [2009] EWCA Civ 23, the appellant appealed against a decision refusing to quash a byelaw which prevented her from camping in the vicinity of the Atomic Weapons Establishment at Aldermaston. The camp had been going for 23 years, with the women assembling on the land for the second weekend of every month. They held vigils, meetings and demonstrations and the protest was always peaceful. The Secretary of State passed a byelaw in 2007 that prohibited camping in the 'Controlled Areas', which included the area where the peace camp had always been held.

The Court of Appeal held that the byelaw's interference with the appellant's rights was far from being weak or insubstantial, and the Secretary of State had to demonstrate under Article 10(2) a substantial objective justification for the particular byelaw, amounting to a pressing social need. In the circumstances, the effect of the 2007 byelaw was to violate the appellant's rights of free expression and association guaranteed by Articles 10 and 11.

Often, as in this case, the two rights are interlinked. The judge regarded Article 11 not as an autonomous claim in its own right, but as underlining the mode of free expression relied on – a communal protest in a camp.

3.6.3 Freedom of association

Article 11 does not merely contain the right to freedom of assembly. It also covers the right to freedom of association. Article 11(1) provides that 'Everyone has the right to ... freedom of association with others'. What does this mean?

The right to freedom of association is designed to protect an individual's right to participate with other people in an organised way in pursuit of a common aim. It applies to a wide variety of bodies, including pressure groups, political parties and religious organisations. In the absence of the right to freedom of association, the state could ban those groups of which it does not approve, such as opposition political parties or movements.

Article 11 is, however, qualified. As with the other qualified rights, the state may lawfully limit the exercise of the right to freedom of association provided that limitation is prescribed by law, is in pursuit of a legitimate aim, and is proportionate to that aim. There are occasions on which a state has sought to proscribe particular political parties or associations. Proscription means that a party or association is banned.

The ECtHR first considered the proscription of political parties in *United Communist Party of Turkey v Turkey* (1998) 26 EHRR 121. The United Communist Party of Turkey was formed in 1990. Turkish law required that all new political parties had to have rules, aims and a political programme that were compatible with the country's constitution. The authorities in Turkey applied to the country's constitutional court to have the United Communist Party dissolved. It was alleged that the Party had violated the Turkish constitution by having incorporated the word 'communist' into its name, and by having carried on activities likely to undermine the territorial integrity of the state, through advocating the establishment of a separate Kurdish nation. In July 1991, the constitutional court made an order dissolving the Party, based on the inclusion in its name of the constitutionally prohibited word 'communist' and the alleged encouragement of Kurdish separatism. The Party and its leaders applied to the ECtHR, complaining that the dissolution of the party infringed their right to freedom of association as guaranteed by Article 11.

The Court found that the dissolution of the Party was permitted under Turkish law and arguably had a legitimate aim – national security. However, the Court found the ban to be disproportionate. The Court said that political parties had an essential role in ensuring pluralism and the proper functioning of democracy, and Article 11 therefore had to be viewed in the light of the protection of freedom of expression as guaranteed by Article 10.

The Court held that a political party's choice of name could not justify its dissolution in the absence of other relevant and sufficient circumstances, and there was no evidence that the United Communist Party represented a real threat to Turkish society or to the Turkish state. Also, a detailed reading of the Party's programme showed that it intended to resolve the Kurdish issue through dialogue, not violence.

The Court accordingly concluded that the drastic measure of dissolving the Party breached Article 11.

In 2003, the European Court of Human Rights considered another Turkish case that involved freedom of association. The case, *Refah Partisi (the Welfare Party) v Turkey* (2003) 37 EHRR 1, was very controversial.

Refah Partisi was a political party set up in 1983. By 1996, it was able to form a government in coalition with another party and its leader was Prime Minister. In 1997, Turkey's state counsel successfully applied to the country's constitutional court for the dissolution of Refah Partisi on the ground that its activities were contrary to the principle of the separation of the state from religious institutions as set out in the Turkish constitution, and also because some of its members had called for the establishment of an Islamic state and the imposition of sharia law in Turkey. Refah Partisi applied to the ECtHR, arguing that the interference with its rights under Article 11 had been violated.

The Court found that the dissolution of the Refah Partisi did not violate Article 11. Although there had been an interference with the party members' rights under Article 11, this was justified as it met the urgent need to protect democracy, for which purpose the state could take pre-emptive steps where necessary. Refah Partisi's commitment to implement the strict requirements of Muslim sharia law was not compatible with Turkey's secular democracy. The Court said that the model of society and government that Refah Partisi wished to introduce would undermine the very basis on which the ECHR rested.

The fact that Refah Partisi could have gone on to implement those policies in government meant that it posed an immediate danger to Turkish democracy. Given the nature and immediacy of the threat, the actions of the Turkish Constitutional Court in dissolving the Party were proportionate.

3.6.4 Unions

Article 11 gives the 'right to form and join trade unions'. This includes the right to strike (*Schmidt and Dahlström v Sweden* (1979–80) 1 EHRR 632), although the state can limit the exercise of this right in certain cases. In *Secretary of State for Business and Trade v Mercer* [2024] UKSC 12, the Supreme Court made a declaration that s 146 of the Trade Union and Labour Relations (Consolidation) Act 1992 was incompatible with Article 11 as it failed to protect workers against sanctions short of dismissal which were intended to deter or penalise trade union members from taking part in lawful strike action.

3.7 Article 1 of Protocol 1 – protection of property

3.7.1 Introduction

Article 1 of Protocol 1 provides:

> Every natural or legal person is entitled to the peaceful enjoyment of his possessions. No one shall be deprived of his possessions except in the public interest and

> subject to the conditions provided for by law and by the general principles of international law.
>
> The preceding provisions shall not, however, in any way impair the right of a State to enforce such laws as it deems necessary to control the use of property in accordance with the general interest or to secure the payment of taxes or other contributions or penalties.

This Article guarantees the right to peaceful enjoyment of possessions (both land (realty) and personal property).

ACTIVITY 3 Possessions

Which of the following do you think would be classified as 'possessions' for the purpose of Article 1 of Protocol 1? Do you think that they should be included?

(1) shares in a company PP

(2) planning permission

(3) a registered trade mark PP

(4) welfare benefits.

COMMENT

Possessions have been widely defined by the ECtHR, and all of the things mentioned would come within the definition. The fact that these things come within the definition, however, means only that the state will need to justify any interference with them. So, for example, planning permission could be withdrawn in certain circumstances.

Note that although entitlement to a welfare benefit would come within the definition of a possession, there is no duty on the state under the ECHR to provide welfare benefits.

Whether you think that certain things should be included as possessions is a matter of personal opinion. However, you may be of the opinion that a right to protection of possessions should not be included in the ECHR at all. Possessions are not distributed equally, and Article 1 of Protocol 1 can be (and has been) widely utilised by commercial entities. Its inclusion was controversial as can be seen by the fact that it was not included in the ECHR as originally drafted. In addition, the right can be interfered with 'in the public interest', which is a broad term.

'Peaceful enjoyment' of property would, on its face, suggest that it covers a wide range of situations. However, only interference which affects the financial value of property or possessions will engage the right to 'peaceful enjoyment' of them. Thus, for example, noise nuisance will only interfere with peaceful enjoyment to the extent that it reduces the value of that property.

3.7.2 Restrictions

There are some situations in which public authorities can deprive people of their property or restrict the way they can use them. This is only possible where the authority can show that its action is lawful and necessary for the public interest. Generally speaking, a 'deprivation of property' under this Article will not be considered to be in the public interest unless the owner receives compensation. The state must strike a fair balance between the interests of a property owner and the general interests of society as a whole.

Accordingly, a public authority wanting to use a compulsory purchase order to acquire property for public purposes must strike a fair balance between the rights of the individual property owners and the rights of the community. A crucial factor in any such balance will be the availability of compensation reflecting the value of the property being compulsorily purchased.

The case of *James v UK* (1986) 8 EHRR 123 concerned legislation giving tenants who were living in houses under long leases and at low rents the right to compulsorily purchase the freehold of the property in certain circumstances. The applicants, who had been made to transfer property to tenants under this legislation, complained of a breach of Article 1 of Protocol 1. The ECtHR stated that the compulsory transfer of property from one individual to another may, depending upon the circumstances, constitute a legitimate means for promoting the public interest. The notion of 'public interest' is a wide one, and the action complained of was within the UK's margin of appreciation. The taking of property without payment of an amount reasonably related to its value would normally amount to a disproportionate interference with rights under Article 1 of Protocol 1. However, there is no guaranteed right to full compensation in all circumstances. The public interest, for example where measures are designed to achieve greater social justice, may call for less than reimbursement of the full market value.

In *R (on the application of L1T FM Holdings UK Ltd) v Chancellor of the Duchy of Lancaster in the Cabinet Office* [2024] EWHC 2963 (Admin), the claimant applied for judicial review of an order made by the Secretary of State for Business, Energy and Industrial Strategy requiring the claimant to divest its shareholding in a broadband company on the basis of national security risks. It claimed that this breached its rights under Article 1 of Protocol 1 on the basis that it would be paid no compensation. The court stated that Article 1 of Protocol 1 does not guarantee a right to full compensation in all circumstances; it all depended on the context. In this case, the court concluded that a fair balance meant that the interests of national security prevailed over the claimant's financial interests. The claimant would obtain the proceeds of sale of the shareholding, and large-scale investors could not be surprised that they may lose money on investments that threaten national security – the risk of such losses was ultimately part of the economic landscape for those operating in the sector. It was not disproportionate, or otherwise in breach of Article 1 of Protocol 1, for the financial burden of the sale to fall on the claimant's shoulders and not on the public purse.

This right does not affect the ability of public authorities to enforce taxes or fines.

3.8 Article 2 of Protocol 1 – the right to education

3.8.1 Introduction

Article 2 of Protocol 1 provides:

> No person shall be denied the right to education. In the exercise of any functions which it assumes in relation to education and teaching, the state shall respect the rights of parents to ensure such education and teaching in conformity with their own religious and philosophical convictions.

In *Belgian Linguistic* (1979–80) 1 EHRR 252 the ECtHR stated that the rights protected in Article 2 of Protocol 1 are:

- a right of access to educational institutions existing at a given time. It does not require the Government to provide or subsidise any particular type of education;
- a right to official recognition of the studies a student has successfully completed.

Schools are allowed to use admission policies so long as they are objective and reasonable.

As the Article itself indicates, parents have a right to ensure that their religious or philosophical beliefs are respected during their children's education. However, this is not an absolute guarantee, and states may determine the content of their school curriculums, provided they are consistent with requirements of objectivity and pluralism and respect the parents' different religious and philosophical convictions.

3.8.2 Exclusions

Pupils who have been excluded from schools for disruptive behaviour have invoked this right, but usually without success, as the right is subject to limitations. In *Ali v United Kingdom* (2011) 53 EHRR 12, the ECtHR held that the right did not preclude disciplinary measures such as expulsion or temporary exclusion, though to be lawful any such measures had to be foreseeable, had to pursue a legitimate aim and had to be proportionate to that aim. In determining whether an exclusion resulted in a denial of the right to education, the court would have to consider whether a fair balance had been struck between the exclusion and the justification for it. However, where an exclusion from a school is permanent, it is likely that states should ensure that pupils of school-going age receive education at another school.

Summary

- Qualified rights can be interfered with by the state when the interference is prescribed by law, is for a legitimate aim and is proportionate.
- *Bank Mellat v HM Treasury* sets out a four part test for proportionality:
  - Is the objective sufficiently important to justify limiting a fundamental right?
  - Is the measure rationally connected to the objective?
  - Could a less intrusive measure be used?
  - Has a fair balance been struck between the rights of the individual and the interests of the community?
- Article 8 protects a person's private life, family life, home and correspondence.
- Freedom of thought, conscience and religion under Article 9 is absolute, but the right to manifest that belief is qualified.
- Freedom of expression may take many forms, but political expression is particularly important. Certain expressions, such as those aimed at undermining others, are incompatible with the values underpinning the ECHR and will not be protected by Article 10.
- Freedom of assembly under Article 11 only protects protests that are peaceful. Freedom of association protects an individual's right to participate with other people in pursuit of a common aim, but this right can be interfered with, and occasionally groups have been banned without this leading to a breach of Article 11.
- Article 1 of Protocol 1 gives a right to peaceful enjoyment of possessions, but this can be interfered with in the public interest.

Figure 3.1 Breach of qualified rights

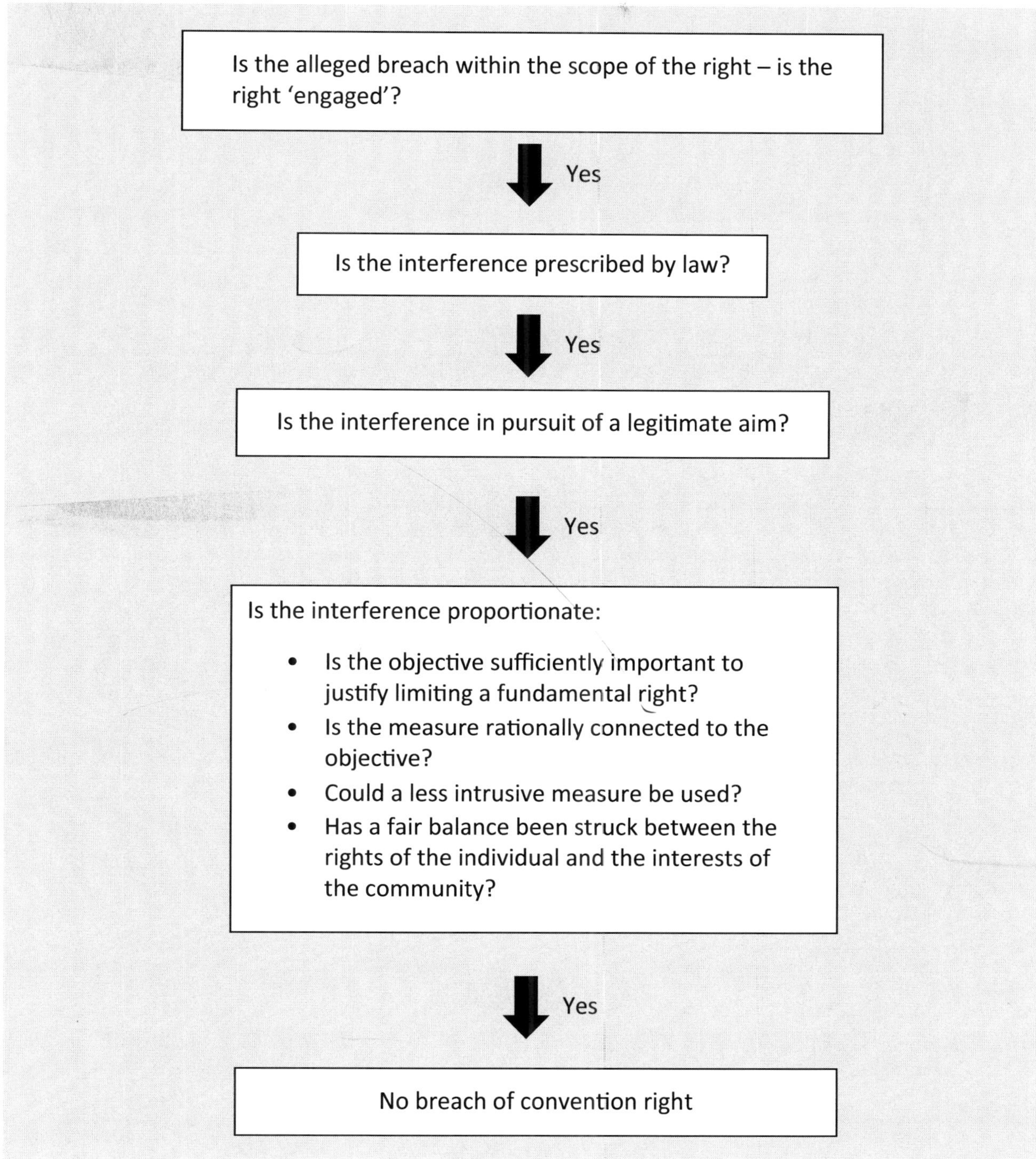

4 Conflict Between Different Rights and Freedoms

Learning outcomes

When you have completed this chapter, you should be able to:

- explain the interrelationship between different rights under the European Convention on Human Rights and how the courts strike a balance in their legal protection;
- analyse the structure adopted by the courts in balancing Articles 8 and 10 and assess that balance;
- explain and analyse the legal controls relating to contempt of court.

4.1 Introduction

One difficulty in setting out a list of fundamental rights is that sometimes rights can conflict with each other. The European Convention on Human Rights (ECHR) does not lay down any strict hierarchy of rights, and therefore the courts have to determine priority on a case-by-case basis. The following activity will introduce you to this problem.

ACTIVITY 1 Conflicts between Convention rights

Consider the following examples. Jot down the Convention rights which you think are in conflict, and which right or rights should have priority in the circumstances. Consider whether any particular type of right should have priority.

1. A person convicted of murder (X) is released after serving his sentence. He changes his name and goes to live in a part of the country where he will not be recognised, as he fears threats to his life. The press have found out where he lives and wish to publish the details.
2. A pop star is photographed emerging from a walk-in HIV and STD/STI Clinic in London. A newspaper has published the photograph.

COMMENT

1. This involves the right to life (Article 2) and the right to respect for private life (Article 8) of X. These are in conflict with the right to freedom of expression (Article 10) of the press. Article 2 is an absolute right, whereas Articles 8 and 10 are qualified rights. In *A v BBC* [2014] UKSC 25 the court held that where there was a conflict between Article 10 and an absolute right, such as Articles 2 and 3, the absolute right would prevail. However, the Court also stated that, given the important role the media plays in a democratic society, the interference with the media's Article 10 rights must be no greater than is necessary.

2. This involves the Article 8 rights of the pop star and the Article 10 rights of the newspaper publishers. As both are qualified rights there is in principle no clear priority between them. The court has to conduct a balancing exercise, asking whether the degree of interference with each right is proportionate to the need to protect the other. In other words, a balance must be struck between the pop star's right to respect for their private life and the rights of others to their freedom of expression.

The need in some cases to strike a balance between Convention rights is only part of the wider problem of deciding whether interference with rights is justified on the basis of wider public interests, such as the need to prevent crime.

4.2 Conflict between absolute rights and qualified rights

4.2.1 Articles 2 and 3

In *Venables and Thompson v News Group Newspapers Ltd* [2001] 2 WLR 1038, Venables and Thompson, who, at the age of 11, had been convicted of the murder of toddler James Bulger, were granted injunctions protecting them from being identified upon their release from detention. This was on the basis that publication of such information would cause their lives to be in danger. The injunction was subsequently amended by the High Court in 2010, so as to prohibit permanently the publication of information which would lead to the identification of Venables, despite it arising from proceedings in open court following his conviction for child pornography offences. The court held that, although there was an understandable and legitimate public interest in the fact of the conviction, there was no reason why Venables' new name should be made public, where the effect of doing so would simply be to assist those who sought to track him down.

In 2005, Maxine Carr, the former girlfriend of Soham murderer Ian Huntley, was granted an indefinite order protecting her new identity by the High Court (*Carr v News Group Newspapers Ltd* [2005] EWHC 971 (QB)). Mr Justice Eady, who granted the order, said it was necessary to protect 'life and limb' as well as Carr's psychological health. Carr's lawyer had argued that such an order was justified on the grounds laid down in the *Venables and Thompson* case, where similar permanent injunctions were granted. The *Carr* case is significant because it is the first such order granted to an adult who has not committed a serious offence (she was convicted of perverting the course of justice with Huntley, but was not involved in the murder of the schoolgirls Holly Wells and Jessica Chapman in August 2002).

In *D v Persons Unknown; F v Persons Unknown* [2021] EWHC 157 (QB), D and F were granted permanent injunctions to protect their identities. D and F were children when they murdered a vulnerable victim. In this case, the source of the risk to life was not others, but D and F themselves.

These cases can be compared with *Tickle v BBC* [2025] EWCA Civ 42 which concerned a reporting restrictions order anonymising the judges in historic care proceedings and private family law proceedings relating to Sara Sharif, who was brutally murdered by her father and step-mother in 2023. The Court found that there was no evidential basis on which to think that the threshold for the application of Articles 2, 3 or 8 had been reached. Any threats to the judges were of the generic kind that were commonly made on social media. To justify anonymisation, it would have to be shown that any risks could not be adequately addressed by security measures. Judges are in a special position as regards open justice, and any risks would need to be so grave that, exceptionally, they provided a justification for overriding the fundamental principle of open justice.

4.2.2 Article 6

Where a media outlet comments on a court case which has not yet been decided, there is a danger that the newspaper report will, for example, influence a jury or put excessive pressure on the judge to decide the case in a particular way. This will interfere with the right to a fair trial protected by Article 6. In *WFZ v BBC* [2023] EWHC 1618 (KB), the court emphasised that the law in this area is not concerned solely with a claimant's right to fair criminal procedure (although it is concerned with that). The law is also concerned with the public's right to fair criminal procedure, and with complainants' rights to fair criminal procedure. English law used to treat such 'trial by Press' as automatically a form of criminal contempt, but the law was reformed in the Contempt of Court Act 1981 to accord with Article 10 of the ECHR. The result is that the court deciding a contempt case has to consider a range of issues before making a finding of contempt.

The Law Commission published a consultation paper on reform of the laws of contempt in July 2024. The consultation focuses on, amongst other things, whether the law of contempt should be codified and simplified, and the scope of court powers in relation to contempt proceedings. The initial consultation ran until November 2024. However, following the murders by Axel Rudakubana of young girls at a dance class, a supplementary consultation paper was published on 3 March 2025. This was to allow further responses in the light of the events following the girls' murders, which saw widespread public disorder. There were suggestions that this disorder was an indirect result of contempt of court laws on the basis that these laws constrained what information public authorities could disclose in relation to the defendant, creating an information vacuum which then filled with misinformation and disinformation. Further responses could be made until 31 March 2025. The Law Commission intends to publish the first part of its report in autumn 2025.

4.2.2.1 Contempt of Court Act 1981

Statutory contempt is regulated by the Contempt of Court Act 1981. Under this Act, liability for contempt of court is strict, meaning that no intention to interfere with court proceedings needs to be shown. This is often known as the 'strict liability rule'.

Under s 2(1) the only sort of publication to which the strict liability rule can apply is a communication addressed to the public at large or a section of the public. So it cannot apply to private communications with a jury. (A private communication with a juror would amount to contempt at common law if the defendant intended to interfere with the course of justice – see **4.2.2.2**.)

The publication must create a substantial risk that the proceedings will be seriously prejudiced (s 2(2)). In *Attorney General v News Group Newspapers* [1987] QB 1 the court made it clear that there were two limbs to s 2(2) – there must be both a 'substantial risk' and the risk should be of 'serious prejudice'. Whether there has been a 'substantial risk' focuses on whether the relevant publication is likely to have been read and remembered by, for example, the jury. So, factors such as whether the publication is local or national (and what locality) and the proximity of the trial will be important. In *Attorney-General v NGN* itself the trial was not for 10 months, and so the court thought there was little likelihood that anyone who had read the article would remember it. For there to be a risk of serious prejudice, the wording of the publication must be capable of seriously prejudicing the trial. One example may be if it refers to the previous convictions of the defendant.

Proceedings must be 'active' to be caught by the strict liability rule (s 2(3) and (4)). The time when proceedings become active differs depending on the type of case. Criminal proceedings will be active from the time the defendant is arrested (or a summons issued for a summary offence). Civil proceedings are active when arrangements for the hearing are made.

Section 3 provides a defence for 'innocent publication'. This is quite narrow and means that the publisher will not be guilty of contempt if they did not know and had no reason to suspect that proceedings were active.

Section 4 provides a defence for contemporary reports of proceedings provided that these are fair and accurate and published in good faith.

Section 5 protects discussions in good faith of public affairs or matters of general public interest if the risk of prejudice is merely incidental. Section 5 is not, strictly speaking, a defence. The House of Lords indicated in *Attorney General v English* [1983] 1 AC 116 that s 5 'stands on an equal footing with s 2(2)' rather than operating as a defence. It is therefore for the prosecution to prove that s 2(2) is satisfied, and that s 5 does not apply. The aim of s 5 is to ensure that discussion of matters of public interest are not shut down just because there is a court case going on which raises those issues. In *Attorney General v English* (above) the *Daily Mail* published an article supporting a pro-life Parliamentary candidate. In the article it alleged that a medical practice had developed whereby severely disabled babies would be caused or allowed to die. The article was published during the trial of a doctor for murder of a disabled baby by starvation. The House of Lords held that the paper could rely on s 5. Any risk of prejudice was an incidental consequence of arguing the main theme. The article did not mention the doctor's trial.

In *HM Attorney General v MGN Ltd (No 2)* [2011] EWHC 2383 (Admin), the Administrative Court found that the publishers of the *Daily Mirror* and the *Sun* had committed contempt of court under the strict liability rule and fined them £50,000 and £18,000 respectively. Both newspapers had published material that created substantial risks for the course of justice in criminal proceedings arising from the murder of Joanna Yeates in Bristol in December 2010. The articles had all been about Miss Yeates's landlord, Christopher Jefferies, who had been arrested on suspicion of her murder. Mr Jefferies was subsequently exonerated and another man, Vincent Tabak, was convicted. The vilification of Mr Jefferies by the newspapers created a substantial risk that the course of justice in any criminal proceedings against him, should he have been charged and tried, would have been seriously impeded by deterring potential witnesses from coming forward to assist the defence.

4.2.2.2 Common law contempt

You have seen how the Contempt of Court Act 1981 deals with 'strict liability' or contempt irrespective of intent. Intentional contempt remains an offence at common law. The offence will be committed where the publication was calculated to impede or prejudice the administration of justice (in other words, the publisher knew of the inevitable consequences of publication). In practice it is a difficult offence to prove.

In *Attorney-General v News Group Newspapers Plc* [1989] QB 110, the Sun newspaper published articles referring to the rape of a girl by a doctor and stated that they would fund a private prosecution of the doctor by the girl's mother. The editor asserted that he lacked intention to interfere with the course of justice. However, the court held that such intention could be inferred from the contents of the articles and the offer to fund a private prosecution.

It is also an offence at common law to impede the judicial process in the courtroom itself. This may take the form of holding a demonstration, shouting or otherwise interfering with the proceedings. For example, in *R v Jordan* [2024] EWCA Crim 229 the defendant, who was outside the court, directed recorded music through a megaphone at the court causing disruption to the jury trial. He was arrested on the orders of the presiding judge and sentenced to prison for 14 days, suspended for 12 months. This type of contempt is known as contempt 'in the face of the court'.

ACTIVITY 2 Common law contempt

Assume that articles about the wife of a serial killer appeared in a satirical magazine. These articles alleged that she had provided a false alibi for her husband, and were published at a time when there was already a libel action between the parties relating to another matter.

Consider the potential liability of the magazine's editor for common law contempt of court.

COMMENT

These facts are based on the case of *Attorney General v Hislop* [1991] 2 WLR 219. Ian Hislop (the editor) and Pressdram Ltd (the publishers of *Private Eye*) were the defendants in a libel action brought by Sonia Sutcliffe, the wife of the 'Yorkshire Ripper', arising out of an article that had appeared in an earlier edition of *Private Eye*. Shortly before the start of that libel trial, the magazine published two more articles about Sonia Sutcliffe. The Court of Appeal held that those later articles were clearly intended to prejudice anyone reading them against Sonia Sutcliffe. Given that defamation actions were tried with a jury, the allegations were such that anyone reading them would remember them and be likely to pass them on. Accordingly, the Court considered that there was a clear intention to pressurise Sonia Sutcliffe into discontinuing the proceedings, or a jury from considering her case impartially or both, and this in turn constituted an intentional contempt.

This case confirmed that 'common law' contempt and 'strict liability' contempt under the Contempt of Court Act 1981 are not mutually exclusive. The defendants were found guilty of both types.

4.2.2.3 Online publication

In *Attorney General v Associated Newspapers Ltd & News Group Newspapers Ltd* [2011] EWHC 418 (Admin) the High Court convicted the *Daily Mail* and the *Sun* newspapers of statutory contempt of court. During his ongoing criminal trial, they had published on their websites a photograph of the accused toting a gun. The implications of this judgment for tweeters and bloggers who comment on ongoing criminal trials are significant as it makes it clear that users of social media run the risk of committing contempt of court if they post comments about such cases.

We would now like you to check your understanding of contempt of court by attempting the following activity. You may find the following flowchart helpful when structuring your answer:

Figure 4.1 Contempt of Court Act 1981 – strict liability

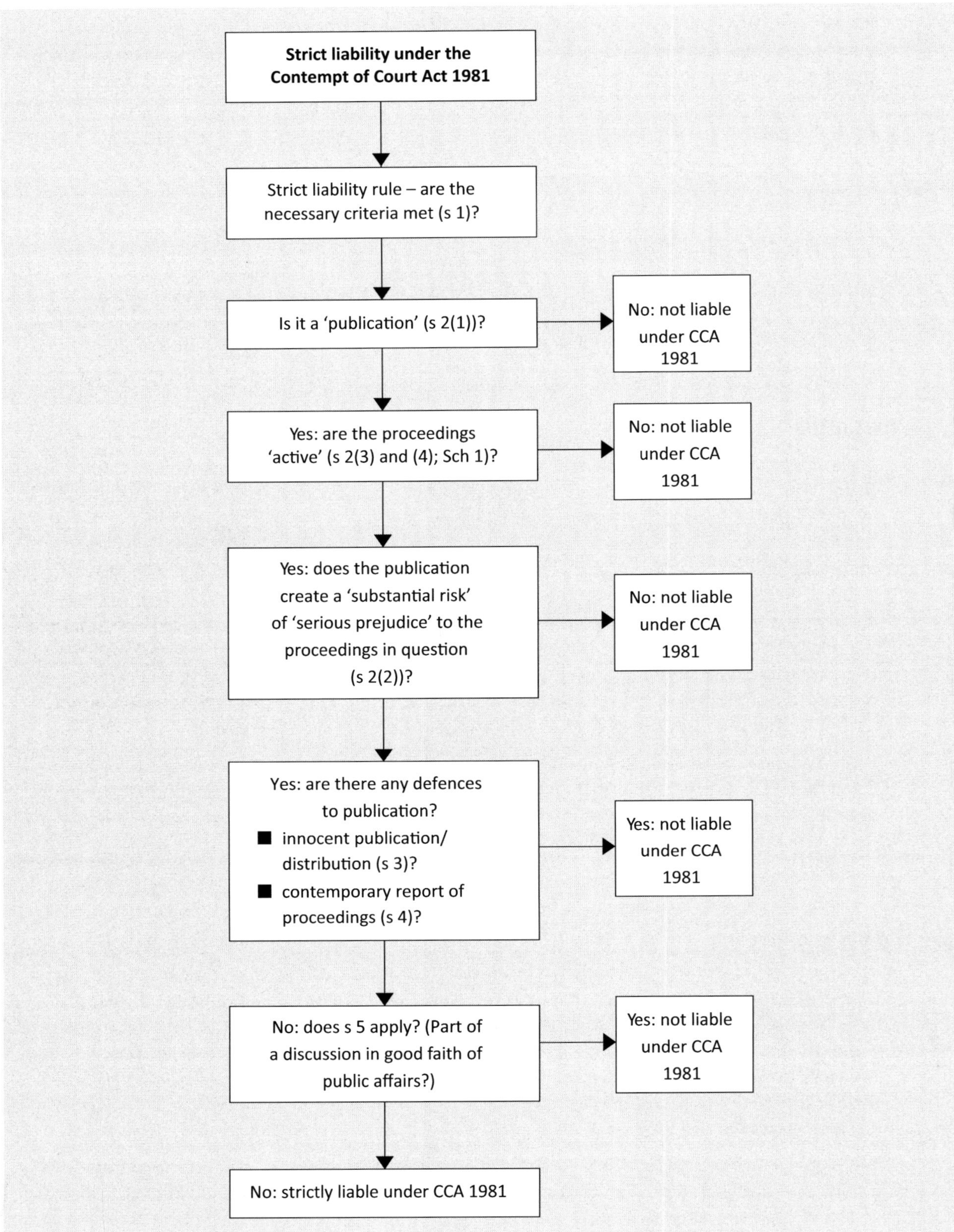

ACTIVITY 3 Contempt of court

Legal proceedings have been commenced against Ahmed in Weyford County Court for non-payment of rent. The hearing date has been set for one month's time. The proceedings have been issued by his landlord, Realhousing plc, a company which provides low-cost housing in deprived areas of the UK. Ahmed faces being evicted from his flat if he loses the case.

Realhousing plc is known for taking a tough stance against tenants who fall behind with their rent. Ahmed has decided to withhold his rent as a publicity stunt to raise awareness of Realhousing plc's tactics. He claims that Realhousing plc causes unnecessary suffering to the poor and underprivileged, who frequently end up homeless as a result of being evicted.

Helen, a journalist with a national newspaper, the *Daily Messenger*, is known to be sympathetic to the methods employed by Realhousing plc. Asserting her right to freedom of expression, Helen plans to publish an article outlining the positive side of Realhousing plc's business. The concluding paragraph of the article will discuss Ahmed's situation and conclude that he is a well-known 'rabble-rouser and layabout' who deserves to be 'thrown out on his ear'.

Consider whether Helen will incur any criminal liability if she publishes the article as planned.

COMMENT

This question involves potential criminal contempt of court. The Contempt of Court Act (CCA) 1981 is relevant here. Provided various criteria are met, Helen (or, more likely, the editor/owner of the national newspaper) could be liable under 'the strict liability rule' contained in CCA 1981, s 1:

(a) Helen's article will clearly be a 'publication' within s 2(1). This requires that any publication must be addressed to the public at large, which, as the *Daily Messenger* is a national newspaper, it will be.

(b) At the time of publication, arrangements for the hearing have been made. This means that for the purposes of s 2(3) and (4), the proceedings are 'active' under para 12 of Sch 1 to the Act (because these are civil proceedings).

(c) Under s 2(2), the strict liability rule applies only to a publication which creates a 'substantial risk' of 'serious prejudice' to the proceedings in question.

In deciding whether there is such a risk, the court will look at the article itself, and also at the nature of the publications and their proximity to the hearing.

It is also relevant that there will not be a jury trial as this is in the County Court. In addition, Helen is proposing to publish one article rather than a series of articles.

There is, however, a clear risk here in view of the words used and the fact that this is a national newspaper. Further, the hearing will take place in one month's time and so is clearly proximate.

Defences? From the content of the article, it appears that Helen knows that the proceedings are active. The defence in s 3(1) is therefore unavailable. (That in s 4 is inapplicable on the facts.)

Under s 5, Helen may escape liability if it can be shown that the publication is part of a discussion 'in good faith of public affairs or other matters of general public interest' and the risk of prejudice is merely incidental. Helen might be able to argue that the article is part of a genuine discussion. However, the specific references to Ahmed in the article may well take her outside the s 5 protection, as it is questionable whether the risk of prejudice to any trial would be 'merely incidental' to the discussion or indeed whether the article could be said to have been written in good faith.

In *Attorney General v English* [1982] 2 All ER 903, it was held to be significant that the article in question made no reference to the specific proceedings.

There may also be enough to show intention for common law contempt, ie there must be a real risk of prejudice of a fair trial and specific intent to create such (*AG v Hislop*).

4.3 Conflict between qualified rights

The main area of conflict of different qualified rights is between Article 10 and Article 8. This often arises when a celebrity claims that articles published by the media have breached their right to privacy.

4.3.1 Human Rights Act 1998, s 12(4)

Section 12(4) of the Human Rights Act (HRA) 1998 is drafted so as to prevent claims of breach of privacy from unduly restricting the freedom of the press. It states that the courts must have particular regard to the right to the freedom of expression. Where proceedings relate to journalistic, literary or artistic material, the court must consider the extent to which the material is already in the public domain, whether publication would be in the public interest and any relevant privacy code.

4.3.2 Proportionality where there is a conflict of qualified rights

A balance must be struck between one person's right to respect for their private life and the right of others to their freedom of expression. There is therefore a challenge to the courts here. We know from **Chapter 3** that where qualified human rights are engaged, the court must apply the test of proportionality. When a claimant brings a case against the state for breach of human rights, the test used is the *Bank Mellat* test. However, where two qualified Convention rights are in conflict, such as Articles 8 and 10, the approach is more complex and instead the test set out by Baroness Hale in the *Campbell case* (see **4.3.2.1** below) should be applied.

4.3.2.1 The *Campbell* case

The House of Lords case of *Campbell v Mirror Group Newspapers Ltd* [2004] UKHL 22 is the leading authority on this area. The *Daily Mirror* had published the following information relating to the supermodel Naomi Campbell:

(i) A claim that she was a drug addict (despite her previous public claims that she did not take drugs).

(ii) The fact that she was receiving treatment for this addiction.

(iii) Details of the treatment she was receiving.

(iv) Covert photographs of Campbell leaving a Narcotics Anonymous meeting.

Campbell sued in the tort of breach of confidence and raised before the court her right to privacy under Article 8 of the ECHR. At trial, Campbell conceded that Mirror Group Newspapers was entitled to publish the fact that she was a drug addict (ie (i) above) since she had previously lied about this. However, she argued that the paper should not have disclosed the other information or the photographs.

Mirror Group Newspapers defended the claim, raising before the court their right to freedom of expression under Article 10 of the ECHR.

The House of Lords stated that in order to decide whether there had been a breach of Article 8, the court first needed to decide whether that article was 'engaged', ie whether Campbell's claim came within the scope of Article 8. The House of Lords said that the appropriate test was whether the complainant (Campbell) had a reasonable expectation of privacy. There are some types of information, such as information about health or finances, which are likely to automatically give rise to a reasonable expectation of privacy. In *ZXC v Bloomberg LP* [2022] UKSC 5, Bloomberg published an article identifying the claimant as the subject of a criminal investigation. The Supreme Court held that, as a legitimate starting point, a person under criminal investigation has a reasonable expectation of privacy in respect of information relating to that investigation prior to charge.

In *Murray v Express Newspapers* [2008] EWCA Civ 446, the Court of Appeal stated that whether or not there was a reasonable expectation of privacy was an objective question. It took account of all the circumstances of the case; these included the attributes of the claimant, the nature of the activity in which they were engaged, the place at which it happened, the nature and purpose of the intrusion, the absence of consent, the effect on the claimant and the circumstances in which, and the purposes for which, the information reached the publisher.

If there is a reasonable expectation of privacy and Article 8 is therefore engaged, the court must carry out a balancing exercise between the conflicting claims of Articles 8 and 10, to decide if there had been a breach of Article 8. The judges in *Campbell* agreed that neither Article 8 nor Article 10 had precedence over the other. Which should assume most importance would depend on the facts of the case.

Baroness Hale set out the following test for balancing the proportionality of interfering with one right against the proportionality of restricting the other:

> This involves looking first at the comparative importance of the actual rights being claimed in the individual case; then at the justifications for interfering with or restricting each of those rights; and applying the proportionality test to each.

Baroness Hale indicated that there are different types of freedom of speech, some of which are more deserving of protection than others. Political speech is particularly deserving of protection, as is artistic speech or impression. Conversely, stories about the intimate details of a celebrity's private life attract less protection.

The crucial factor in *Campbell* was that the model was photographed and the text identified her as leaving Narcotics Anonymous meetings, which, being a medical matter, made the issue particularly private. Publication might even deter someone in these circumstances from having further treatment. Baroness Hale added that the fact that the information may have been 'leaked' from a member of the group could make Campbell think she had been followed or betrayed and may deter her from going back again.

Baroness Hale distinguished the subject matter of the photograph in this case from a photograph of Campbell simply walking down the street to go shopping. She stated that people would obviously be interested to see how the supermodel looked if and when she pops out to the shops for a bottle of milk. There is nothing essentially private about that information nor can it be expected to damage her private life.

Here, the House of Lords found that photographs of Campbell attending a Narcotics Anonymous meeting had a far greater effect than just words and so had invaded her right to respect for her private life. Indeed, had it not been for the publication of the photographs, the majority of the House of Lords would have been inclined to regard the balance between Articles 8 and 10 as about even.

It is clear from *Campbell*, therefore, that it is not whether the individual action occurred in the public or private domain that is the determining factor as to whether the individual has a reasonable expectation of respect for their private life.

The *Mirror* subsequently appealed to the ECtHR. In *MGN Ltd v United Kingdom* (Application No 39401/04) 29 BHRC 686, the ECtHR upheld the House of Lords' decision, stating that the publication of details about the nature of Campbell's Narcotics Anonymous treatment and covert photographs taken outside the clinic had been harmful to her continued treatment, and that there was a lack of any compelling need for the public to have this information.

4.3.2.2 The balancing exercise

The case of *ZXC v Bloomberg LP* [2022] UKSC 5 set out factors that need to be taken into account in the balancing exercise. The Supreme Court stated that the decisive factor is an assessment of the contribution which the publication of the relevant information would make to a debate of general interest. The court must also bear in mind the essential role the press plays as a 'public watchdog'. Finally, the court must take into account the factors identified by the ECtHR in the case of *Axel Springer AG v Germany* (2012) 55 EHRR 6, namely:

(1) contribution to a debate of general interest (ie the decisive factor mentioned above);

(2) how well known is the person concerned and what is the subject of the report;

(3) the prior conduct of the person concerned;

(4) the method of obtaining the information and its veracity;

(5) the content, form and consequences of publication; and

(6) if publication has been restrained, the severity of any sanction imposed.

4.3.3 Photographs

A year after *Campbell*, the ECtHR considered the position of photographs in the case of *Von Hannover v Germany (No 1)* (2005) 40 EHRR 1. The *Von Hannover* case involved a successful claim brought by Princess Caroline of Monaco that a variety of photographs taken of her by the paparazzi were in breach of her Article 8 right to respect for her private and family life. The Princess's claim was successful, despite the fact that the photographs showed her shopping, skiing, and riding with her children.

In striking the balance between privacy and freedom of expression, the ECtHR ruled that the decisive factor was the contribution that the published photos and articles made to a debate of general interest. Since the applicant exercised no official function and the photos and articles related exclusively to details of her private life, they made no such contribution.

It is therefore clear from *Von Hannover (No 1)* that the fact that someone is a public figure does not mean that they have no right to respect for their private life when in a public place.

However, in *Von Hannover v Germany (No 2)* (2012) 55 EHRR 15, the ECtHR may have retreated slightly from the stringent approach to photographs that it took in *Von Hannover (No 1)*. *Von Hannover (No 2)* concerned the publication in a German magazine of a photograph showing Princess Caroline and her husband on a skiing holiday in St Moritz in Switzerland. Accompanying the photograph was an article about the health of Prince Rainier, Princess Caroline's father and then reigning prince of Monaco. The information about Prince Rainier's health was a matter of public interest due to his status, and the public were legitimately interested in how his children 'reconciled their obligations of family solidarity with the legitimate needs of their private life'. Moreover, even if Princess Caroline did not perform any official functions, she and her husband were not ordinary private individuals, but were public figures.

The link between the photograph and accompanying article was close enough to justify its publication, particularly as there was no evidence that the photographs were taken in either a covert or intrusive manner. The judgment in *Von Hannover (No 2)* indicates that the ECtHR may be allowing states a greater margin of appreciation in this type of case. Nonetheless, the judgment does not clear the way for the press to publish photographs of celebrities carrying out everyday activities; the photographs must contribute to a genuine debate of general interest.

Murray (by his Litigation Friends) v Express Newspapers [2008] EWCA Civ 446 concerned the Article 8 rights of the 18-month-old son of the author JK Rowling and her husband. A photograph had been taken of the boy, using a long-range lens, when he was in the street with his parents. The photograph was taken without the consent of the parents, and in 2005 it was used by Express Newspapers in its *Sunday Express* magazine alongside a quotation from JK Rowling about motherhood. The court, following *Campbell*, confirmed that, in deciding whether there had been an infringement of Article 8, the first question to be asked was whether there was a reasonable expectation of privacy. The reason for this is that Article 8 needed to be engaged before the balancing act between Articles 8 and 10 becomes relevant.

If there was a reasonable expectation of privacy, then the second question was how the balance should be struck as between the claimant's right to respect for their private life and the publisher's right to publish. It was at least arguable that the appellant had a reasonable expectation of privacy. The fact that he was a child was of great significance. Although the Press Complaints Commission had ruled that the mere publication of a child's image could not breach its Editors' Code of Practice when the picture was taken in a public place and unaccompanied by private details that might embarrass the child, everything depended on the circumstances.

The Court expressed the view that there might well be circumstances, even after *Hannover*, in which there would be no reasonable expectation of privacy. However, it all depended on the circumstances of the case. It was not possible to draw a distinction between activities that were part of a person's private recreation time and publication of which would be intrusive, and other activities such as a walk down the street or a trip to the grocer to buy milk. It was not necessarily the case that such routine activities should not attract any reasonable expectation of privacy; everything depended on the circumstances. Generally, however, the law should protect children of parents who were in the public eye from intrusive media attention, at least to the extent of holding that the child had a reasonable expectation that they would not be targeted in order to obtain photographs in a public place for publication, where the taking of such photographs would be objected to on the child's behalf.

In the 2009 decision of *Reklos and Davourlis v Greece* (Application No 1234/05), the ECtHR held that a photograph taken of a baby in a special care baby unit by a photographer for the parents, but without their consent, violated the baby's Article 8 rights. This ruling would suggest that a parent could object to another parent taking pictures of their child in any public place without their consent – for example the filming of a school production.

In the case of *RocknRoll v News Group Newspapers Ltd* [2013] EWHC 24 (Ch), the judge granted an injunction to the husband of the actor, Kate Winslet, preventing publication by a newspaper of photographs which had been posted on Facebook by a friend of his.

4.3.4 Other case law since *Campbell*

Mosley v News Group Newspapers [2008] EWHC 1777 (QB) concerned Max Mosley, the head of Formula 1 motor racing, who claimed that his right to privacy under Article 8 had been infringed after the *News of the World* published a story alleging that he had engaged in a Nazi-themed sado-masochistic orgy with a group of prostitutes. The court found that Mosley's rights under Article 8 were clearly engaged – the activities had taken place in private and only come to light because one of the prostitutes sold her story. The real issue in the case was whether there was sufficient public interest so as to justify the publication of the story. The High Court found that there was not, because the newspaper failed to demonstrate that the activities did actually have a Nazi theme. The judge suggested that, had the activities had a Nazi theme, there may have been a public interest in allowing publication. This was because of Mr Mosley's position as President of the FIA (the governing body of Formula 1) and son of the wartime fascist Oswald Mosley. Although the case essentially involved the court applying the test set out in *Campbell*, it does suggest that the courts may be more willing than previously to protect the sex lives of those in the public eye. As Eady J said:

> ... it is not for the state or for the media to expose sexual conduct which does not involve any significant breach of the criminal law. That is so whether the motive

> for such intrusion is merely prurience or a moral crusade. It is not for journalists to undermine human rights, or for judges to refuse to enforce them, merely on grounds of taste or moral disapproval.'

Although Mr Mosley was awarded damages by the High Court, he continued to campaign to oblige newspapers to notify their 'victims' before exposing their private lives. He took his case to the ECtHR. However, the Court ruled that newspapers were not required to give such prior notice.

In *LNS v Persons Unknown* [2010] EWHC 119 (QB), the High Court overturned a so-called 'super-injunction' which had prevented a newspaper from reporting on an alleged extramarital affair of John Terry, who was, at that time, the England football team captain. 'Super-injunctions' not only prevent the publication of the story in question, but also forbid any reference to the fact that the injunction itself exists, and they have been criticised as a significant block to freedom of speech. Justice Tugendhat said that:

> Freedom to live as one chooses is one of the most valuable freedoms. But so is the freedom to criticise – within the limits of the law – the conduct of other members of society as being socially harmful, or wrong.

In the instant case, he said it was likely that Terry's main concern was protecting his financial arrangements (eg sponsorship deals), rather than the protection of his private life. An injunction was not necessary or proportionate having regard to the level of gravity of the interference with the footballer's private life in the event of publication.

In *Ferdinand v MGN Ltd* [2011] EWHC 2454 (QB), another case involving an England football team captain, Rio Ferdinand claimed that a newspaper article about his relationship with a woman, which allegedly continued even once he had become engaged, breached his privacy. The court found that since Ferdinand had stated that he was a family man, there was a public interest in demonstrating that this image was false, particularly since he was by then captain of the England football team.

Lastly, in *PJS v News Group Newspapers Ltd* [2016] UKSC 26, the *Sun on Sunday* proposed to publish the story of PJS's sexual encounters with AB, including a three-way sexual encounter involving PJS, AB and AB's partner. PJS sued for breach of confidence and breach of privacy and asked for an injunction to prevent publication. The story had already been published in the USA (and some other places) and on numerous websites. PJS argued that an injunction was necessary to protect himself, his partner and their young children.

The majority of the Supreme Court was of the view that, should the injunction be refused, there would be a 'media storm' in England and that an injunction was necessary to protect PJS, his partner and especially their children.

This case has proved controversial. Details of the story had been published in the USA but, as the celebrities involved were not so well known there, had not been widely taken up. There were further articles in Canada and in a Scottish newspaper and the details then started to appear on numerous websites. On this basis, Lord Toulson (who dissented) would not have granted the injunction.

4.3.5 Taking action against private bodies

The cases you have studied at **4.3** involve private bodies as respondents, usually newspapers, and not 'public authorities' for the purposes of s 6 of the HRA 1998. However, individuals have nevertheless been able to bring claims against such bodies under the 'horizontal effect' principle as developed in cases such as *Venables and Thompson v News Group Newspapers* (see **4.2.1**) and *Douglas v Hello! Ltd* (see **4.3.6** below). This principle allows individuals to bring a case based on an existing cause of action, for example breach of confidence or misuse of private information, which acts as the 'vehicle' which brings the HRA 1998 issues before the court. The court, as a public authority under s 6 of the HRA 1998, is then under a duty to act compatibly with Convention rights. In this context, this means that the courts have developed the law on breach of confidence/misuse of private information to give effect to both Article 8 and Article 10 rights.

4.3.6 Is there a new tort of invasion of privacy?

In *Douglas v Hello! Ltd (No 1)* [2001] 2 WLR 992, the actors Michael Douglas and Catherine Zeta-Jones had granted *OK* magazine exclusive rights to publish photographs of their wedding, and wedding guests were asked not to take photographs. However, *Hello!* magazine obtained some photographs that had been taken in secret despite security measures.

An interim injunction was granted to restrain publication by *Hello!* pending trial. In the appeal, which concerned whether the interim injunction should remain in force, breach of confidence was relied on as the cause of action, but the court also considered Article 8 of the ECHR, being itself a public authority under s 6 of the HRA 1998. Sedley LJ stated that 'English law will recognise and will appropriately protect a right of personal privacy'.

In *Wainwright and another v Home Office* [2003] UKHL 53, Lord Hoffman stated:

> I do not understand Sedley LJ to have been advocating the creation of a high-level principle of invasion of privacy. His observations are in my opinion no more ... than a plea for the extension ... of ... breach of confidence ... There [is] a great difference between identifying privacy as a value which underlies the existence of a rule of law (and may point the direction in which the law should develop) and privacy as a principle of law in itself.

However, the jurisprudence of the higher courts has developed since then as there has clearly been some judicial dissatisfaction with the need to 'squeeze' breach of privacy claims within the cause of action of common law breach of confidence.

The Court of Appeal in *Vidal-Hall v Google Inc* [2015] EWCA Civ 311 held that there was now a tort of misuse of private information, distinct from the equitable claim for breach of confidence. Moreover, in *PJS v News Group Newspapers Ltd* [2016] UKSC 26 the majority of the Supreme Court held that publication of private sexual encounters 'will on the face of it constitute the tort of invasion of privacy' and that 'repetition ... on further occasions is capable of constituting a further tort of invasion of privacy'. In *Abbasi v Newcastle upon Tyne Hospitals NHS Foundations Trust* [2025] UKSC 15, the Supreme Court referred to the tort of invasion of privacy. It stated that this cause of action had developed in recent times, partly to secure rights relating to privacy in English law as required by Article 8 of the ECHR, while also giving effect to freedom of expression in accordance with Article 10. Thus it seems that a tort of invasion of privacy has now been developed by the courts.

Summary

- The rights contained in the ECHR may come into conflict and, where they do, the court will need to strike a balance between them.
- Where an absolute right and a qualified right come into conflict, the absolute right will prevail. However, interference with the qualified right, especially if this is Article 10, should be no greater than is necessary.
- The most common qualified rights to come into conflict are Article 8 and Article 10. Neither of these Articles has precedence over the other and which should assume most importance will depend on the facts of the case.
- In *Campbell v MGN*, Baroness Hale set out the test for balancing the proportionality of interfering with one right against the proportionality of restricting the other, that is that you

should first look at the comparative importance of the actual rights being claimed in the individual case; then at the justifications for interfering with or restricting each of those rights; and finally apply the proportionality test to each.

- The case of *Murray v Express Newspapers* stated that in deciding whether Article 8 was engaged - whether there was a reasonable expectation of privacy - the court would take into account all the circumstances of the case including the attributes of the claimant; the nature of the activity in which they were engaged; the place at which it happened; the nature and purpose of the intrusion; the absence of consent; the effect on the claimant and the circumstances in which, and the purposes for which, the information reached the publisher.
- When deciding where the balance lies between Article 8 and Article 10, the decisive factor is the contribution which the publication would make to a debate of general interest.
- The Contempt of Court Act 1981 creates the strict liability rule. It will be contempt of court where a publication creates a substantial risk that the proceedings will be seriously prejudiced. For this to apply, the proceedings must be active. There are some defences, such as innocent publication, and s 5 allows discussion of matters of general public interest provided that any risk of prejudice to proceedings is incidental to that discussion.
- Common law contempt takes place where a publication is intended to prejudice the administration of justice.

Figure 4.2 Conflict of qualified Convention rights

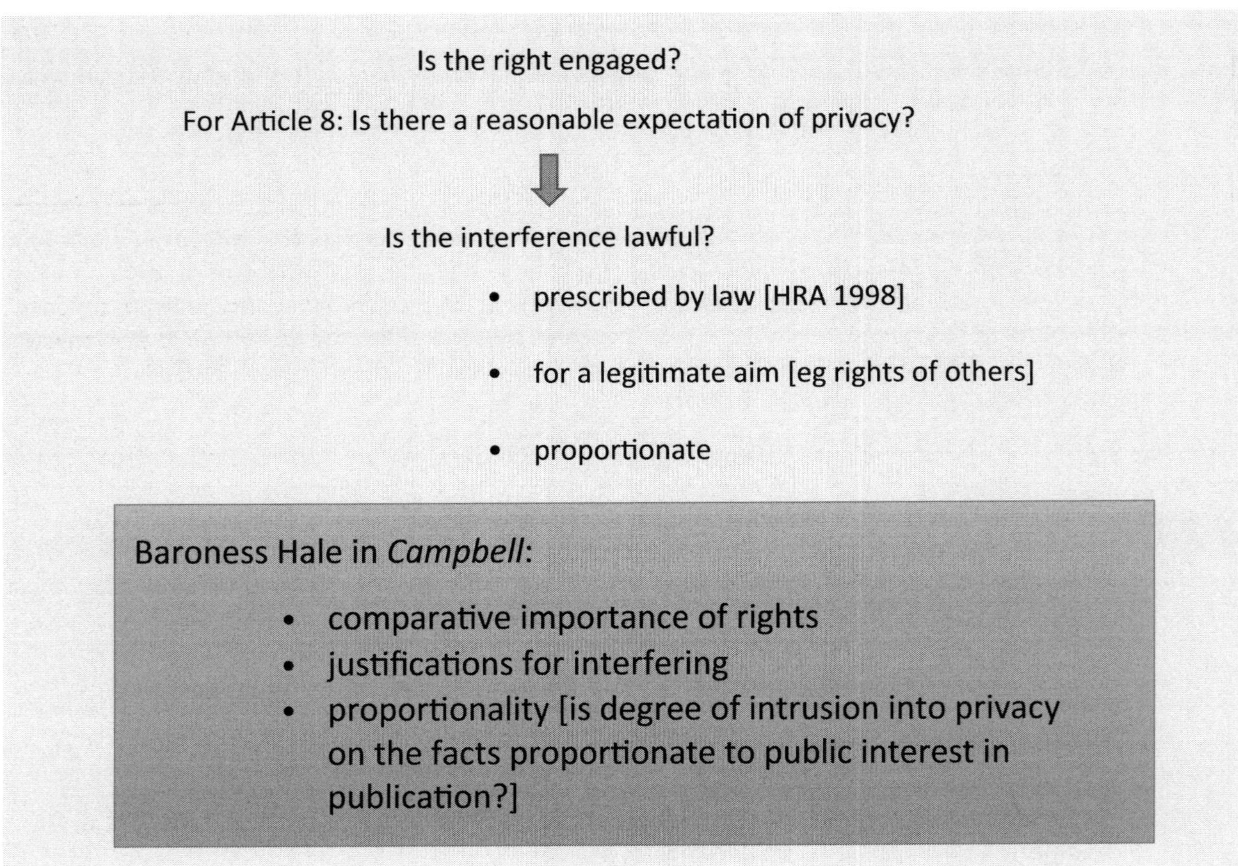

5 Introduction to Judicial Review and the Grounds of Judicial Review

Learning outcomes

When you have completed this chapter, you should be able to:

- explain what is meant by judicial review and assess how judicial review can be justified;
- identify the grounds under which judicial review claims may be brought;
- explain and analyse the ways in which a public body may act illegally;
- understand and explain the concept of irrationality;
- explain and analyse the principles of procedural fairness (ie the rules of natural justice: the right to a fair hearing and the rule against bias) and the consequences of breaching a procedural requirement contained in legislation;
- in factual problems, analyse in a critical and structured manner the availability of both the substantive and the procedural grounds of review, and give a reasoned assessment of their likely chances of success.

5.1 Introduction to judicial review and the grounds of claim

In this chapter, you will begin your study of judicial review, and the diagram below is a 'road map' to assist you. The topics you are studying in this chapter are set out under the heading '2. If so, what are C's likely grounds of challenge?', in boxes highlighted in bold.

5.2 What is judicial review?

Judicial review is the mechanism by which the courts ensure that public bodies act within the powers that they have been granted. In deciding judicial review cases, the judiciary is making sure that the executive branch of government does not exceed or abuse those powers and so does not breach the rule of law.

A court which judicially reviews the actions of a public body is *not* concerned with the merits of that body's decision. Judicial review involves the courts making sure that public bodies make decisions in the 'right way'. If the court became concerned with the merits of the decision, this would encroach on the role of the legislative or executive branches of state and would contravene the doctrine of the separation of powers.

Figure 5.1 Judicial review: an overview

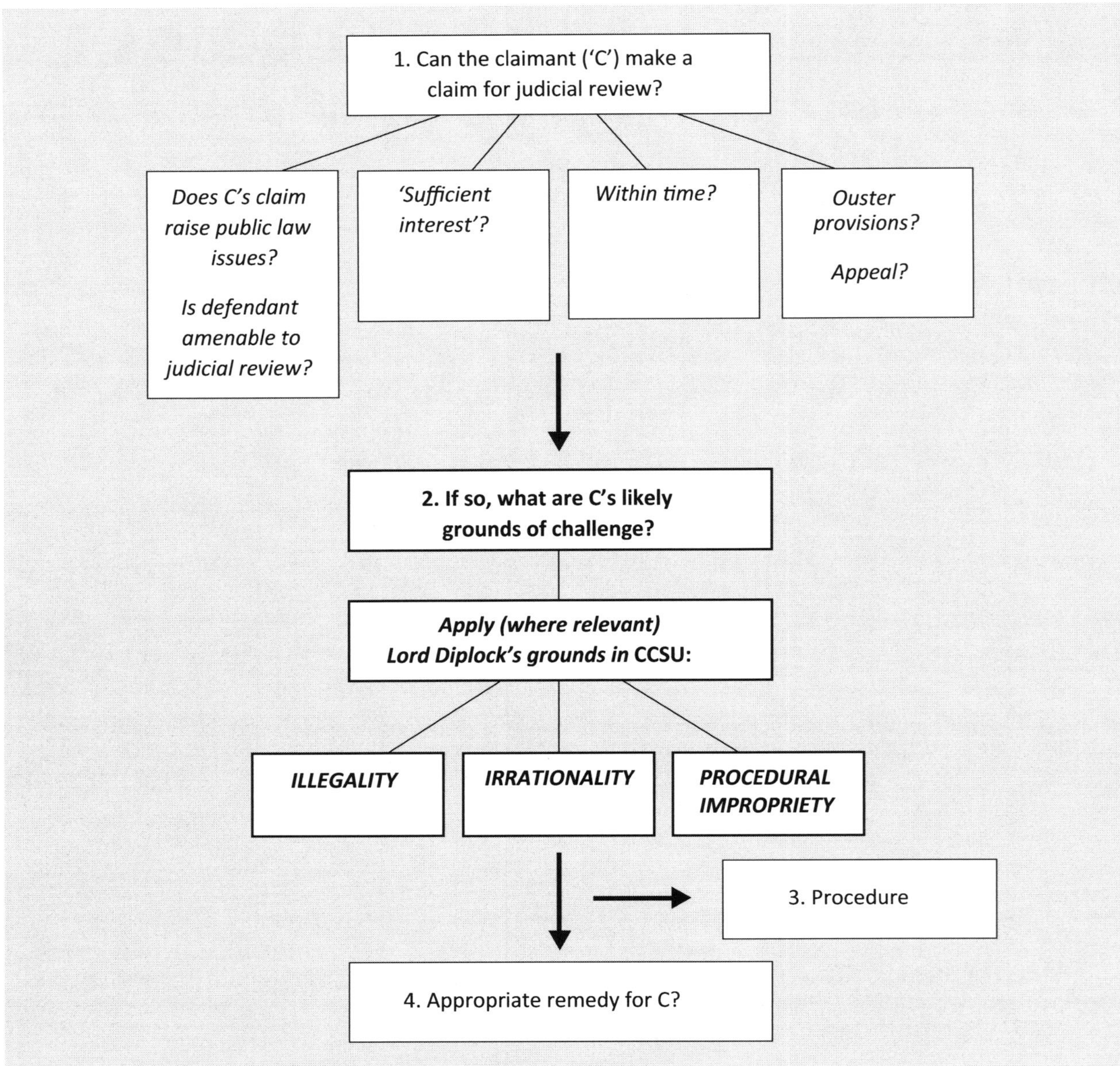

5.2.1 What powers can the court judicially review?

5.2.1.1 Powers under statute and delegated legislation

Most powers exercised by public bodies are powers which have been given to them by statute. Thus, for example, local authorities are given wide-ranging powers by statute, such as the Local Government Act 1972. Immigration officers act under statutory powers (most commonly the Immigration Act 1971, as amended), and the police use statutory powers, in particular under the Police and Criminal Evidence Act 1984 (PACE) and the Public Order Act 1986. In addition, government Ministers are often given powers under statute to make delegated legislation. The use of all these powers can be reviewed by the courts to ensure that the public bodies have acted lawfully. Due to the doctrine of Parliamentary supremacy, courts do not generally have the power to judicially review primary acts of Parliament. However, delegated legislation is made by the executive, rather than Parliament, and so the courts can review, and potentially strike down, delegated legislation.

5.2.1.2 Prerogative powers

In the past, the courts would not review decisions of the executive taken under prerogative powers. The seminal case of *CCSU v Minister for Civil Service* [1984] AC 374 held that any executive powers, including prerogative powers, could be reviewed, provided that the subject matter of those powers was suitable for review by a court. So, for example, case law has shown that a court could review the exercise of the royal prerogative power to grant a passport (*R v Secretary of State for Foreign and Commonwealth Affairs, ex p Everett* [1989] QB 811). However, some prerogative powers were said to be 'non-justiciable', that is, not appropriate for review by the court. This means that the courts are not prepared to review executive decisions such as those relating to treaty-making, national security or the defence of the realm. These types of powers are highly political and should be decided by the executive, who are politically accountable.

The following figure may help to explain the role that judicial review plays in the relationship between the three branches of government:

Figure 5.2 Judicial review and the branches of government

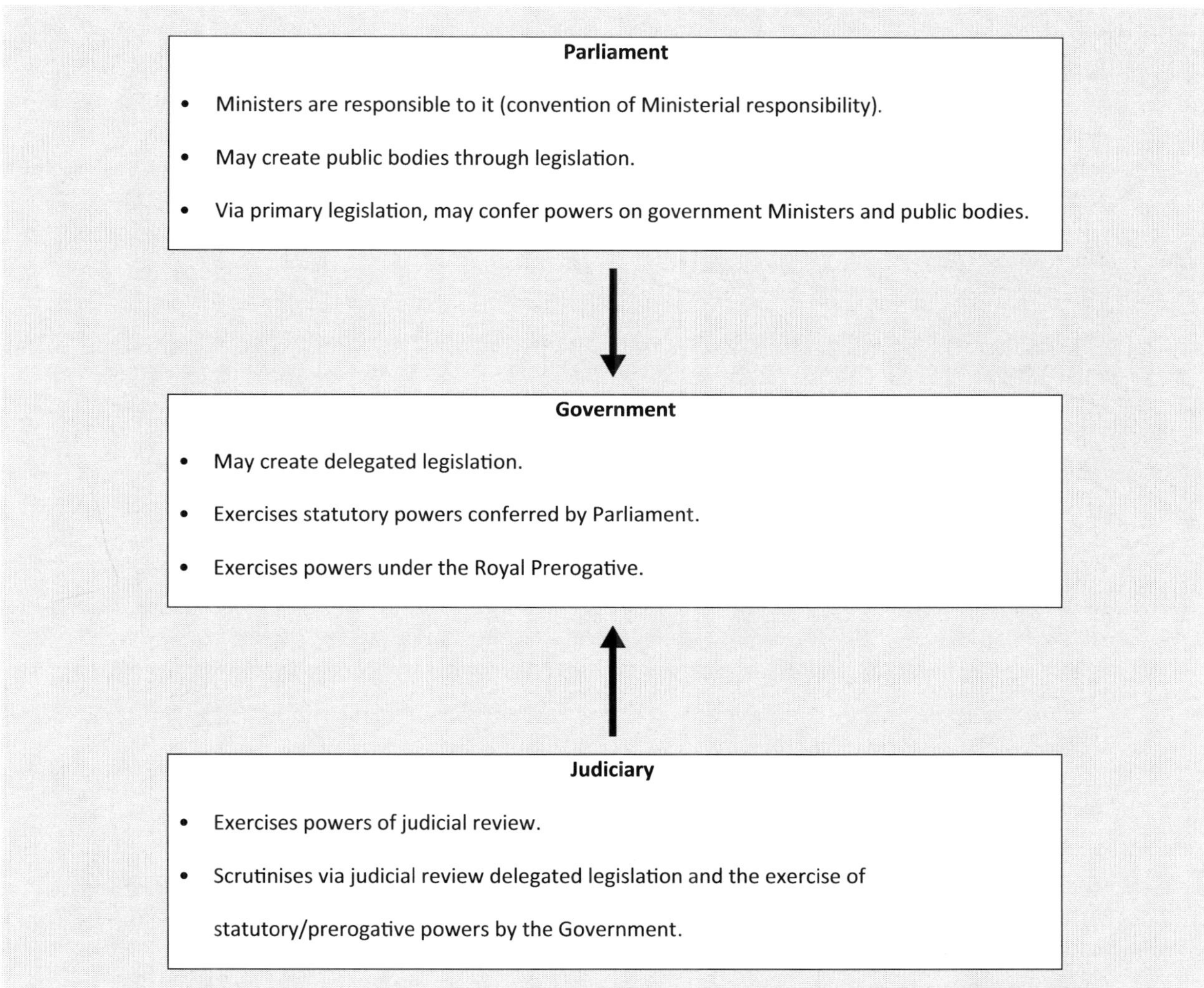

5.2.2 Judicial review compared to appeals

It is often said that judicial review is 'supervisory not appellate'. What this means is that the courts in judicial review are checking to make sure that public bodies 'play by the rules', that is, act lawfully. The court will be concerned with the 'decision-making process' – looking at whether the decision-maker has stayed within their powers and followed a fair procedure.

If the court finds against the public body in a judicial review case, it will not substitute its own decision for that of the public body. Instead, the court will refer the matter back to the public body to make the decision again, this time in a lawful manner. Compare this with an appeal, where the appeal court can look at whether a decision is right or wrong and usually substitute its own.

Many rights of appeal are statutory, but judicial review comes from the common law and has developed over time in line with the increase in government activities. As judicial review has developed through the common law, the relevant principles are contained in the decisions of judges and, in studying judicial review, you will need to consider a large number of cases.

5.3 How is judicial review justified?

As you have seen, judicial review involves the judiciary reviewing decisions of public bodies, often government ministers. What justifies the unelected judiciary reviewing the decisions of a democratically elected government which is accountable to Parliament? There are three main academic theories about this: the *ultra vires* theory; the common law theory; and the modified *ultra vires* theory. We will now consider each of these briefly.

5.3.1 *Ultra vires* theory

Ultra vires means 'beyond the powers'. This theory holds that the justification for judicial review lies in the fact that it is upholding the supremacy of Parliament. When they exercise their powers of judicial review, the courts are ensuring that public bodies do not act beyond those powers conferred upon them by Parliament. This is the 'traditional' justification for judicial review.

5.3.2 Common law theory

This theory emphasises judicial review as arising from the common law. Although it does not dispute that most public bodies derive their powers from Parliament, this theory holds that the grounds for judicial review are judge-made, and that the basic justification for judicial review lies in the principles of good and fair administration. An example of this would be the development of the rules of natural justice – the right to a fair hearing and the rule against bias (see **5.7**). Such rules appear to be rooted in the desire to ensure that decisions are made in a fair manner.

Both the *ultra vires* and common law theories have been subjected to criticism. This has led to the development of a third theory – the modified *ultra vires* theory.

5.3.3 Modified *ultra vires* theory

This theory has been developed by Forsyth and Elliott. They accept that, in carrying out judicial review, the courts are upholding Parliamentary supremacy as it is Parliament that grants discretionary powers to public bodies. However, in addition, they assert that the courts ensure that such discretionary powers are exercised fairly and in accordance with the rule of law. Thus this theory arguably neatly draws together both the *ultra vires* and common law theories.

We will now go on to consider the grounds for judicial review. While doing so, it is worth reflecting on the three theories mentioned above to decide which you find most persuasive.

5.4 Identifying the grounds of review

This chapter focuses on the 'domestic' grounds of judicial review. Lord Diplock, in the case of *CCSU v Minister for Civil Service* [1984] 3 All ER 935, identified three grounds of domestic judicial review. These grounds are:

(a) illegality;

(b) irrationality; and

(c) procedural impropriety.

Illegality and irrationality are referred to as the substantive grounds of review. This is because they focus on the 'substance' of the decision under review.

Procedural impropriety focuses instead on the procedure followed in arriving at the decision under review.

In addition to these three domestic grounds, judicial review claims can also be made under two further 'European' grounds:

(a) breach of the European Convention on Human Rights (ECHR); and

(b) breach of retained EU law.

Breach of the ECHR has been considered in **Chapters 1–4**. Breach of retained EU law will not be considered in detail in this textbook.

5.5 Illegality

5.5.1 How might illegality occur?

An action is illegal or *ultra vires* if it is beyond the powers of the public body in question either because the powers claimed do not exist, or because they are exceeded or abused in some way.

We will now consider in turn the various heads of illegality.

5.5.2 Acting without legal authority

Public authorities cannot act without legal authority, as confirmed by the House of Lords in the case of *R v Richmond-upon-Thames LBC, ex p McCarthy and Stone (Developments) Ltd* [1992] 2 AC 48.

McCarthy and Stone were developers who consulted with the planning officers of Richmond LBC before deciding whether to make a planning application. They were charged for the informal consultation. Richmond LBC argued that it was entitled to levy a fee for this under a power contained in s 111 of the Local Government Act 1972 to do 'anything incidental to the discharge of any of [its] functions'. McCarthy and Stone applied to the High Court for judicial review, claiming that s 111 did not allow Richmond LBC to charge a fee, so that the council was acting without legal authority.

Both the High Court and the Court of Appeal found for Richmond LBC, but the House of Lords found for McCarthy and Stone. The Law Lords stated that the charges imposed for providing informal pre-application planning advice were *ultra vires* because of the lack of a relevant power. The difference between the courts illustrates that, although deciding whether or not something is within the powers of a public body should simply involve applying the words of the statute, this is not always straightforward.

5.5.3 The rule against delegation

5.5.3.1 The rule

There is a general rule that decision-making powers, once given by Parliament, cannot then be further delegated, or 'sub-delegated'.

This rule was confirmed in the case of *Vine v National Dock Labour Board* [1957] AC 488. In this case, the Dock Workers (Regulation of Employment) Order 1947 gave local dock labour boards the power to take disciplinary action against dock workers. A complaint was made against Vine, alleging that he had regularly reported late for work. The relevant local dock labour board appointed a committee to deal with the complaint. After hearing evidence, the committee terminated Vine's employment. The House of Lords held that the decision to dismiss Vine was void because the duty of the local board could not be delegated to a separate committee. Lord Somervell commented:

> There are ... many administrative duties which cannot be delegated. Appointment to an office or position is plainly an administrative act. If under a statute a duty to appoint is placed on the holder of an office, whether under the Crown or not, he would, normally, have no authority to delegate ...

5.5.3.2 Exceptions to the rule against delegation

There are two important exceptions to the general rule against delegation, namely the '*Carltona* principle' and s 101 of the Local Government Act 1972.

(i) The '*Carltona* principle'

In the case of *Carltona v Commissioners of Works* [1943] 2 All ER 560, the relevant legislation specified that the power to requisition factories during World War II was exercisable by the Minister of Works and Planning. A factory owner whose factory had been requisitioned argued that the requisition was invalid because the order had not in fact been signed by the Minister, but by a civil servant within the Ministry.

In the judgment, Lord Greene MR confirmed that government Ministers sub-delegating decision-making powers to civil servants in their departments provides an exception to the general rule against delegation. He stated that, under the convention of individual Ministerial responsibility, government Ministers are ultimately responsible to Parliament for their departments, so there is an expectation that they act through their civil servants in taking even major decisions. Public business could not be carried on if that were not the case.

In *R v Adams* [2020] UKSC 19, the Supreme Court stated that, exceptionally, the *Carltona* principle would not apply if it was clear from the wording of the statute that the decision was one for the Minister alone. Whether this was the case would be decided by studying both the words used and the context. In *Adams*, the decision was a crucial one, relating to whether a suspect could be detained without trial, possibly for a limitless period. In addition, the evidence showed that placing a duty on the individual Minister to take the decision would not place an excessive burden on them. Thus, the court concluded, the *Carltona* principle would not apply.

(ii) Local Government Act 1972, s 101

Under s 101 of the Local Government Act 1972, local authorities may delegate decision-making powers to committees (or to an individual officer), provided they make a *formal resolution so to do.*

5.5.4 'Fettering' of discretion

As a general principle, if Parliament provides a public body with a discretionary power, the courts will not permit that body to restrict or 'fetter' such discretion.

'Fettering' of discretion may occur in two ways:

(a) acting under the dictation of another; or

(b) applying a general policy as to the exercise of discretion in too strict a manner.

We shall look at each of these further below.

5.5.4.1 Acting under the dictation of another

Public authorities cannot act under the dictation of another person or body. In the case of *Lavender & Sons Ltd v Minister of Housing and Local Government* [1970] 1 WLR 1231, Lavender & Sons were refused planning permission to extract sand and gravel from high-grade agricultural land. The company therefore appealed to the Minister of Housing and Local Government, who, in line with a general policy, sought the view of the Minister of Agriculture. The Minister of Agriculture believed that such high-grade land should be preserved for agricultural purposes, so the Minister of Housing and Local Government rejected Lavender & Sons' appeal. The letter containing the Minister's decision stated that he would not grant permission for mineral extraction 'unless the Minister of Agriculture is not opposed to [mineral] working' and that as, in the present case, the agricultural objection had not been waived, he had decided not to grant permission. Lavender & Sons sought judicial review of the rejection of their appeal.

The court found for Lavender & Sons, stating that although the Minister was entitled to formulate a general policy, this decision had not been based on a general policy but on another Minister's objection. The Minister of Housing and Local Government had fettered his discretion by not opening his mind to Lavender & Sons' application.

5.5.4.2 Applying a general policy as to the exercise of discretion in too strict a manner

Sometimes Parliament requires public authorities to exercise powers in large numbers of similar cases. For example, local authorities have to decide numerous planning applications. Fairness requires that like cases should be decided in like ways, and so public authorities may formulate their own policies to help them take consistent decisions. Such policies will be lawful, provided that they are consistent with the statute and applied in such a way that the public authority does not fetter its discretion.

In the case of *British Oxygen v Minister of Technology* [1971] AC 610, the Minister had the statutory power to award industrial grants. To deal with a large number of applications, he formulated his own general policy of awarding grants for businesses to invest in plant and machinery only if the item in which the business was to invest cost at least £25. British Oxygen invested £4 million in oxygen cylinders, but each cylinder cost only £20. The Minister rejected British Oxygen's application for a grant.

The House of Lords held that the Ministry of Technology did have the right to formulate its own general policy, but only provided the policy did not preclude the Ministry from considering individual cases. If the policy had been applied over-rigidly, the Minister would effectively have tied his own hands, preventing him from considering each case on its merits. Lord Reid stated that anyone who has a statutory discretion must not shut his ears to an application and *must be always willing to listen to anyone with something new to say.* On the facts, however, the Minister had considered what British Oxygen had to say and so its claim was dismissed.

5.5.5 Using powers for an improper or unauthorised purpose

Public authorities will be acting illegally if they use their powers for an improper or unauthorised purpose.

In *Congreve v Home Office* [1976] QB 629, the Home Secretary announced that the TV licence fee would be increased from £12 to £18. Congreve was one of over 20,000 people who took out a new licence before the old one expired, so as to avoid paying the extra cost. The Home Office wrote to all of those who had taken out overlapping licences asking them to pay the extra fee and telling them that, if they did not, their licence would be revoked. Congreve sought judicial review of the threatened revocation.

The Court of Appeal found for Congreve, stating that the Home Office had no authority to revoke the licences. The purpose of revoking the licence was simply to raise revenue, in a way not provided for by Parliament. The Court of Appeal added that this would represent a misuse of the power conferred on the Government by Parliament.

5.5.6 Dual purposes

What happens in situations where a public authority arrives at a decision based on more than one consideration, one of which is relevant to the purpose of the power it is exercising, the other of which is irrelevant?

Over a century ago, the House of Lords established the 'primary purpose' test in the case of *Westminster Corporation v LNWR* [1905] AC 426. The London and Northern Western Railway Company (LNWR) sought judicial review of the Westminster Corporation's decision, under public health legislation, to build underground lavatories at Whitehall. The lavatories could be accessed from either side of the street, effectively creating a subway. The LNWR argued that the main reason behind the Corporation's decision to build the toilets had not been to provide conveniences but, rather, to build a subway, which the legislation had not authorised.

The House of Lords found in favour of the Westminster Corporation, deciding that the primary object of the Corporation was the construction of the conveniences and, provided that they acted in good faith and reasonably, their decision could not be interfered with. Their Lordships held that where there are dual purposes behind a decision, provided the permitted/authorised purpose is the 'primary' purpose, then the decision is not *ultra vires* and should stand.

In *R v Inner London Education Authority, ex p Westminster City Council* [1986] 1 WLR 28, the court used a different formulation. The Inner London Education Authority (ILEA) had statutory power to 'arrange for the publication within [its] area of information on matters relating to local government'. ILEA mounted a publicity campaign costing £651,000 concerning the Government's proposals for rate-capping, which would limit the amount it could raise in local taxation and thus spend on education. Westminster City Council sought a declaration that this was unlawful.

The High Court held that ILEA had sought to achieve two purposes:

(i) Giving information about rate-capping and its results; this was an authorised purpose.

(ii) Persuading the public to support ILEA's views on rate-capping; this was not an authorised purpose.

The test that the High Court applied when there were two purposes, one authorised and one unauthorised, was as follows: 'Was the authority pursuing an unauthorised purpose, which materially influenced the making of its decision?'

The High Court considered that the unauthorised purpose was one of the purposes, if not the major purpose, of the decision to launch the campaign. The unauthorised purpose had therefore materially influenced the making of the decision and therefore the decision was unlawful, because ILEA had taken into account an irrelevant consideration.

Although the High Court thought that the 'material influence' test was consistent with the 'primary purpose' test in the 1905 case, the two tests are not easy to reconcile.

5.5.7 Taking account of irrelevant considerations or failing to take account of relevant considerations

A public authority must both disregard irrelevant considerations and take into account relevant considerations when exercising its powers. The case of *Roberts v Hopwood* [1925] AC 578 is authority for both requirements.

Poplar Borough Council had exercised its power under statute to pay its employees such wages 'as it saw fit'. It set a generous minimum wage and applied the minimum to female workers in the same way as it did to male workers. The District Auditor ordered that the Council make good the financial losses caused by paying its employees so generously. The Council sought judicial review of the District Auditor's order.

The House of Lords found for the District Auditor, first because the Council had taken account of irrelevant considerations, namely, 'socialist philanthropy' and 'feminist ambition', and, secondly, because the Council had also disregarded relevant considerations, namely the wage levels in the labour market and the burden which would be placed on the ratepayers as a consequence of its decision.

It need not always be the case that a public authority both takes into account an irrelevant consideration and fails to take into account a relevant consideration. It may simply do one or the other, as the case of *Padfield v Minister of Agriculture* [1968] AC 997 shows.

Legislation gave the Minister of Agriculture the discretionary power to order an investigation into complaints made by those in the farming industry about the conduct of the Milk Distribution Board, a public body set up to regulate the distribution of milk products.
A number of farmers made a complaint to the Minister, alleging that the Board had fixed milk prices in a way which was prejudicial to their interests. The Minister refused to order an investigation, stating that if the complaint were upheld, he would be expected to give effect to the committee's recommendations. The House of Lords held that the Minister had taken into account an irrelevant consideration in deciding not to exercise his discretion to order an investigation.

The potential political embarrassment to the Minister was not a matter the Minister ought to have taken into account when refusing to consider the complaint.

The following activity will enable you to apply the heads of illegality you have considered so far.

ACTIVITY 1 Heads of illegality

Assume that the Public Transport Act 2016 ('the Act') (fictitious) empowers local authorities to give financial assistance in the form of grant aid to organisations involved in operating any form of public transport. The aim of the Act is to encourage the use of public transport to get people to work.

Greenborough District Council (GDC) has created a policy as to how it will deal with applications for grant aid. The policy provides, amongst other things, that applications from minibus operators should not be considered as there is no evidence that such vehicles are regularly used in travel to and from work, and exhaust emissions from minibuses are harmful to the environment.

Ted has operated a minibus company for the past five years. He has recently secured contracts with two large employers in the area to provide transport for their workforce. His application for a grant has been refused without consideration, on the basis of GDC's policy.

Joe is a taxi cab licence holder and has applied for a grant to expand his business into operating minibuses. His application was also refused. The decision was made by GDC's Transport Sub-Committee.

Consider whether Ted and/or Joe have grounds for judicial review.

COMMENT

Ted and Joe are seeking to challenge the decisions of GDC in respect of their applications for grant aid. Ted is already operating a minibus business and is seeking to expand it, whereas this is a new area of work for Joe.

Ted could rely on illegality as a category of review. The statute has created discretion in respect of the award of grant aid to organisations. Any discretion must be exercised reasonably in accordance with the aims of the statute (you will look at the requirement of reasonableness later). GDC has created a policy as to how applications for grant aid should be processed. There is no objection in principle to the formulation of such a policy by a public authority, provided the policy itself is consistent with the statute. Furthermore, any policy must not be applied in an overly rigid manner so as to fetter GDC's discretion.

In this particular case, Ted can first argue that the policy itself is not consistent with the statutory purpose. The policy seeks to prevent applications from minibus operators because, amongst other things, exhaust emissions are harmful to the environment. The environmental issue is not clearly a purpose the legislation was aimed at achieving, and therefore GDC has taken into account an irrelevant consideration (*Padfield v Minister of Agriculture* [1968] AC 997). Putting this another way, if GDC has tried to use the statute to further environmental objectives, it is using the statute for an improper purpose (*Congreve v Home Office* [1976] 1 QB 629).

This could, alternatively, be a case of mixed motives, whereby GDC has in fact achieved two objectives, one of which is authorised (preventing use of private minibuses) and one of which is not (promoting environmental issues). If the primary purpose is lawful then obtaining an incidental advantage may not invalidate the exercise of the power (*Westminster Corporation v LNWR* [1905] AC 426), but much will depend on what the primary purpose was here. Furthermore, in more recent case law, the courts have considered whether the unauthorised purpose 'materially influenced' the decision (*R v ILEA, ex p Westminster City Council* [1986] 1 WLR 28). Ted would need to establish that the environmental issues materially influenced GDC's formulation of its policy.

Even if the policy itself is lawful, Ted could argue that it has been over-rigidly *applied* in his particular case. Although he operates minibuses, he should be treated as an exception to it, having secured contracts from two employers in the area to transport their workers (*British Oxygen v Minister of Technology* [1971] AC 610).

The only issue that Joe can raise is the fact that the decision was taken by the Transport Sub-Committee. However, under s 101 of the Local Government Act 1972, councils are allowed to delegate their decision making to committees or sub-committees of the Council. If the Council has formally delegated its functions in this case, Joe would not have any grounds of review.

5.5.8 Errors of law/errors of fact

5.5.8.1 Errors of law

Errors of law which affect a decision will always be amenable to judicial review, as confirmed in the case of *Anisminic Ltd v Foreign Compensation Commission* [1969] 2 AC 147.

The Foreign Compensation Commission (FCC) had statutory responsibility for deciding on claims for compensation made by UK companies which had suffered losses as a result of war damage overseas. Under the relevant legislation, the owners of damaged property and their 'successors in title' had to be UK subjects. Anisminic was a UK company which, as a result of the Suez Crisis in 1956, had been forced to sell property it owned in Egypt to an Egyptian business for less than its market value. Anisminic applied to the FCC for compensation.

The FCC rejected the claim, on the basis that Anisminic had sold its property to a non-UK business. The House of Lords held that, as a matter of law, a purchaser was not a successor in title. A majority of their Lordships held that such an error of law made the FCC's decision not just wrong but outside of its jurisdiction. An error of law will always therefore be amenable to judicial review.

5.5.8.2 Errors of fact

Public bodies dealing with the same issues on a daily basis develop expertise in assessing facts, and it would overload the courts if they had to decide all the factual disputes which arise from executive decisions. So the courts are more reluctant to allow judicial review for errors of fact than errors of law. Some errors of fact are, however, amenable to judicial review.

'Jurisdictional' errors of fact

Alleged 'jurisdictional' errors of fact are reviewable by the courts, as confirmed in the case of *R v Secretary of State for the Home Department, ex p Khawaja* [1984] AC 74. The Immigration Act 1971 allowed the Home Secretary to order the removal from the UK of 'illegal entrants'. The Home Secretary made such an order in respect of a Mr Khera. Khera's lawyer sought judicial review of the order on the grounds that the Home Secretary had got a central fact wrong, in that Khera had not, as the Home Secretary had thought, tried to hide his entry into the UK, and he was therefore not in the UK illegally.

The House of Lords decided that the matter was amenable to judicial review and found for Khera. Their Lordships stated that decisions based on alleged errors of fact which go to the root of a public body's capacity to act (ie 'jurisdictional' or 'precedent' facts) are reviewable. This was such an error of fact, since the Home Secretary would not have been able to rely on the Act if Khera had been legally in the UK.

Material error of fact leading to unfairness

In *E v Secretary of State for the Home Department* [2004] EWCA Civ 49, E was refused asylum on the basis that he would not be at risk of persecution if returned to Egypt. He appealed, but the Appeal Tribunal refused to accept in evidence two recent reports which made it clear that E would be at risk if returned. The Court of Appeal allowed his appeal on the basis that there had been a mistake of fact giving rise to unfairness. The court stated that four conditions would need to be satisfied to give rise to this ground:

(1) There must have been a mistake as to an existing fact (including a mistake as to the availability of evidence on a particular matter).

(2) The fact must be uncontentious and objectively verifiable.

(3) The person seeking review must not have been responsible for the mistake.

(4) The mistake must have played a material part in the decision-maker's reasoning.

Other errors of fact

Other errors of fact are not usually amenable to judicial review. The courts will defer to the decision of the decision-maker designated by statute.

The example exercise that follows will help you to distinguish between error of law and fact.

Example

A local authority has a statutory power to buy land compulsorily unless it is residential land, including parks and gardens. The authority makes a compulsory purchase order in respect of some farmland. The owner asserts that the land is part of a park.

Is this an error or law or of fact, and, if the latter, is it amenable to judicial review?

Whether farmland is part of a park and therefore 'residential land' depends on evidence and is therefore a question of fact. Assuming that it has made an error, the local authority decision can be challenged on the basis that it has made a 'jurisdictional' error of fact in reaching a decision. Under the statute, the local authority did not have the jurisdiction to make a compulsory purchase order if the land was in fact part of a park. This is a 'precedent fact' relevant to the exercise of the power (R v Secretary of State for the Home Department, ex p Khawaja [1984] AC 74). Alternatively, provided that the land being part of a park is objectively verifiable and the owner was not responsible for any mistake, the decision could be challenged on the basis that the local authority had made a material error of fact and this had led to unfairness (the compulsory purchase of the owner's land) (E v Secretary of State for the Home Department [2004] EWCA Civ 49).

5.6 Irrationality

Successful challenges under the irrationality ground of review require proof of a very high degree of unreasonableness. This is possibly due to concerns on the part of the judiciary that ruling on irrationality will open the courts up to accusations of judging the merits of a decision rather than whether the decision was arrived at lawfully.

As the courts have used different tests over the years, we need to consider how the test for irrationality has developed.

5.6.1 The '*Wednesbury* principle'

The concept of irrationality has its roots in the landmark Court of Appeal case of *Associated Provincial Picture Houses Ltd v Wednesbury Corporation* [1948] 1 KB 223. The owners of a cinema were granted a licence by a local authority to show films on Sundays, but only on condition that no under-15s were admitted (whether with an adult or not). The owners challenged the decision on the grounds that the condition was unreasonable. The test laid down by Lord Greene MR was whether the decision-maker came to a conclusion that was 'so unreasonable that no reasonable authority could ever have come to it'. Lord Greene made it clear that this was not what the court considers unreasonable. The court may well have different views from the decision-maker on policy issues, but this would not be sufficient to give rise to a ground for review. In this instance, the Court of Appeal found for the authority (on the basis that it had made no error of law and its policy was not 'manifestly unreasonable'), but the importance of the case is the test that it established.

Before the test was further developed in 1984, irrationality was more commonly referred to as the '*Wednesbury* principle', or '*Wednesbury* unreasonableness'.

5.6.2 Developments post-*Wednesbury*

The *Wednesbury* test stood unaltered until *CCSU v Minister for Civil Service* [1984] 3 All ER 935, in which Lord Diplock stated that, to be irrational, a decision needed to be 'so outrageous in its defiance of logic, or of accepted moral standards, that no sensible person could have arrived at it'.

Although irrationality can be hard to establish, it is not impossible. Public authorities may still fail the test, as happened in the case of *Wheeler v Leicester City Council* [1985] AC 1054. Leicester City Council opposed sporting links with South Africa, which at the time was ruled by a white minority government that imposed oppressive apartheid policies on its population. Three players from Leicester, one of the top rugby clubs in the country, were selected by England to tour South Africa. The club said that it condemned apartheid, but it was up to the players to decide whether they should go on the tour with the national side. The players concerned did travel to South Africa, and the Council decided to ban the club from using a council-owned recreation ground.

The club's application for judicial review succeeded. According to the House of Lords, the club could not be punished because it had done nothing wrong; it was not illegal for the players to take part in the England rugby tour of South Africa. By using its powers to punish someone who had acted legally, the council had misused them and so had acted unlawfully and *Wednesbury* unreasonably. However, as is often the case, the House of Lords also justified the decision on an alternative ground, in this instance, procedural unfairness.

A more recent example of the application of the test for irrationality is the case of *R (on the application of Gardner and another) v Secretary of State for Health and Social Care* [2022] EWHC 967 (Admin). This case was brought by the children of two residents of care homes who died of Covid-19 during the first wave of the pandemic in 2020. They argued that certain policy documents issued by the Secretary of State breached their fathers' rights under Article 2 and Article 8 of the ECHR and were irrational. The claims based on the ECHR failed but the court held that it was irrational not to have advised that, where an asymptomatic patient (other than one who had tested negative for Covid-19) was admitted to a care home, they should, as far as practicable, be kept apart from other residents for 14 days. The drafters of the documents had failed to take into account the risk to elderly and vulnerable residents from non-symptomatic transmission which had been highlighted by the Chief Scientific Adviser (amongst others).

The example exercise that follows will give you an opportunity to apply the various tests for irrationality, as well as considering aspects of illegality.

Example

Assume that, to combat traffic congestion in urban areas, Parliament passed the Parking Restrictions Act 2019 ('the Act') (fictitious), giving local authorities power to ban parking of cars 'in such areas as they think fit'.

Herbert lives near a busy main road in the centre of Redton. He has received a letter from the 'Transport Officer' of Redton Borough Council stating that he is no longer allowed to park his car on his driveway.

Consider whether Herbert can challenge this decision on grounds of irrationality. Could any other ground(s) of challenge be relevant?

Irrationality

Although there is a statutory power to ban parking of cars 'in such areas as [Redton Borough Council] think[s] fit', the aim of the legislation was to combat traffic congestion in urban areas. Herbert will argue that banning him from parking on his own driveway is not a rational exercise of that power.

Applying the Wednesbury principle from Associated Provincial Picture Houses Ltd v Wednesbury Corporation [1948] 1 KB 223, the court must ask itself if it is a decision that no reasonable local authority could have arrived at and, bearing in mind Lord Diplock's terminology in CCSU v Minister for Civil Service [1984] 3 All ER 935, if it could be regarded as 'outrageous in its defiance of logic'.

Other grounds of challenge?

The following challenges might be considered under the ground of illegality:

1. *Delegation. On the face of it, the exercise of the power by the officer breaches the rule against delegation. However, s 101 of the Local Government Act 1972 allows powers given to local authorities to be exercised by officers on their behalf.*
2. *Unauthorised purpose. As noted above, the power was conferred by Parliament to combat traffic congestion. Preventing Herbert from parking on his driveway does not seem to be part of that purpose (Congreve v Home Office [1976] 1 QB 629).*

5.7 The procedural grounds of judicial review

Procedural grounds of review differ from the substantive grounds in that they focus not on the decision itself, but instead on the *procedure* followed in arriving at the decision under review.

The next example exercise will enable you to distinguish between 'substantive' and 'procedural' grounds of challenge.

Example

Assume that a statute sets up a tribunal to determine appeals from welfare benefit claimants who have had their claims rejected.

Which of the following complaints would be procedural and which substantive? Why should claimants be able to use procedural grounds of challenge?

(a) Claimant A says that the tribunal has made findings about their private life which they had no chance to contest before the tribunal.

(b) Claimant A also says that the findings about their private life are wrong.

(c) Claimant B says that they have not been told by the tribunal why their appeal was refused.

(d) Claimant C says that a member of the tribunal deciding their case is a neighbour with whom they have quarrelled in the past.

All the above complaints are procedural apart from (b). What they have in common is that they are about the steps leading to and the circumstances surrounding the tribunal's decision, rather than the decision itself. Procedures should be open to challenge because the claimant needs to know that their case was handled fairly, quite apart from whether the decision affecting them was right or wrong.

Many procedural requirements, on which a decision's validity depends, are found in the statutes which confer the decision-making powers. To breach such requirements is said to be 'procedurally *ultra vires*'.

Other requirements are derived from the common law rules of natural justice or, as it is now widely known, the doctrine of 'procedural fairness'. We shall examine the common law procedural requirements first.

5.7.1 Procedural fairness – the rules of natural justice

The development of the rules of natural justice has led to some controversy. They are common law rules, meaning that they were created by the judiciary, an unelected body. The legal doctrine of Parliamentary supremacy requires that it should be the legislature, rather than the judiciary, that makes law. The rules of natural justice have, however, become an accepted part of administrative law. In the case of *Fairmount Investments Ltd v Secretary of State for the Environment* [1976] 1 WLR 1255, Lord Russell stated that:

> It is to be implied, unless the contrary appears, that Parliament does not authorise by the statute the exercise of powers in breach of the rules of natural justice and that Parliament does ... require compliance with those principles.

There are two rules of natural justice:

(a) the rule against bias (which provides that a decision-maker should have no personal interest in the outcome of their decision); and

(b) the right to a fair hearing.

5.7.2 The rule against bias

The application of the rule against bias depends on whether the interest the decision-maker has in the outcome of the decision is 'direct' or 'indirect'.

This distinction is important because, where the interest is direct, the court is normally obliged automatically to 'quash' the decision as bias on the part of the decision-maker is presumed.

5.7.2.1 Direct interests

In *Dimes v Grand Junction Canal Proprietors* (1852) 10 ER 301, the House of Lords established that an interest which may lead to financial gain falls into the direct interest category.

In that case, the Lord Chancellor at the time, Lord Cottenham, awarded various injunctions to Grand Junction Canal Proprietors in their ongoing litigated dispute with Mr Dimes. Dimes then discovered that Lord Cottenham had, for 10 years, held significant shares in Grand Junction Canal Proprietors. Dimes therefore appealed to the House of Lords against the injunctions. The House of Lords found for Dimes, stating that Lord Cottenham should have been disqualified from hearing the case because he had a direct interest in the outcome.

In *R v Bow Street Metropolitan Stipendiary Magistrate and Others, ex p Pinochet Ugarte (No 2)* [2000] 1 AC 119, the House of Lords added a new element to this principle.

General Augusto Pinochet was indicted for human rights violations committed in his native country whilst he was the head of the military dictatorship that ruled Chile between 1973 and 1990. He was indicted by a Spanish magistrate on 10 October 1998 and arrested in London six days later. Initially, he was successful in the courts, with the Lord Chief Justice, Lord Bingham, ruling that he was 'entitled to immunity as a former sovereign'.

The House of Lords disagreed, ruling by a majority of three to two that state immunity applied only to acts which international law recognised as being amongst the functions of a head of state, and this did not include torture or hostage taking (*R v Bow Street Metropolitan Stipendiary Magistrate, ex p Pinochet Ugarte* [2000] 1 AC 61). Lord Hoffmann agreed with the judgment, but it subsequently became apparent that he had been an unpaid director and chairman of Amnesty International Charity Ltd (AICL) since 1990. AICL was wholly controlled by Amnesty International (AI), which had been allowed to intervene in the appeal. Pinochet sought to have the decision set aside on the basis that Lord Hoffmann had an interest that disqualified him from taking part in the case.

The court stated that the principle that a person may not be judge in their own cause included cases of non-pecuniary interest, where the decision-maker is involved in promoting the same cause as a party to the case. The Law Lords in the *Pinochet* case thought that the public could not have complete faith that bias had played no part in the original decision because Lord Hoffmann had an apparently direct interest, albeit one from which he did not stand to benefit financially, which should have disqualified him from sitting on the panel. The decision was therefore overturned.

5.7.2.2 Indirect interests

So when does an interest fall short of amounting to a direct interest and amount instead to an indirect interest? An example might be where it is a relative of the decision-maker who has the interest.

In such cases, the reviewing court cannot simply quash the decision automatically; it has to investigate the relationship between the indirect interest and the decision and decide whether the decision should be quashed on the basis of apparent bias.

The leading case on this issue is *Porter v Magill* [2002] 2 AC 357. This case concerned Dame Shirley Porter, the Conservative leader of Westminster City Council. As the 1990 local authority elections approached, she offered council house tenants the opportunity to buy their homes. She was accused of deliberately targeting tenants in marginal wards to try to increase her prospects of re-election.

Magill was the auditor who investigated claims that this was an abuse of power by Porter. Before the very lengthy investigation was complete, Magill called a press conference, at which he said initial results of the investigation suggested strongly that Porter would be found guilty of abuse of power. Porter was eventually found guilty and ordered to pay a large fine.

However, Porter challenged the finding on the ground that it breached the common law rule against bias. She argued that Magill had, through having stated at the press conference that all the signs were that she would be found guilty, put irresistible pressure on himself to ensure that the final verdict would indeed be that she was guilty, so as not to lose face.

The House of Lords agreed that it had been unwise of Magill to call a premature press conference, but disagreed that there was any evidence of bias. The Law Lords were satisfied that Magill had not unwittingly created for himself an indirect interest in the outcome of the investigation.

The House of Lords said that the following test should be applied in cases of indirect bias: *would a fair-minded and informed observer conclude that there had been a real possibility of bias?* The court does not ask whether the decision was in fact affected by the bias of the decision-maker, but how the decision would appear to the observer.

A case that illustrates the application of this rule is *R v Pintori* [2007] EWCA Crim 170. The appellant was convicted of possessing a Class A drug after several police officers had raided his flat. Following the trial, it became apparent that one of the jurors was a civilian working for the police who knew some of the officers involved in the raid reasonably well. The appellant appealed against his conviction on the ground that there was a real possibility that the juror and therefore the jury as a whole was biased against him.

The Court of Appeal allowed the appeal, holding that the appellant did not have a fair trial because the fact that the juror knew the officers would, of itself, have led the fair-minded and informed observer to conclude that there was a real possibility of bias on her part. Such a person would have concluded that the juror was disposed to find the appellant guilty simply because she knew the officers, had worked with them, and therefore wanted (consciously or unconsciously) to support them in the prosecution. Although the deliberations of a jury are secret, the fair-minded and informed observer would also have concluded that there was a real possibility that the juror had influenced her fellow jurors, leading to the conclusion that there had been a 'real possibility' of bias.

5.7.3 The right to a fair hearing

The right to a fair hearing is the second common law rule of natural justice. In *Board of Education v Rice* [1911] AC 179, Lord Loreburn stated that there is a duty on decision-makers to act in good faith and listen fairly to both sides.

It is important to note that the right to a fair hearing is flexible and depends on the context of each individual case.

5.7.3.1 Fairness and the claimant's interest

What precisely is required to be done in order to achieve 'fairness' will depend partly upon the nature of the claimant's interest.

A key determining factor applied by the courts in deciding whether a hearing has been fair is the question of how much the claimant had to lose (ie the nature of the claimant's interest).

In *McInnes v Onslow-Fane* [1978] 1 WLR 1520, Megarry V-C established three categories of claimant, depending on the nature of their interest:

(a) Megarry labelled cases where the claimant had the most to lose, such as their livelihood or job, as *forfeiture cases*. These involve the claimant having been deprived of something they previously enjoyed. Such claimants are entitled to expect a lot more from their hearing for it to be considered to amount to a fair hearing.

(b) Megarry highlighted as the second category of claimant one who seeks the renewal or confirmation of some licence, or membership or office which they have held previously. He labelled these cases as *legitimate expectation cases*, since it was legitimate for the claimant to expect that an established practice would continue. This category also includes those seeking renewal of some form of payment (such as state benefits).

(c) Megarry's third category of claimant is the first-time applicant who merely seeks a licence, membership or office which they have not held previously. Megarry labelled such cases as *application cases*. Such claimants are entitled to expect a lot less from their hearing for it to be considered to amount to a fair hearing.

In the next activity you will consider into which category a potential claimant falls.

ACTIVITY 2 Classes of claimant

Under the Factory Safety Act 2013 (fictitious), the Factory Approval Board ('the Board') is given the power to regulate matters of health and safety in factories. Any person wishing to open a new factory must apply to the Board for a licence. All existing factory owners must apply to the Board for a licence to continue operating.

1. Faisal applies to the Board for a licence to open a new factory to manufacture industrial lathes. Faisal has never previously operated any factory premises.
2. Charlotte has operated a factory making garden ornaments for 10 years. When she applies for a licence to continue operating her factory, she is informed by the Board that her factory is to shut forthwith.
3. Paul applies to the Board to renew the licence for his factory which manufactures computer components.

Identify whether Faisal, Charlotte and Paul respectively fall into the category of forfeiture, legitimate expectation or mere applicant.

COMMENT

1. Faisal is a mere applicant. He is seeking a licence which he has not held previously.
2. Charlotte's case is one of forfeiture. She is being deprived of something (ie the right to use her factory) which she already has.
3. Paul has a legitimate expectation as his is a renewal case.

Forfeiture cases

For an example of a *forfeiture case*, consider *Ridge v Baldwin* [1964] AC 40. Ridge was the Chief Constable of Sussex. Together with some more junior officers, Ridge was accused of conspiracy to obstruct the course of justice. The other officers were found guilty, but Ridge was acquitted. Despite his acquittal, the trial judge criticised Ridge for not having set a good example to the junior officers. Ridge was dismissed the following day, apparently on the strength of the judge's comments. He was given no warning and was not told of the case against him. Ridge applied for judicial review of the decision to dismiss him on grounds of procedural unfairness.

The House of Lords held that the outcome of the decision was of special importance in this case, since Ridge stood to lose (or 'forfeit') his pension rights as well as his livelihood. Consequently, he was entitled at the very least to know the case against him. The Law Lords declared the decision to dismiss Ridge unlawful.

Legitimate expectation cases

The express promise, or existence of a regular working practice, might give rise to two different types of legitimate expectation:

(1) *procedural* legitimate expectation in which a decision-maker has failed to follow a normal procedure; and

(2) *substantive* legitimate expectation where the decision-maker has led someone to believe that they will receive a benefit.

Here, we will examine the first of these: procedural legitimate expectation. *R v Liverpool Corporation, ex p Liverpool Taxi Fleet Operators* [1972] 2 QB 299 provides an example of a procedural legitimate expectation case. Three hundred existing Liverpool taxi licence holders were given a written assurance by the City Council that they would first be consulted if the Council decided to grant any new licences to more taxi drivers. However, the Council then passed a resolution to grant more licences without consulting existing taxi drivers, who challenged the decision on grounds of a broken written promise.

The Court of Appeal held that it had been legitimate for the existing taxi drivers to expect the Council to honour its written undertaking. The Council was not at liberty to disregard its promise.

A more recent example is *R (Save Britain's Heritage) v Secretary of State for Communities and Local Government* [2018] EWCA Civ 2137 where the Court of Appeal stated that there was a legitimate expectation that the Secretary of State would provide reasons for refusing to call in a planning application. A ministerial promise to give reasons in such circumstances was made in 2001, repeated in 2012 and had not been withdrawn.

What if a procedural policy, such as internal guidance within a government department, has not been published publicly and therefore the claimant has no knowledge of it? In *Mandalia v Home Secretary* [2015] UKSC 59 the Supreme Court held that the public body should apply that policy unless it had a good reason not to do so. It stated that this principle ensured that cases would be dealt with fairly and consistently. Such a principle was related to legitimate expectation but was 'freestanding'.

Application cases

For an example of an *application case*, see *McInnes v Onslow-Fane* [1978] 1 WLR 1520. McInnes made six applications to the Boxing Board of Control for a licence to manage boxers. On each occasion his application was refused, with no oral hearing being granted and no reasons being given. McInnes applied for judicial review on the basis that he had not received a fair hearing.

The court found for the Boxing Board as McInnes was a mere first-time applicant. All that natural justice therefore required of the Board was that it should act honestly and without bias.

Another example of an application case is *R v Gaming Board, ex p Benaim and Khaida* [1970] 2 QB 417. Applications to magistrates for gaming licences could be made only once potential applicants had obtained a certificate of consent from the Gaming Board. The Board refused to grant such a certificate to Benaim and Khaida. The Board gave them an opportunity to make representations and disclosed information which had led them to doubt the applicants' suitability, referring to criteria laid down by statute. Benaim and Khaida sought judicial review of the Board's decision.

The Court of Appeal found in favour of the Board. The Board was under a duty, even with first-time applicants, to give applicants a sufficient indication of the objections against them to enable them to answer those objections. However, it had done this. It had no further duty to give reasons for its decisions.

5.7.4 Does the right to a fair hearing always apply?

The 'right to a fair hearing' may not apply in certain situations, for example if a decision which has been made is merely 'preliminary'.

For example, in the case of *Lewis v Heffer* [1978] 1 WLR 1061, there had been a struggle for power in the local branch of the Labour Party in Newham North-East. The struggle became so intense that the national party intervened through the National Executive Committee, suspending all officers and committees of the local party and taking over control itself. The Committee gave the disputing members no opportunity to be heard before suspension. The suspended officers sought judicial review of the decision to suspend them.

The Court of Appeal held that the officers had not yet been dismissed, merely suspended. Since the investigation was only at a preliminary stage, and the final decision had not yet been made, the officers did not have the right to seek judicial review.

The right to a fair hearing may also be overridden by national security concerns. In *CCSU v Minister for Civil Service* [1984] 3 All ER 935, the right of the trade union to be consulted before a change was made to the terms and conditions of staff at GCHQ yielded to considerations of national security. In *R (on the application of Begum) v Secretary of State for the Home Department* [2021] UKSC 7 Shamima Begum left the UK in 2015 aged 15 to join ISIL (the Islamic State of Iraq and the Levant). She was deprived of her British citizenship in 2019 and wished to enter the UK to appeal against that decision. Entry was refused and she applied for judicial review of that refusal decision. The Supreme Court held that the requirements of national security prevailed over Shamima Begum's right to a fair hearing to determine the lawfulness of the Home Secretary's decision to deprive her of British citizenship.

5.7.5 Content of the fair hearing rule

What does the right to a fair hearing include? This depends largely on whether it is a forfeiture, legitimate expectation or mere application case.

The case of *Fairmount Investments Ltd v Secretary of State for the Environment* [1976] 1 WLR 1255 is a good example of a forfeiture case and illustrates how natural justice requires that claimants in such cases should *know the case against them and have the right to reply at each stage of the decision-making process.*

The facts of the case were as follows. Fairmount requested reasons for the receipt of a compulsory purchase order (CPO) as part of the Government's slum clearance programme. An inspector who later visited the site said the decision to make the CPO had been based on a factor (defective foundations) that had not come to light prior to his visit. Fairmount therefore sought judicial review on the ground that the decision was made before they had had a chance to reply.

The House of Lords found for Fairmount on the ground that natural justice requires that an individual should know the case against them and have the opportunity to respond at each stage of the decision-making process. Viscount Dilhorne stated that it had been on account of his belief as to the inadequacy of the foundations, along with other defects, that the inspector ruled out rehabilitation. The inspector had attached great weight to a factor which formed no part of the council's case, of which the respondents had not been given notice and with which they had been given no opportunity of dealing.

In legitimate expectation cases, the nature of a fair hearing depends very much on the expectation that the decision-maker created. For example, in *ex p Liverpool Taxi Fleet Operators* it should have first consulted with the existing taxi drivers before issuing new licences.

In mere application cases, *McInnes v Onslow-Fane* shows that as a general rule applicants are merely entitled to have their cases heard honestly and without bias. However, in *ex p Benaim and Khaida*, as the refusal of the licence cast doubt on their good character, the applicants were entitled to know the gist of the case against them.

Every claimant, however, regardless of the category of case, is entitled to a hearing which is *fair and reasonable* in all the circumstances – *Lloyd v McMahon* [1987] AC 625. Prior to the council tax, the Government raised money by imposing 'rates' on local residents. The District Auditor (DA) twice warned Liverpool City Councillors that they were in danger of missing the deadline imposed by the Government for setting their rates. When the Councillors did then miss the deadline, the DA fined them just over £100,000. Although the DA did not offer the Councillors a full oral hearing, he did provide detailed reasons for the fine and offered to consider written appeals. The Councillors nonetheless sought judicial review of the decision and lack of oral hearing.

The House of Lords found for the DA. The Councillors had been warned twice and had not requested an oral hearing. The DA had therefore acted fairly in not offering them one, and the Councillors had not been prejudiced by not having been granted an oral hearing.

Lord Bridge stated that:

> what the requirements of fairness demand ... depends on the character of the decision-making body, the kind of decision it has to make and the statutory or other framework in which it operates.

In other words, what fairness requires will depend on the particular circumstances of each case, but every claimant, regardless of the category of case, is entitled to a hearing which is fair and reasonable in all the circumstances.

5.7.6 The right to reasons

Statute may well impose on a decision-maker a duty to provide reasons for their decision. Where, however, there is no statutory duty, does the right to a fair hearing include the right to receive reasons for a decision?

As you have seen at **5.7.3** above, the right to know the case against you is a standard requirement of a fair hearing. However, the law has not yet accepted that public authorities also have a general duty to give reasons for their decisions. In the case *R (on the application of Hasan) v Secretary of State for Trade and Industry* [2008] EWCA Civ 1311, the High Court held that the law did not recognise a general duty to give reasons for an administrative decision. However, exceptions do exist.

Where the decision appears aberrant

One exception is when a decision is taken which, in the absence of reasons, looks 'aberrant' (ie completely wrong). For example, in *R v Civil Service Appeal Board, ex p Cunningham* [1991] IRLR 297, Cunningham was dismissed, unfairly in his opinion, from the prison service, whose members had no right to claim unfair dismissal. Cunningham's only option was to apply to the Civil Service Appeal Board for compensation. The usual award in circumstances where, as here, dismissal was considered unfair was around £15,000, but Cunningham was awarded only £6,500. He therefore sought judicial review of the Board's decision to award him such a small amount.

The Court of Appeal ruled that natural justice requires that a decision-maker should give reasons for a decision where fairness requires that a claimant should have an effective right to challenge a decision which looks wrong; where, in the words of Lord Donaldson MR, the decision 'cries out for explanation'. This inexplicably low award amounted to such a case.

Importance of the right at stake

In *R v Secretary of State for the Home Department, ex p Doody* [1994] 1 AC 531, the applicants were convicted of murder and received mandatory sentences of life imprisonment. The Parole Board could only consider applications for a parole once the prisoner had served a minimum period of imprisonment. This period, known as the tariff, was set by the Home Secretary following recommendations by the trial judge. In the cases involving the appellants, the Home Secretary decided not to follow recommendations of the trial judges and set longer tariffs. The applicants were not consulted but they were told the tariffs they would have to serve before a review of their sentences. The applicants claimed that the Home Secretary had acted unlawfully by failing to give reasons for his decisions.

The House of Lords expressly accepted that there is no general duty to give reasons for an administrative decision. However, such a duty may in appropriate circumstances be implied. In this case, the length of the tariff was of crucial importance to the prisoners. To give effect to the fundamental considerations of procedural fairness, it was necessary to ensure, firstly, that every life prisoner should have the opportunity to make written representations as to the appropriate minimum period in their case and, secondly, those representations should be informed by a full knowledge of any relevant judicial recommendations and comments. This meant that, although the Home Secretary was not obliged to adopt the judicial view of the tariff, if he departed from it he had to give reasons for doing so. Moreover, since the Home Secretary's decision was susceptible to judicial review, it would only be possible to mount an effective attack on it if his reasoning was known.

Ability to challenge legality of decision

R (Citizens UK) v Secretary of State for the Home Department [2018] EWCA Civ 1812 concerned the process for assessing the eligibility of unaccompanied asylum-seeking children to be transferred to the UK when the makeshift encampment in Calais, known as 'the Jungle', was demolished. Those refused were given sparse, often one-word, reasons. The Court of Appeal held that the applicants should be given sufficient reasons to enable them to challenge the legality of the decisions. Singh LJ stated that this 'is one of the fundamental reasons why the law imposes a duty to act fairly: the ability to challenge the legality of a decision and so to vindicate the rule of law'.

A general duty to give reasons?

The law in this area is developing and there have been some recent comments from judges which suggest that a wider duty to give reasons may be imposed in the near future (see for example *R (Citizens UK)* above).

Currently, however, it is clear that in some circumstances, reasons will not be required. An example of this is *Higher Education Funding Council, ex p Institute of Dental Surgery* [1994] 1 WLR 242. In this case the Higher Education Funding Council awarded research grants to institutions, according to the quality of their research, based on the results of a research assessment exercise it conducted. The Council gave the Institute of Dental Surgery a low rating, resulting in a reduction of £270,000 in the amount granted. The Council gave no reasons as to why it had reduced the Institute's rating. The Institute applied for judicial review. The court held that as the instant case involved no more than the informed exercise of academic judgment and there was nothing inexplicable about the decision itself, fairness did not require the giving of reasons.

5.7.7 Right to an oral hearing and cross-examination of witnesses?

Does the right to a fair hearing give parties the right to a full oral hearing? No, not in every case, although, as already mentioned, a claimant in a 'forfeiture case' is entitled to expect far more of a hearing for it to be considered to amount to a fair hearing, and this might include a full oral hearing.

A significant case involving cross-examination of witnesses is *R v Hull Prison Board of Visitors, ex p St Germain (No 2)* [1979] 1 WLR 1401. The case arose out of a prison riot, which took place in 1976, and the serious damage which occurred as a consequence. The prisoners were charged with disciplinary offences under the Prison Act 1952 and brought before the prison's board of visitors. The prisoners subsequently argued that they had not been given a proper opportunity to present their cases as they had not been allowed to call witnesses. Furthermore, the board had acted on statements made during the hearing by the governor which were based on reports by prison officers who had not given oral evidence. The court held that there was a discretion to refuse to allow witnesses to be called or cross-examined, but that discretion must be exercised reasonably and on proper grounds. The overriding obligation was to provide a fair hearing. On the facts, the court held that fairness required the calling of evidence and witnesses. Cross-examination of witnesses was also required to enable the prisoners to contest hearsay evidence.

5.7.8 The making of delegated legislation

The rules of natural justice do not apply where the decision-maker has a legislative rather than a judicial function, as confirmed in the case of *Bates v Lord Hailsham* [1972] 1 WLR 1373.

Under s 56 of the Solicitors Act 1957, a committee was empowered to make orders (a type of delegated legislation) relating to the payment of solicitors. Using these powers, the committee published a draft order bringing in changes to the way solicitors were paid for conveyancing work. On behalf of the committee and as required by s 56 of the Solicitors Act 1957, Lord Hailsham sent a draft of the order to The Law Society, allowing a month's consultation period before the proposal would be finalised. The Law Society published the proposal in the *Law Society Gazette*.

Bates was a solicitor who was also a member of the British Legal Association (BLA). The BLA asked Lord Hailsham to extend the one-month consultation period to three months. Lord Hailsham refused the BLA's request. Bates sought judicial review of the refusal to extend the consultation period and sought an injunction against the proposed order becoming finalised.

The court found for Lord Hailsham on the grounds that the committee's function was legislative rather than judicial, and so the rules of natural justice did not apply. The court said one month was sufficient for solicitors to consider the proposal.

The reason why the rules of natural justice do not apply to legislative functions is that delegated legislation usually affects the public or a section of the public as a whole, rather than having a separate effect on each individual's rights. Fairness could not require that each member of the public should be heard before legislation is made.

5.7.9 Procedural *ultra vires*

5.7.9.1 'Mandatory' or 'directory' requirements

Having considered the common law procedural requirements placed upon decision-makers by the rules of natural justice, we now turn to the statutory procedural requirements sometimes placed upon decision-makers by the wording of the legislation which gives them their powers.

Such statutory procedural requirements have historically been classified as being either 'mandatory' or 'directory'. The distinction is important, because failure to comply with a mandatory requirement rendered the decision invalid on grounds of procedural *ultra vires*, but failure to comply with a directory requirement did not.

Bradbury v London Borough of Enfield [1967] 1 WLR 1311 provides an example of a mandatory procedural requirement. Section 13 of the Education Act 1944 required local education authorities to give notice to the public if they closed down existing schools, opened new schools, or changed the nature of a school. Enfield had failed to provide the required notice to the public when it carried out a major reform of local schools. It tried to justify its failure to give notice on the grounds that, had it done so, educational chaos would have ensued. Eight ratepayers nonetheless sought judicial review of the borough's failure to provide notice.

The Court of Appeal found in favour of the eight ratepayers. In other words, the Court considered non-compliance with s 13 in this case to have been a breach of a mandatory requirement, rather than a breach of a merely directory requirement.

Conversely, the case of *Coney v Choyce* [1975] 1 All ER 979 provides an example of a directory procedural requirement. There, the North Nottinghamshire Local Education Authority announced plans for two Roman Catholic schools to become comprehensive schools.

Section 13(3) of the Education Act 1944 specifically required that notice should be given to the public in a local newspaper, in some conspicuous places and at or near the main entrance of the school concerned. The Authority did comply with the first two notice requirements but not with the third.

The changes meant that parents of pupils over 13 years of age might have to travel much further to deliver their children to school. Three hundred parents therefore petitioned the Secretary of State for Education against the planned changes, but the changes went ahead regardless. The parents therefore sought judicial review of the Authority's failure to comply in full with the notice requirements.

The court found in favour of the Authority. In other words, the court considered non-compliance with s 13 in this case to have been breach of a merely directory requirement, rather than breach of a mandatory requirement.

How does the court decide whether a procedural requirement is mandatory or directory? One of the factors the court will take into account is the wording of the statute itself. However, given that both of the above cases turned on the same section of the Education Act, this is clearly not the only factor they consider. A closer inspection of any distinguishing facts between the two cases illustrates what other factors the courts take into account.

In *Bradbury*, the London Borough of Enfield had failed to give any notice at all. It had made no effort to comply with any of the notice requirements contained in s 13. The Court of Appeal decided that the Borough had thereby substantially prejudiced claimants, who were significantly affected by the major reforms. The Court found that the requirements of the Act were an important procedural safeguard for those likely to be affected by the school closures.

By contrast, in *Coney*, the North Nottinghamshire Local Education Authority had placed notices both in the local newspaper and in some conspicuous places. It had even placed notices around the schools but had simply not done so at or near the main entrances. The court decided the Authority had not thereby substantially prejudiced claimants, who, the court felt, had every prospect of seeing one of the many notices, despite their absence from the school entrances.

A comparison of these two cases, then, shows that:

(a) the extent to which the public authority had attempted to comply with the procedural requirements; and

(b) whether or not a claimant is substantially prejudiced by non-compliance with an important procedural safeguard,

are both factors for the courts to take into account in determining whether a statutory requirement is mandatory or merely directory in addition to the wording of the statute.

5.7.9.2 Subsequent developments

In *R v Soneji* [2006] 1 AC 340, Lord Steyn suggested that, rather than trying to make a rigid distinction between mandatory and directory requirements, courts should instead consider the consequences of non-compliance with a statutory procedure. Lord Steyn held that the correct procedure for the court to adopt was to put itself in the position of those who had enacted the legislation – would Parliament have intended the consequence of non-compliance with the relevant statutory requirement to be the invalidity of the decision that had been taken?

In the same case, Lord Carswell suggested that the distinction between mandatory and directory requirements remained a useful starting point, but ultimately the question for the court was whether it had been the intention of Parliament that failure to comply with the procedural requirement would render the decision unlawful.

5.7.10 Legitimate expectations

As you have seen (at **5.7.3.1**), an express promise or existence of a regular working practice may give rise to two different types of legitimate expectation: procedural and substantive. Having already considered procedural legitimate expectation, we will concentrate here on substantive legitimate expectation.

A substantive legitimate expectation may occur where the decision-maker has led someone to believe that they will receive a benefit. The leading case in this area is *R v North and East Devon Health Authority, ex p Coughlan* [2001] QB 213. The claimant, having been injured in a road accident, was severely disabled. She consented to be moved to a new care facility, Mardon House, on the basis that she had been assured by the health authority that this would be her home for life. However, a few years later, the authority decided to close Mardon House on the basis that it was too expensive to run. Lord Woolf CJ analysed the court's role when dealing with legitimate expectation cases. He stated that there are at least three possible outcomes:

(1) The court may decide that the public authority is only required to bear in mind its previous policy or other representation. It must give this the weight it thinks right, but no more, before deciding whether to change course. Here the court is confined to reviewing the decision on *Wednesbury*, that is, irrationality, grounds. It will only be in exceptional cases that irrationality will be found. An example where the decision-maker

was found to be irrational was *R v IRC, ex p Unilever plc* [1996] STC 681. In this case the loss relief which the company claimed was technically time-barred. However, the Inland Revenue had always accepted such claims by the company in the past. The court held that, on the basis of the Revenue's past practice, refusal to grant the relief would be irrational.

(2) The court may decide that the promise or practice induces a legitimate expectation of, for example, being consulted before a particular decision is taken. This is the 'procedural legitimate expectation' which you considered at **5.7.3.1**.

(3) The court may decide that the promise or practice has induced a legitimate expectation of a substantive benefit and that to frustrate the expectation is so unfair that it would amount to an abuse of power. In these cases, the court will have the task of weighing the requirements of fairness to the individual against any overriding public interest relied on by the public body for its change of policy.

Mrs Coughlan's case fell into the third category. She had received both oral and written assurances from the health authority that she could live at Mardon House for as long as she chose to do so. She had interpreted this to mean for the remainder of her life. The court had to consider the 'compelling reasons' put forward by the health authority for closure of Mrs Coughlan's home, ie that Mardon House had become 'a prohibitively expensive white elephant'. The court decided that Mrs Coughlan did have a substantive legitimate expectation to remain in Mardon House for the remainder of her life. This expectation had arisen in her mind as a result of words and actions of the local authority, which had not properly weighed all the considerations before making its decision. There was no overriding public interest to justify the breach of her legitimate expectation. The decision to close Mardon House was therefore quashed.

The danger exists that in requiring a decision-maker to honour a substantive legitimate expectation, the courts are usurping the role of the decision-maker. However, in *R (on the application of Niazi) v Secretary of State for the Home Department* [2008] EWCA Civ 755, Laws LJ stressed that a substantive legitimate expectation (in Lord Woolf's third category) would only arise where the public body concerned had made a specific undertaking, directed at a particular individual or group, that the relevant policy would be continued. Such undertakings are likely to be directed at a small class of people. Laws LJ stressed that the type of legitimate expectation found in *Coughlan* was likely to be exceptional. Public bodies will not normally be legally bound to maintain a policy which they have reasonably decided to change. In addition, the consequences of requiring the authority to keep to its promise in this case were financial only – and as the group of people was small, the impact on public finances would not be severe.

Legitimate expectation is rather difficult to classify under the traditional judicial review grounds, and it would appear to span all three of Lord Diplock's 'domestic' grounds in the *CCSU* case. In the first of Lord Woolf's categories, a claimant's ground of challenge would appear to be irrationality, in the second procedural impropriety, and in the third 'abuse of power', a type of illegality. Some academics argue that legitimate expectation constitutes a new ground of review. However, so far the courts seem to have squeezed it into the traditional categories.

5.7.11 Summary

Figure 5.3 Procedural impropriety

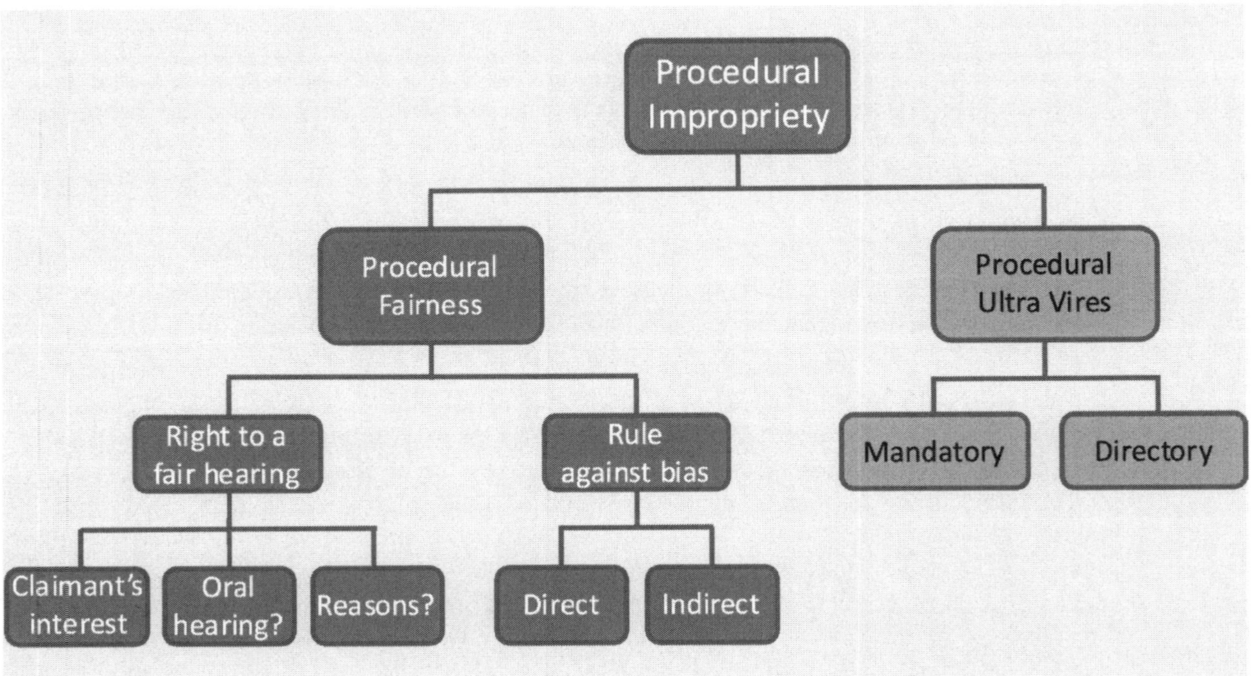

5.8 Conclusion

To check your understanding of the grounds for judicial review, attempt the following activity and compare your answer with the commentary given.

ACTIVITY 3 The grounds for judicial review

Assume that the Terrorist Bomb Damage Act 2020 ('the Act') (fictitious) gives power to the Secretary of State to assess claims for property damage arising out of terrorist bomb attacks and to award financial compensation. The Act provides that claims must be lodged within 28 days of the relevant bomb attack and permits a maximum award of £100,000 to be made.

1. 'Anarchy CDs', a specialist CD shop, was destroyed in a bomb attack. The shop's claim for compensation was rejected on the basis of the Secretary of State's policy not to award compensation to organisations which promote anti-social activity.
2. 'Club Wear', a clothes shop, suffered minor damage in the same bomb attack. The shop applied for £2,000 compensation. The Secretary of State referred the claim to Sveta, a civil servant, to deal with. Sveta has been made responsible for assessing all claims for under £5,000. Sveta rejected the shop's claim as having been made outside the statutory time limit.
3. 'City Crisis Action', a charity which provides temporary accommodation for the homeless, had its premises destroyed in the same bomb attack. It applied to the Secretary of State for compensation of £100,000 to go towards the cost of rebuilding.

It was awarded compensation of only £5,000. No reasons were given by the Secretary of State for the size of the award. Before applying for compensation, the charity consulted the Secretary of State's department and was sent a copy of a departmental circular which states 'when awarding compensation, a full award will normally be given to charitable organisations providing care to the under-privileged'.

Consider whether Anarchy CDs, Club Wear and City Crisis Action have any grounds for making a claim for judicial review.

COMMENT

1. Anarchy CDs
   (a) *Illegality*. The Minister has taken into account an irrelevant consideration (not awarding any compensation to organisations which promote anti-social activity) in reaching his decision (*Padfield v Minister of Agriculture* [1968] AC 997). As a result, the Minister is also using their statutory discretion for an improper purpose (*Congreve v Home Office* [1976] 1 QB 629). Lastly, Anarchy CDs may be able to argue here that the Minister has fettered their discretion by an over-rigid application of their policy (*British Oxygen v Minister of Technology* [1971] AC 610).
   (b) *Irrationality*. This could also be raised if it could be established that the policy and decision are so unreasonable that no reasonable authority could have come to them (*Associated Provincial Picture Houses Ltd v Wednesbury Corporation* [1948] 1 KB 223). Alternatively, the decision is 'outrageous in its defiance of logic' (*CCSU v Minister for Civil Service*). However, this is a difficult test to satisfy due to the high threshold.
2. Club Wear

   Club Wear does not appear to have any grounds for review. Generally, the decision-making power cannot be delegated by public authorities, but a Minister is permitted to delegate powers to a civil servant under the *Carltona* principle (*Carltona v Commissioners of Works* [1943] 2 All ER 560). This is permitted even where there is no express authority in the statute. The exception to the *Carltona* principle in *R v Adams* would not apply on the facts – the decision is not a crucial one and it would place an excessive burden on the Secretary of State to consider such small claims.
3. City Crisis Action (CCA)

   Procedural impropriety. CCA is entitled to a fair hearing. On the face of it, it is a first-time applicant for compensation (*McInnes v Onslow-Fane* [1978] 1 WLR 1520), which may impact on what is expected of the decision-maker in order to achieve fairness. However, the statement in the circular is likely to create a substantive legitimate expectation that its application will be successful.

   It is then necessary to analyse whether this case falls within the first or third of Lord Woolf's categories in *Coughlan*. It is likely to fall within the first category as it involves the payment of money rather than a basic need such as healthcare. CCA would therefore have to rely on irrationality. As no reasons have been given for reducing the award of compensation from £100,000 to £5,000, CCA has a strong argument that the *Wednesbury* threshold of irrationality has been reached.

   Although there is no general requirement for Ministers to give reasons for their decisions, the courts may require this if the decision appears wrong. Here, they may require reasons to enable the charity to ascertain whether the Minister took all relevant circumstances into account in reaching their decision (*R v Civil Service Appeal Board, ex p Cunningham* [1991] IRLR 297). In this case, the size of the award may appear unjustifiably low, and if so, the decision could be quashed for the failure to give reasons.

Summary

By studying this chapter, you should have gained an understanding of what judicial review can achieve, how a claim can be established by reference to grounds of challenge, and an understanding of the difference between substantive and procedural grounds. This will provide a basis for you to go on in the next chapter to explore in detail how a claim for judicial review is made.

- Illegality is a ground for challenge. The main categories of illegality are:
  - Acting without legal authority (*ultra vires*): The decision-maker exceeds the powers given by statute (*ex p McCarthy and Stone*).
  - Error of law: the decision-maker misunderstands its powers (*Anisminic*).
  - Error of fact: where either the decision-maker makes a mistake as to a fact that must be in place to trigger the use of the power (*ex p Khawaja* [1984] AC 74) or has made a material error of fact leading to unfairness (*E v Secretary of State for the Home Department*).
  - Unlawful delegation: a decision-maker cannot further delegate its powers, unless it is a local authority and has made a formal resolution to do so (Local Government Act 1972, s 101) or they are a Minister delegating to a civil servant within their department (*Carltona*).
  - Fettering discretion by applying a policy too rigidly: a decision-maker must not close its ears to an applicant who has something new to say (*British Oxygen*).
  - Fettering discretion by acting under the dictation of another: a decision-maker must not allow another person to make the decision for it (*Lavender & Son*).
  - Improper or unauthorised purpose: the decision-maker must use its powers for the correct purpose (*Congreve*).
  - Dual purpose: the decision-maker should not use its powers to cover two or more different purposes, if one or more of those purposes was unlawful and materially influenced the decision. If, on the other hand, the authorised purpose was the dominant purpose, then the decision will stand (*LNWR/ILEA*).
  - Considerations: a decision-maker must not take irrelevant considerations into account when making its decision and must not ignore relevant considerations (*Roberts v Hopwood; Padfield*).
- Irrationality is a ground for challenge where a decision is 'so unreasonable' that 'no reasonable authority could ever have come to it' (*Associated Provincial Picture Houses v Wednesbury Corporation*) or 'so outrageous' in its defiance of logic that 'no sensible person' could have reached it (*CCSU*). Whilst the threshold for irrationality is high, cases such as *Gardner* show it can be reached.
- Procedural impropriety is a ground for challenge based on the way in which a decision has been reached ('procedure').
- The two common law rules of procedural fairness, or natural justice, are:
  - The right to fair hearing: the rules of natural justice demand that a hearing should be fair in all the circumstances (*Ridge v Baldwin*), although what constitutes a fair hearing depends on factors such as the nature of the interest of a party adversely affected by a decision (*McInnes v Onslow-Fane*).
  - The rule against bias: an individual has the right to a fair and independent tribunal, so they can challenge decisions where the decision-maker is biased or appears to be biased. There are two categories of bias:
    - Direct interest: the decision-maker should not judge in their own cause. If they receive a pecuniary advantage as result of their decision, it will automatically be void (*Dimes v Grand Junction Canal Co.*). The same principle applies if they

are involved in promoting the same cause as one of the parties in the case (*ex p Pinochet Ugarte (No 2)*).

- Indirect interest: the test is whether a fair-minded and informed observer would conclude that there was a real possibility of bias (*Porter v Magill*).

- ◦ Breach of statutory procedural requirements, or procedural *ultra vires*: according to *R v Soneji*, whether a procedure set within a statute should be followed depends on Parliament's intention in the face of its breach.

- A legitimate expectation, either procedural or substantive, can arise as a result of a promise made by a decision-maker. The promise should be honoured unless public interest prevails (*ex p Coughlan*).

6 Judicial Review - Procedure and Remedies

Learning outcomes

When you have completed this chapter, you should be able to:

- explain in outline the principle of 'procedural exclusivity';
- assess whether a decision-maker is one against whom judicial review claims may be brought;
- explain the legal principles relating to standing in judicial review claims and analyse whether a claimant is likely to be deemed to have sufficient standing to bring a judicial review claim;
- explain the legal principles relating to time limits and analyse whether a court is likely to permit a judicial review claim which is brought neither promptly nor without undue delay;
- assess whether attempts by Parliament to oust the judiciary from participating in a judicial review claim are likely to succeed;
- consider what remedies a successful claimant is likely to be granted.

6.1 Introduction

Judicial review procedure is governed by primary legislation (s 31 of the Senior Courts Act 1981) and by rules of court contained in Part 54 of the Civil Procedure Rules (CPR) 1998. In this chapter, you will study the procedure required to obtain judicial review and the remedies available.

Set out below is the overview diagram, to which you were introduced in **Chapter 5**. As before, the topics you are studying are in boxes highlighted in bold.

6.2 Is judicial review the appropriate procedure to use?

As you know, judicial review is a process carried out by the courts to ensure that the government and other public bodies act within their legal powers. That means that a claim for judicial review can only be brought against a public body. In addition, judicial review is only used to challenge a public law decision. As an introduction to this area, please attempt Activity 1 below.

Figure 6.1 Judicial review: an overview

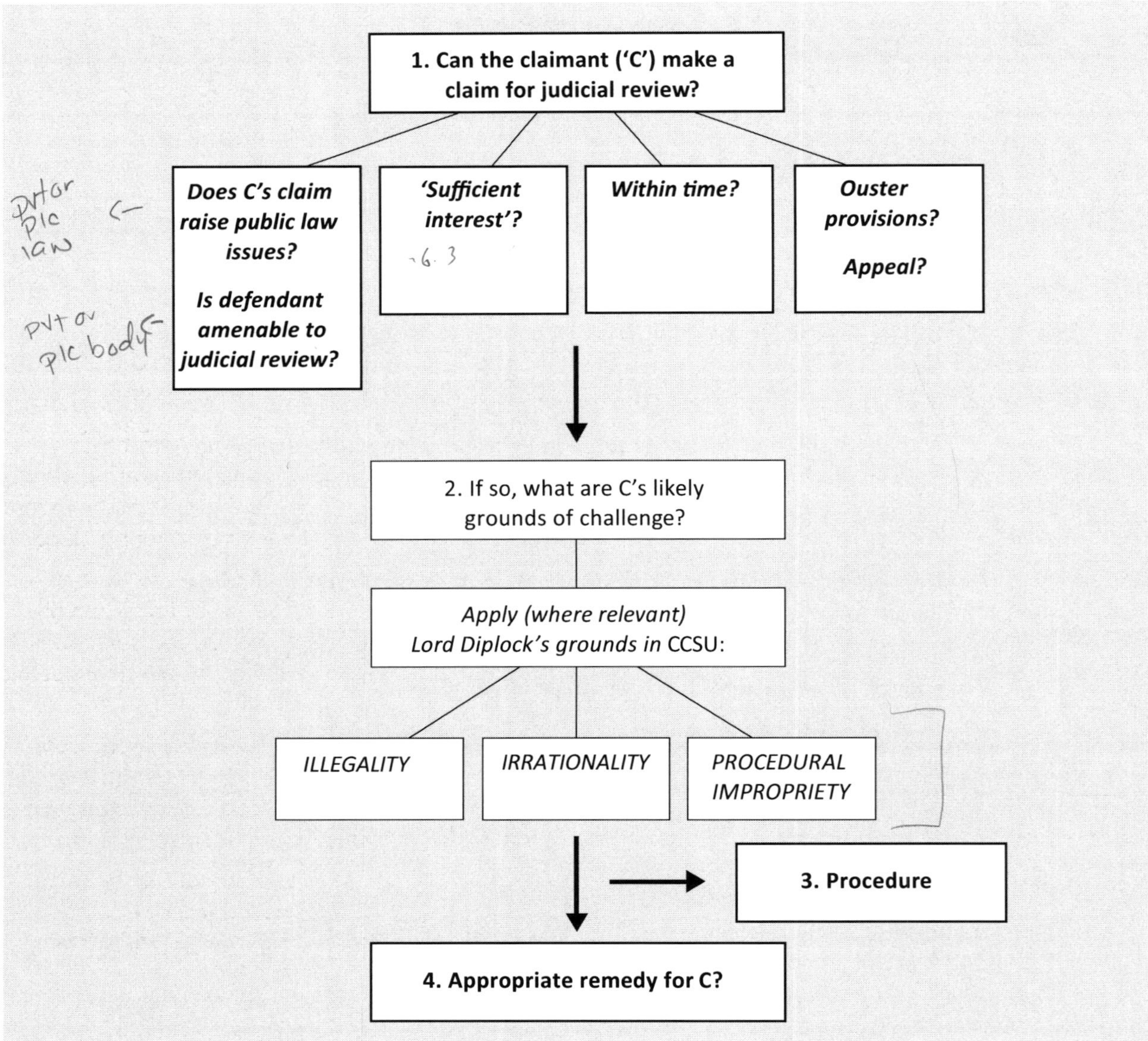

ACTIVITY 1 Is judicial review the appropriate procedure?

Consider which of the following claims you would expect to be brought by way of judicial review proceedings:

1. A private care home has told an elderly woman that it is terminating her care contract and will remove her from the home. She wishes to challenge the decision.
2. Your client has been given negligent advice by a council planning officer, leading him to spend money on a planning application which has failed. He wishes to recover compensation.
3. You act for an electricity company which has been told that the Government is revising its national power strategy in favour of nuclear power sources. The company feels that it was not properly consulted.

COMMENT

Only claim 3 would be brought via judicial review proceedings, as it involves a challenge to a public body (the Government) on public law grounds (fair hearing).

Claim 1 involves a challenge to a private body (the care home) on private law grounds (breach of contract).

Claim 2 involves a claim against a public body (the local authority) but on private law grounds (claim in tort for negligent misstatement).

6.2.1 Public law v private law: the principle of 'procedural exclusivity'

We first need to consider when judicial review is the appropriate procedure to use.

The principle of procedural exclusivity requires that, in a 'public law case', the judicial review procedure *should normally* be followed, rather than the ordinary private law procedure.

In *O'Reilly v Mackman* [1983] 2 AC 2370, the claimants were four prisoners who were charged with, and found guilty of, disciplinary offences by the board of visitors to the prison. They were seeking a declaration that the disciplinary decisions affecting them were void, but by means of a private law action rather than via an application for judicial review.

Lord Diplock stated that the claimants were not complaining about a breach of their private rights because their private right to personal liberty had been taken away by the sentence of the court. They were complaining that they should be entitled to remission of sentence, but this was a matter of discretion rather than right.

He went on to say that the prisoners had a legitimate expectation, based on past practice, that good behaviour would earn remission. This gave them a sufficient interest to challenge the board's decision, using public law grounds of challenge. Thus they could have brought a judicial review claim.

The House of Lords found for the board of visitors as the claimants had brought the wrong type of claim. The Law Lords stated that it would, as a general rule, be contrary to public policy and an abuse of process of court to allow a claimant to seek to enforce public law rights by way of ordinary action rather than by judicial review.

Lord Diplock gave the following reasons for using judicial review:

(a) By using private law procedures, the plaintiffs were 'evading the safeguards' imposed in the public interest against 'groundless, unmeritorious or tardy' attacks on the validity of decisions (eg the permission and delay rules which affect an application for judicial review; see **6.4.2** and **6.6.2** below).

(b) The judicial review procedure had been reformed in 1978 to remove the defects of the old procedures.

6.2.2 Cases involving both a public law and a private law element

An exception to the 'procedural exclusivity' principle is where a case involves both private and public law.

This was so in *Roy v Kensington Family Practitioner Committee* [1992] AC 624. Dr Roy, a GP, argued that he was entitled, under NHS regulations, to be paid the 'full rate' on the fee scale provided by the Kensington Family Practitioner Committee. Such a rate was available to any GP where the Committee was satisfied that they were devoting a substantial amount of their time to general practice.

The Committee believed that Dr Roy did not satisfy this criterion and so paid him 20% less than the 'full rate'. This was a public law decision, challengeable via judicial review. Dr Roy sued the Committee for the balance, alleging breach of contract and pursuing ordinary private law procedure. The Committee argued that he should have sought judicial review and that his private law claim should therefore be dismissed.

The House of Lords found that where a claim is based on a mixture of private rights and public law grounds, the public law element may be raised in private law proceedings.

In *R (on the application of Shashikanth) v NHS Litigation Authority* [2024] EWCA Civ 1477, a GP had a dispute with an NHS clinical commissioning group ('CCG'). The contract the GP had with the CCG was a non-NHS contract which created contractual rights and liabilities. A dispute arose and the GP exercised his right under the contract to refer the dispute to the Secretary of State to be determined by an adjudicator. The adjudicator found against the GP, and the GP challenged their decision by way of judicial review. The Court of Appeal stated that the adjudicator had acquired jurisdiction under statute, and the procedure for determining the dispute was also regulated by statute. This gave rise to a presumption that this was a public law function amenable to judicial review. Although the adjudicator was determining issues involving private law, those rights arose in a statutory context. The reality of the situation was that the statutory disputes process in relation to this contract did involve a public function and thus judicial review was available.

However, it remains the case that exclusively public law issues must be determined in judicial review proceedings, and exclusively private law issues must be determined in ordinary private law proceedings. The principle of procedural exclusivity was confirmed (notwithstanding some academic criticism) in *Trim v North Dorset District Council of Nordon* [2010] EWCA Civ 1446. In this case, the applicant had challenged the validity of a notice of breach of planning condition using private law proceedings. Citing *O'Reilly v Mackman* as authority, the Court of Appeal held that the applicant's case was a matter of public law and should therefore have been commenced by way of judicial review.

Examples of the most common types of public law cases include challenges to the making of a compulsory purchase order over land, challenges to the grant (or refusal) of a licence permitting a particular type of activity to be carried out, and challenges to the refusal of discretionary financial grants.

A public law issue may also be raised as a defence in private law proceedings, through the principle of 'collateral challenge', as illustrated in the cases of *Wandsworth London Borough Council v Winder* [1985] AC 461 and *Boddington v British Transport Police* [1998] 2 WLR 639.

In *Wandsworth v Winder* the Council had increased council rents substantially and sued a council tenant who had refused to pay the increase. The defendant claimed, as a public law defence, that the increase in rent was *ultra vires*. The Council argued that he should have used judicial review.

The House of Lords confirmed that a defence alleging the invalidity of a public law decision may be raised either in private law proceedings or through judicial review. In this case, the public law issue is said to arise 'collaterally' in the private law proceedings.

In *Boddington* the House of Lords extended the concept of collateral challenge to criminal cases. Mr Boddington had been prosecuted for smoking on a train in breach of a by-law. His defence was that the by-law itself was unlawful. Although he failed to establish this, the House of Lords found that a defendant to a criminal charge may normally use a public law issue as a defence.

The next example will enable you to consolidate your understanding of this area.

Example

1. *Aruna is a self-employed accountant who provided some accountancy services to the Constantia District Council. The Council has refused to pay her bill, arguing that it is too high.*

How should Aruna proceed?

Aruna has a private law (contractual) relationship with the Constantia District Council. She needs to proceed by way of a private law claim for damages, not by way of judicial review.

2. *A group of protesters is being sued for trespassing on common land in contravention of a local authority by-law. The protesters claim that the by-law is ultra vires and therefore that they were not trespassing.*

   Will the protesters be able to assert their claim that the by-law is ultra vires as a defence against the claim for trespass? Would your answer differ if the protesters were instead being privately prosecuted for criminal trespass?

   By way of exception to the general principle in O'Reilly v Mackman, the protesters should be able to challenge the validity of the by-law as part of their defence to what appears to be a civil claim for trespass (rather than a criminal prosecution) as they are raising a public law defence to private law proceedings (Wandsworth LBC v Winder).

   If the protesters were defending a private prosecution for criminal trespass, they could still raise the invalidity of the by-law as a defence, but the appropriate authority for this is Boddington v British Transport Police.

6.2.3 Identity of the decision-maker

Claimants can seek judicial review only of decisions made by *public* bodies. Decisions of private bodies must be challenged under private law proceedings.

Lloyd LJ established a two-part test to determine what constitutes a public body in the case of *R v Panel on Takeovers, ex p Datafin plc* [1987] 2 WLR 699. In this case the applicants challenged a decision of the Panel on Takeovers and Mergers. Initially, the applicant was refused permission to apply for judicial review on the basis that the Panel's decision was not susceptible to judicial review. The company appealed to the Court of Appeal which stated that the decision of a body could be susceptible to judicial review if it fulfilled one or both elements of the following two-part test.

The first part of the test is the *source of power* test. Under this, if the body making a decision has been set up under statute or delegated legislation, or derives its power under a reviewable prerogative power, then it is a public body.

If this part of the test is not satisfied then the court goes on to apply the second part, the *nature of power* test. Under this, if the body making the decision is exercising a public, governmental, function, it may still be a public body. To decide whether a power is 'governmental', the court will usually ask what the situation would be if the body did not exist. If the answer is that the government would step in and create a body with similar functions, then that body will be a 'public body'. So, for example, in the *Datafin* case itself, had the Panel on Takeovers and Mergers not existed, the government would probably have set up its own body to carry out the Panel's functions as the Panel was carrying out wide-ranging and important functions which affected a large number of people. On that basis, the Panel was a public body whose decisions could be challenged by way of judicial review. In contrast, the court in *R (on the application of Tortoise Media Ltd) v Conservative and Unionist Party* [2023] EWHC 3088 (Admin) held that the Conservative party was not performing a public function when it chose a new leader, mid Parliamentary term. The party was not appointing a new Prime Minister since this was something which could only be done by the monarch. Thus the news outlet failed in its claim to review the Conservative party's refusal to provide information regarding its leadership voting system.

The next example will enable you to check your understanding of this area.

Example

Under the Advertising Regulation Act 2019 (fictitious) the Advertising Conduct Commission (ACC) is established to regulate the advertising industry. Under the Act, a business wanting to set up a new advertising agency must obtain a licence from the ACC.

Is the ACC amenable to judicial review?

The ACC was created by statute, namely, the Advertising Regulation Act 2019. It therefore satisfies the first element of the two-part test, ie the source of power test, established in R v Panel on Takeovers, ex p Datafin plc [1987] 2 WLR 699. Consequently, it is a public rather than a private body and, as such, is amenable to judicial review.

6.3 Standing in claims for judicial review

6.3.1 The requirement of 'sufficient interest'

The courts will deem a claimant to have standing to bring a judicial review claim only if they have 'sufficient interest in the matter to which a claim relates', as required by s 31(3) of the Senior Courts Act 1981. This will not present a problem if a claimant is personally affected by a decision, but may be an issue if the claimant has no personal interest. The leading case on this issue is *R v Inland Revenue Commissioners, ex p The National Federation of Self-Employed and Small Businesses Ltd* [1982] AC 617. For many years casual workers employed by Fleet Street newspapers had avoided paying tax by using false names. The Inland Revenue granted them an amnesty and agreed not to pursue the workers for arrears of tax provided they paid tax in the future. The National Federation of Self-Employed and Small Businesses applied for judicial review of this arrangement, claiming that it was unlawful. The Revenue argued that the Federation lacked sufficient interest to have standing.

As explained at **6.6.2** below, judicial review is a two-stage process. The House of Lords explained that the purpose of the first stage, the permission stage, was to weed out weak and frivolous claims. It was therefore correct at this stage to hold that the Federation did have standing, as its claim was not obviously unmeritorious. However, the issue of standing could not be separated from the merits of the case. At the second stage, the substantive hearing where the facts and legal issues would be considered in depth, the court should re-examine the claimant's standing with regard to the merits of the claim and the claimant's relationship to the merits. As the Federation had been unable to prove any wrongdoing on the part of the Revenue, it did not have sufficient interest because in general one taxpayer has no legitimate interest in the affairs of another.

However, if the Federation had shown serious wrongdoing on the part of the Revenue, then it is likely that it would have been granted standing. Accordingly, the question of standing is closely linked to the merits of the case; the courts are unlikely to reject a valid judicial review claim simply on the grounds of a lack of standing.

Although the Federation failed to establish the requisite standing, it is clear from the judgment that in principle pressure groups may in the right circumstances have standing, and even perhaps a single 'public-spirited individual'. So, when will pressure groups have standing to bring a judicial review claim?

6.3.2 Pressure groups and judicial review proceedings

The case of *R v Secretary of State for Foreign Affairs, ex p World Development Movement Limited* [1995] 1 WLR 386 gave guidance on the factors that should be taken into account when deciding whether a pressure group has sufficient standing to bring a claim for judicial review.

In the early 1990s, the Foreign Secretary granted aid to Malaysia towards the building of a hydro-electric power station at the Pergau Dam. He granted the aid under s 1(1) of the Overseas Development and Co-operation Act 1980, which required that any donations were 'for the purposes of promoting the development or maintaining the economy of a country'.

The World Development Movement (WDM) was a pressure group which argued that the Foreign Secretary had known that the Pergau Dam project was economically unsound, and that the money was really a payment for the supply of arms by the UK to Malaysia.

The WDM sought judicial review of the granting of the aid. The Foreign Secretary argued that WDM, as a pressure group, lacked standing to seek judicial review.

The Divisional Court found for WDM, and set out the five relevant factors a court should consider in deciding whether a pressure group has standing to bring a judicial review claim.

The five factors are:

(1) the need to uphold the rule of law;

(2) the importance of the issue raised;

(3) the likely absence of any other responsible challenger;

(4) the nature of the alleged breach of duty; and

(5) the role of the pressure group.

The court emphasised the fifth factor as being particularly relevant, pointing out WDM's expertise and prominence in promoting and protecting aid to developing nations.

Sometimes a number of people who are personally affected by a decision may form a grouping to oppose that decision (for example, a group of local residents who join together to oppose the building of a nuclear power station in their area). Such a grouping would *not* ordinarily need to satisfy the factors set out in *ex p World Development Movement* since each individual member of the group would be personally affected by the decision and would therefore have sufficient standing under s 31(3).

In recent years the courts have appeared to adopt a liberal approach to standing, but there are indications of a possible tightening as shown by *R (Good Law Project and Runnymede Trust) v Prime Minister and Secretary of State for Health & Social Care* [2022] EWHC 298 (Admin). The Good Law Project (GLP) is a non-profit campaign organisation with a mission to achieve change through the law, while Runnymede is a race equality think tank. They challenged some senior healthcare appointments that the Government made in the early days of the Covid-19 pandemic on the grounds that the appointment process was (i) indirectly discriminatory, (ii) breached the public sector equality duty (PSED) requiring public bodies to eliminate unlawful discrimination and advance equality of opportunity, and (iii) was procedurally unfair and breached the rule against bias. The High Court held that Runnymede had standing regarding the second issue, the alleged breach of the PSED, as it was an organisation whose specific aims included promoting racial equality, but it did not in relation to the other two issues as Employment Tribunals were the appropriate forum for the claims in question. However, the GLP did not have standing at all due to its broad remit, and moreover Runnymede was a better placed challenger regarding the alleged breach of the PSED. There have been suggestions following this judgment that public bodies should be more willing to challenge the standing of claimants than they are presently.

The next example exercise will illustrate how you apply the requirement that a claimant has 'sufficient interest' to be entitled to bring judicial review proceedings.

Example

You will recall from the previous example that, under the Advertising Regulation Act 2019 (fictitious) (as above), a business wanting to set up a new advertising agency must obtain a licence from the ACC. The ACC has granted a licence to KoVert Marketing Ltd (KoVert).

The UK Consumer Forum (the Forum), a well-known pressure group which campaigns for better standards in the advertising industry, objects to the grant of the licence as the ACC appears to have ignored the fact that one of KoVert's major shareholders and its chief executive have both recently been convicted and fined substantially under legislation prohibiting misleading advertisements.

Does the Forum have standing to bring a judicial review claim?

The courts will deem a claimant to have sufficient standing to bring a judicial review claim only if they have 'sufficient interest in the matter to which a claim relates', as required by s 31(3) of the Senior Courts Act 1981.

The statute contains no definition of 'sufficient interest'. Instead the courts apply factors developed through case law. In the Forum's case, the courts will apply the five factors set out in ex p World Development Movement. The alleged breach of duty appears serious - the ACC has ignored a relevant consideration and granted a licence to an unsuitable business. The Forum is well-known and is likely to have a high level of expertise in this area. There is no other challenger obvious from the facts. Thus, if the Forum is denied standing, what appears to be an unlawful decision will go unchallenged, potentially breaching the rule of law. On the basis of this the courts are likely to consider that the Forum has 'sufficient interest' in the decision to grant KoVert a licence to apply for judicial review.

6.4 Making a claim for judicial review

6.4.1 The Administrative Court

Judicial review is dealt with by the Administrative Court, a specialist court within the High Court.

6.4.2 Time limits

6.4.2.1 What is the rule?

A claimant seeking judicial review must start their claim within the given time limits. These time limits are usually strictly applied as it is generally in the public interest for decisions of public bodies to be final. Public bodies themselves need to be in a position to act on the decisions they make, and third party interests may also be affected by such decisions.

Section 31(6) of the Senior Courts Act 1981 allows a court to refuse a claim where it feels there has been '*undue delay*'. In addition, CPR r 54.5 requires that a claim form must be filed promptly, and in any case within a *maximum* of three months after the ground to make the claim first arose. Amendments to r 54.5 effective from July 2013 have reduced the standard time limit for cases within the 'planning acts' to six weeks from the date of the decision. The 'planning acts' are defined within s 336 of the Town and Country Planning Act 1990, and this reduced time limit will only apply to planning decisions which come within this definition. The 2013 amendments also reduced the time limit for public procurement cases (ie those where a public authority acquires supplies or services) to 30 days. Rule 54.5(4) provides that the requirement that the application be made 'promptly' does not apply in such planning or public procurement cases. Presumably this is because the reduced time limit necessitates promptness.

Rule 54.5(3) emphasises that the time limits in the Rule are without prejudice to any statutory provision which shortens the time limit for making a claim for judicial review, a point we shall revisit when considering ouster clauses at **6.5** below.

It is important to appreciate that this is far from saying that every claimant will have the full standard time limit to bring a claim. Three months is the maximum time a court will allow; less in planning and public procurement cases. In *Finn-Kelcey v Milton Keynes Borough Council and MK Windfarm Ltd* [2008] EWCA Civ 1067, the appellant appealed against the refusal by the Administrative Court to grant him permission to apply for judicial review of the grant of planning permission for a wind farm. The appellant was a local landowner who objected to the construction of the wind farm. He issued an application for judicial review just within the three-month period under CPR r 54.5(1) (note that this case pre-dated the reduction in time limits for planning cases).

The appeal was dismissed. The Court of Appeal held that the appellant had been aware of the decision of the local authority's planning committee to grant permission as soon as that decision had been made, and there was therefore no reason for delaying issuing proceedings until the end of the three-month period. The application had not been made promptly.

R (British Gas) v Secretary of State for Energy Security and Net Zero [2025] EWCA Civ 209 concerned the transfer of business of one retail energy supplier (Bulb) to another (Octopus). Three other energy suppliers, including British Gas, sought to challenge the decision of the Secretary of State. Their applications were made between three weeks and one month from the relevant decision. The Court of Appeal stated that, in deciding whether the claimants had delayed too long in bringing their application, everything depended on the context. A quashing order, which would undo the effect of the decisions under challenge, would be catastrophic for third parties who were affected. In such circumstances, delay should be measured in days. However, if the remedy sought was a financial remedy, such as damages, the potential for harm to third parties was significantly reduced. Consequently, the reasons for measuring delay in days are removed.

6.4.2.2 Can the courts extend the time limit?

The courts do reserve a discretion to extend the time limit, but only for a good reason. For example, in *R v Stratford-upon-Avon DC, ex p Jackson* [1985] 1 WLR 1319, the claimant applied for leave (now known as permission) to seek judicial review of the granting of the planning permission for a supermarket eight months after it was granted. She gave three reasons for the delay in applying for leave to submit her claim form. They were that:

(a) she had had to await the outcome of her request to have the Secretary of State for the Environment 'call the matter in' for his consideration;

(b) she had encountered difficulties in obtaining legal aid; and

(c) she had also encountered difficulties in obtaining permission from the copyright holders for use of the plans and drawings, which she wished to use in her application for judicial review.

The claimant's application for leave to apply late for judicial review was dismissed at first instance, but the Court of Appeal upheld her appeal on the grounds that, although her application had not been made promptly or even within three months (the time limit that then applied), these were good reasons for the delay.

However, a court is not obliged to allow time extensions, as was seen in *Hardy v Pembrokeshire CC* [2006] EWCA Civ 240. The court stated that whilst the importance of public safety issues *is* capable of justifying a grant of permission where there has been delay, it remained for the judge to conclude whether the merits of allowing a claim outweighed the undue delay and prejudice that would be caused by granting the permission.

Note also that in *R (Kigen) v Secretary of State for the Home Department* [2015] EWCA Civ 1286 the court stated that, due to changes which had occurred since the decision in *ex p Jackson*, it was no longer appropriate to treat delay in obtaining legal aid as a complete answer to a failure to comply with procedural requirements. However, it may still be a factor that can be taken into account.

Finally, in *R v Dairy Produce Quota Tribunal, ex p Caswell* [1990] 2 All ER 434, the court stated that, even if permission was granted and the case proceeded to a full hearing, a remedy could be refused if the application had been made outside the three-month time limit.

The next example exercise will enable you to check your understanding of time limits in judicial review.

Example

Under the Advertising Regulation Act 2019 (fictitious) (as above), a business wanting to set up a new advertising agency must obtain a licence from the ACC.

Adgreen Ltd made an application to the ACC for a licence, which was rejected. At the time of the rejection, none of the directors of Adgreen Ltd knew of the existence and availability of judicial review. Six months later, one of the directors discovered that it was possible to ask the High Court to review decisions by public bodies such as the ACC.

Is it too late for Adgreen Ltd now to bring a claim for judicial review?

A claimant for judicial review must make its claim promptly and without undue delay. At the very latest, the claim must be made within three months of the date on which the decision being challenged was made. It is entirely within the court's discretion to decide that a period of less than three months is insufficiently prompt.

However, the court also has a discretion to extend the maximum time period beyond three months where it is satisfied that the claim form was submitted late for a good reason (R v Stratford-upon-Avon DC, ex p Jackson [1985] 1 WLR 1319). In the case of Adgreen Ltd, though, it is unlikely that the court would consider ignorance of the availability of judicial review to be a good reason. If leave were granted, the delay might result in refusal of a remedy (R v Dairy Produce Quota Tribunal, ex p Caswell [1990] 2 All ER 434).

6.5 Exclusion of the courts' judicial review jurisdiction

6.5.1 Ouster clauses

A further potential pitfall for a judicial review claimant is the presence of an ouster clause in the 'enabling' Act of Parliament which grants the public body the power to make decisions in the first place.

Ouster clauses are inserted by Parliament into such Acts where it wishes to exclude any right of challenge once a decision has been made by a public body.

6.5.2 Full ouster clauses

A full ouster clause is one which purports to allow no right of challenge at all, and which attempts to exclude the courts from playing any role in review of the decision.

An example of a case with a full ouster clause is *Anisminic v Foreign Compensation Commission* [1969] 2 AC 147, which you considered in **Chapter 5**. You may recall that, in this case, the House of Lords held that the Foreign Compensation Commission (FCC) had made an error of law in deciding that a purchaser of business property amounted to a 'successor in title'.

The House of Lords was prepared to consider this case even though the statute which created the FCC contained a provision which stated that any decision made by the FCC 'shall not be called into question in any court of law.' The House of Lords stated that, due to the error of law, the 'decision' was unlawful and therefore invalid and not a 'decision' at all. The ouster clause (which applied to decisions) did not apply to it.

The rationale of their Lordships in *Anisminic* was that, whenever a body which had been created by statute had misunderstood the law which regulated its decision-making powers, any decision based on such a misunderstanding had to be *ultra vires* and a 'nullity'. Parliament, in enacting the statute which gave the body its powers, could not have intended decisions which were legally incorrect to be immune from challenge, and therefore any ouster clause would be ineffective in protecting such decisions.

The judgment of the House of Lords in *Anisminic* means that full ouster clauses will not protect decisions that were never legally valid, and it is up to the court to review a decision to decide whether it is legally valid or invalid.

In the case of *R (Privacy International) v Investigatory Powers Tribunal* [2019] UKSC 22, Lord Carnwath, who gave the lead judgment, stated that the courts' treatment of ouster clauses was 'a natural application of the constitutional principle of the rule of law'. The Supreme Court accepted that it may be possible to exclude judicial review by the use of very clear and explicit words. However, to date, no legislation has been passed containing a full ouster clause with sufficiently 'clear and explicit words' to be upheld by the courts when challenged.

6.5.3 Partial ouster clauses

A partial ouster clause provides some opportunity for a decision to be challenged by way of judicial review.

The case of *R v Secretary of State for the Environment, ex p Ostler* [1977] QB 122 shows that the courts are more amenable to partial ouster clauses than to full ones. In May 1974, the Secretary of State confirmed a compulsory purchase order, or CPO, as he was authorised to do under the Highways Act 1959, over land near Ostler's house. The Act included a statutory time limit of six weeks for anyone to challenge such an order. Only 19 months later, in December 1975, did Ostler apply for judicial review of the CPO. He argued that his delay in objecting had been due to a belief that the scheme would not affect his premises.

The clause which imposed the time limit for bringing a claim stated as follows:

> An aggrieved person has the right to challenge the validity of a compulsory purchase order within six weeks from the date of the publication of the order. Subject to that right, the order shall not be questioned in any legal proceedings whatsoever.

This is a partial ouster clause rather than a full ouster clause because it does allow a challenge, but only if made within six weeks. It simply shortened the time period from that usually allowed to bring a judicial review claim.

The Court of Appeal upheld the validity of the partial ouster clause. Ostler should have applied to the High Court within six weeks of the date of the publication of the notice of confirmation. The court had no jurisdiction to entertain an application made outside such time limit, whatever the claimant's grounds. Moreover, unlike situations where the time limits set out in CPR r 54.5 apply, the courts have no discretion to grant an extension even if there are good reasons for the delay (*Smith v East Elloe Rural District Council* [1956] AC 736). There has been some academic debate about whether the courts would uphold an unreasonably short time limit, but there is no direct authority on this point.

In *R (Privacy International) v Investigatory Powers Tribunal* [2019] UKSC 22, Lord Carnwath stated that, in the cases on ouster clauses, the courts have tried to find an appropriate balance between the statutory context and the inferred intention of the legislature on the one hand, and the rule of law on the other. He went on to state that 'there is no difficulty in holding that the six-week time limit provides a proportionate balance between effective judicial review, and the need for certainty to enable such decisions to be acted on with confidence'.

The use of partial ouster clauses appears to be on the increase. The case of *R (LA (Albania)) v Upper Tribunal (Immigration and Asylum Chamber)* [2023] EWCA Civ 1337 concerned s 11A of the Tribunals, Courts and Enforcement Act 2007 (inserted by s 2 of the Judicial Review and Courts Act 2022). This section prevents judicial review of a decision of the Upper Tribunal to refuse permission to appeal from a decision of the First-Tier Tribunal save in very limited situations. These include that the Upper Tribunal acted in bad faith or 'in such a procedurally defective way as amounts to a fundamental breach of the principles of natural justice'. The Court of Appeal held that the partial ouster clause in s 11A was clear and effectively excluded judicial review in the circumstances of the case. A similar partial ouster clause is contained in s 51 of the Illegal Migration Act 2023, although this section will be repealed by the Border Security, Asylum and Immigration Bill 2024–25 currently progressing through Parliament.

6.5.4 Other remedies

The provision of an adequate statutory remedy for an aggrieved party, such as a right of appeal, may impliedly oust the courts' judicial review jurisdiction.

This can be seen in the case of *R v Epping and Harlow Commrs, ex p Goldstraw* [1983] 3 All ER 257. Goldstraw considered that his estimated income tax assessments had been too high, so he appealed under the Taxes Management Act (TMA) 1970, but failed to attend or be represented at the hearing. The Inland Revenue Commissioners (IRC) informed him that they had confirmed his tax assessments in his absence. The TMA 1970 gave Goldstraw 30 days to appeal, but he did not make his appeal for almost three months. The IRC refused to consider his appeal application, so Goldstraw sought leave of the court to apply for judicial review.

The Court of Appeal held that where a claimant had failed to make a proper use of an appropriate statutory procedure for obtaining a remedy, the court would not generally exercise its discretion to allow an application for judicial review.

However, the alternative remedy must be a suitable one. In *Re McAleenon* [2024] UKSC 31, the appellant (Ms McAleenon) lived near a landfill site. She claimed that she and her family had been made ill by the noxious fumes coming from the site. She brought judicial review proceedings against the relevant local authority and the Environment Agency alleging that they had failed to comply with their statutory duties and, as a result of this, had breached her rights under Article 8 ECHR. The defendants argued that Ms McAleenon should have pursued alternative remedies such as a private prosecution or claim for nuisance against the owners of the site. The Supreme Court reiterated that judicial review is a remedy of last resort and that, where Parliament had enacted a statutory scheme for appeal, then a claimant should normally appeal rather than apply for judicial review. However, in this case, there was no statutory right of appeal. Ms McAleenon's objective in bringing her claim was to compel the defendants to carry out their public law duties as regulators. Neither a private prosecution nor a claim for nuisance against the owners of the site could be regarded as a suitable alternative remedy. These other types of action would neither address the issue nor give a remedy in relation to it.

The following activity will enable you to check your understanding of the preliminary hurdles a claimant will need to cross to be able to apply for judicial review.

ACTIVITY 2 Preliminary matters in a judicial review application

In order to address concerns about the behaviour of nightclub doormen in controlling patrons, Parliament passed the (fictitious) Nightclubs Act 2022 ('the Act'). The Act empowers local authorities to grant licences to individuals, and every doorman must hold a licence from the relevant local authority to work in that district.

Liam, who has worked as a licensed doorman for several years in Manchester, has recently moved to Weyford. He has excellent references from his last nightclub but his application has been rejected by Weyford District Council on the grounds that, to protect jobs for local residents, it will only grant licences to those who have lived in the district for at least three years.

The Nightclub Workers' Association is concerned about the fee that Weyford District Council is asking its members to pay on applying for their licences. It wishes to challenge this on their behalf.

Consider whether Liam and the Nightclub Workers' Association can make a claim for judicial review in respect of the decisions of Weyford District Council.

COMMENT

In order to seek judicial review of a decision, there must be a public body carrying out a public function. The grant of licences is a public law issue and Weyford District Council is empowered to grant licences under the Act, so both parts of the test in *ex p Datafin* (see **6.2.3** above) are satisfied.

Liam is a rejected applicant for a licence so clearly has a 'sufficient interest' (Senior Courts Act 1981, s 31) to challenge the decision affecting him.

The Nightclub Workers' Association is a body representing a number of members but, not being able to apply for a licence, is not itself directly affected by the decision. As such, it will have to show that it has 'sufficient interest' to challenge the decision relating to application fees, and the factors from the *World Development Movement* case [1995] 1 WLR 386 will assist. The court will consider the need to uphold the rule of law, which here involves what may be an arbitrary attempt to impose a fee. The importance of the issue, which in this instance is whether or not power is given in the statute to charge a fee, and the facts of the case, which suggest that the challenge by the Association would decide a point of interest to a number of different applicants, would also be relevant. It is also unlikely that its members would themselves have the resources to mount an individual challenge. As such, the Association may be permitted to seek judicial review.

Both challengers must comply with the time limits and must seek permission promptly within three months after the grounds arose (CPR Part 54) and with no undue delay (SCA 1981, s 31). No details of the timeframe are given here, but clearly neither of the parties should delay in bringing their claim. [There does not appear to be an ouster clause in the Act.]

6.6 Procedure for bringing a judicial review claim

6.6.1 Outline of procedure

Before starting proceedings, the claimant should follow the Pre-Action Protocol for Judicial Review. The Protocol needs to be followed in all cases except for very urgent ones, such as where someone is about to be deported. This involves sending a letter before claim to the decision-maker to give the latter 14 days to reconsider its decision and, if possible, to avoid unnecessary legal proceedings. If the decision-maker's response satisfies the claimant, that ends the matter. If not, the claimant should start formal proceedings. Courts will take into account any failure to follow the Protocol when awarding costs.

Bringing a judicial review claim is a two-stage procedure. The first stage is known as the permission stage, the second the substantive hearing. The detailed rules regarding what the parties must do at each stage are contained in CPR Part 54.

6.6.2 Stage 1: the permission stage

It is at the permission stage that the court considers whether the claimant has standing and whether the claim was begun in sufficient time. Primarily, however, the purpose of this stage is to allow the courts to save time by weeding out hopeless claims before they reach the second stage. Under s 31(3C) of the Senior Courts Act 1981 (inserted by the Criminal Justice and Courts Act 2015) the court must not grant permission to apply for judicial review where the improper conduct complained of would be highly likely not to have resulted in a substantially different outcome for the claimant. The court may, however, disregard this requirement for reasons of exceptional public interest.

6.6.3 Stage 2: the hearing of the claim for judicial review

The substantive hearing is before a judge in the Administrative Court. The hearing is usually confined to arguments on points of law, as the facts will rarely be in issue. Following the hearing, the judge will give their ruling.

Figure 6.2 Outline of procedure for judicial review

The claimant issues a claim form in the Administrative Court

The claim form must:

- state that the claimant is requesting permission to proceed with a claim for judicial review and the remedy/remedies sought;
- state, or be accompanied by a detailed statement of, the claimant's grounds for making the claim, the facts relied on and the supporting evidence.

↓

The claim form is 'served' on the defendant (and any other interested party)

Note: if the judicial review proceedings are contested, the defendant should respond to the claim form, indicating the grounds for contesting the claim.

↓

The court will then decide whether to grant permission to the claimant to proceed with the claim

Note:

- Permission will not be granted if the claimant cannot demonstrate a 'sufficient interest' in the claim; if the claimant has been guilty of unjustified delay; or if the conduct complained of would be highly likely not to have resulted in a substantially different outcome for the claimant.
- Permission decisions will often be made 'on the papers' (ie without hearing the parties).

↓

If permission is granted, the defendant (and any other interested party) will file its evidence. The court will now proceed to 'Stage 2', the substantive hearing of the claim for which it will fix a date.

6.7 Remedies in judicial review

Judicial review remedies are discretionary, so a claimant may be able to show that a decision-maker has acted improperly but the court may nonetheless decide not to grant a remedy. Under s 31(2A) of the Senior Courts Act 1981 (inserted by the Criminal Justice and Courts Act 2015) the court must refuse a remedy if it appears to the court to be highly likely that the outcome to the claimant would not have been substantially different if the conduct complained of had not occurred. The court may, however, disregard this requirement for reasons of exceptional public interest. It appears that cases where a remedy is withheld on the basis of this provision are rare.

6.7.1 Public law remedies: the 'prerogative orders'

Prerogative orders are the main court orders that a judicial review claimant can seek and comprise:

(a) a 'quashing order';

(b) a 'prohibiting order';

(c) a 'mandatory order'.

Prerogative orders are available against public bodies only.

6.7.1.1 Quashing order

A quashing order 'quashes' a decision which is *ultra vires* (ie deprives the decision of legal effect). The original decision is thereby nullified. However, the court does not usually substitute its own decision but remits it to the decision-maker who must reconsider the decision in light of the court's judgment. The decision-maker may reach the same decision again. However, this time the decision-maker is more likely to reach a lawful decision as it will now have the benefit of the judgment of the court.

Section 1 of the Judicial Review and Courts Act 2022, which came into force on 14 July 2022, allows the court to make suspended quashing orders (SQOs) and prospective quashing orders (PQOs). A SQO will not take effect until the date specified in the order although, once it does take effect, that effect can be retrospective. A PQO removes or limits any retrospective effect of the quashing order. Both types of order can be subject to conditions imposed by the court in its discretion. The 2022 Act sets out a number of factors the court must take into account when deciding whether to make a SQO or PQO, including the nature and circumstances of the unlawfulness in question; the detriment to good administration that would result from exercising or failing to exercise the power; and any other matter that appears to the court to be relevant.

R (on the application of ECPAT UK (Every Child Protected against Trafficking)) v Kent CC; R (on the application of Kent CC) v Secretary of State for the Home Department [2023] EWHC 2199 (Admin) involved two protocols concerning unaccompanied asylum-seeking children who had arrived in the UK, usually by small boats. The court held that Kent County Council had acted unlawfully by failing to accommodate and look after all such children when notified of their arrival by the Home Office. The court also held that the Home Secretary had acted unlawfully by, amongst other things, accommodating such children outside of the care system in hotels. The court quashed the protocols which gave effect to these practices but suspended the order for three weeks. This would give the local authority time to renegotiate arrangements to enable it to discharge its duties towards the children and the Home Secretary time to complete arrangements for the transfer of responsibility for children who were currently accommodated in hotels. The court also attached a number of conditions to the order.

A situation where a prospective only order might be appropriate is where a public body has set up a scheme pursuant to which it has made thousands of small payments to individuals. If a court were to find the scheme unlawful, it would cause considerable administrative inconvenience if the public body had to re-open all the payments it had made pursuant to the scheme. As the amount paid to each individual concerned was modest, this would cause a considerable burden with little corresponding benefit. However, although the court may make a prospective only quashing order, it is difficult to foresee a situation when a claimant would request such an order. It would be unlikely to benefit them and also make it difficult for them to fulfil the 'substantially different outcome' test in s 31(3C) of the Senior Courts Act 1981 (see **6.6.2**).

6.7.1.2 Prohibiting order

A prohibiting order will order a public body to refrain from illegal action. Such orders are comparatively rare as claimants prefer to apply for injunctions (see **6.7.2.2** below). The case of *R v Liverpool Corporation, ex p Liverpool Taxi Fleet Operators' Association* (see **5.7.3**) provides a good example of a prohibiting order. The council had decided to issue new taxi licences, breaching an assurance that existing licence holders would first be consulted. The court granted a prohibiting order preventing the council from implementing its decision pending consultation with existing licence holders.

6.7.1.3 Mandatory order

A mandatory order is designed to enforce the performance by public bodies of their duties. For example, if a public body has refused even to consider an application for a benefit or licence, a mandatory order would compel the body to consider the application.

6.7.2 Private law remedies: the 'non-prerogative orders'

Although prerogative orders are the main orders used in judicial review proceedings, it is also possible to apply for the following private law remedies in judicial review proceedings.

6.7.2.1 Declaration

A declaration is a court order confirming, but not changing, the legal position or rights of the parties. It is a non-coercive remedy so can be ignored without any legal sanctions. Nonetheless, declarations do perform a useful function. For example, in *Royal College of Nursing v Department of Health and Social Security* [1981] AC 800, a government circular asserted that nurses could lawfully undertake part of a procedure for terminating a pregnancy without a doctor's supervision. The claimants applied for a declaration that the government circular was wrong in law, as its own guidance had pointed in the opposite direction. A quashing order would not have been appropriate as there was no act or decision that could be quashed; however, it was desirable in the interests of nurses and the public for the correct legal position to be established. This was the case even though, in the absence of any prosecutions of nurses, it was an abstract point of law. The Government in turn counterclaimed for a declaration that its guidance was not wrong in law and in fact was granted a declaration in those terms.

6.7.2.2 Injunction

An injunction is a court order performing essentially the same function as a prohibiting order (see **6.7.1.2**), namely, to restrain a person or body from illegal action. One of their main benefits is that it is possible to obtain an interim, as well as a final, injunction. Temporary injunctions, for example preventing a decision from being implemented pending the court's final ruling on the decision's lawfulness, can be very useful. For example, a court may grant an interim injunction preventing an asylum seeker's deportation pending judicial review of the lawfulness of the decision to deport them. This may be essential to guarantee that the person concerned has not been deported by the time the court determines the lawfulness of the decision.

6.7.2.3 Damages

Under s 31(4) of the Senior Courts Act 1981, the Administrative Court can award damages on a claim for judicial review where the claimant is seeking other relief (eg a quashing order) and damages could have been awarded in a civil claim. This means that the claimant must have a *private law* cause of action (eg in tort or contract) or a claim for breach of a Convention right under s 6 of the HRA 1998 (when damages can be awarded under s 8 of the HRA 1998 – see **1.8.6**). Damages cannot be awarded just because the claimant has a ground of challenge. This was confirmed in the cases of *Dunlop v Woollahra Municipal Council* [1982] AC 158 and *R v Knowsley MBC, ex p Maguire* (1992) 142 NLJ 1375.

In the *Maguire* case, the claimant was a taxi driver who had been refused a taxi licence by his local council. He sought judicial review of this and the court found in his favour, quashing the decision. Maguire also sought damages, claiming he had suffered losses as a result of the unlawful refusal of the licence. The court ruled that no damages were available.

The court found that Parliament had not intended an individual to have a private right of action in respect of a failure by a licensing authority properly to exercise its powers under the Act. In the absence of any negligence or breach of contract, there was therefore no right to damages. So there is no general right in law to damages for maladministration.

The next activity will enable you to check your understanding of this area.

ACTIVITY 3 Damages in judicial review claims

A market is held each week in Porchester. Stallholders are licensed annually by Porchester Borough Council. Stefan was awarded a licence in March. In June, following allegations made to the Council's trading standards department that Stefan was selling fake 'Rolex' watches, the Council revoked Stefan's licence with immediate effect, without giving him any opportunity to respond to the allegations (which he denies). Stefan says he has incurred significant losses through being unable to trade.

Consider what remedies (if any) may be available to Stefan on a successful claim for judicial review, and whether he would be likely to obtain damages for his losses.

COMMENT

Assuming Stefan makes a successful claim for judicial review (on the basis of procedural impropriety), he would seek a quashing order. This would quash the revocation and allow him to continue trading under the licence.

Stefan is unlikely to obtain damages. Because of s 31(4) of the Senior Courts Act 1981, damages are in effect available in a claim for judicial review only where the claimant is seeking another remedy (as here) and, in addition to breach of public law rights or legitimate expectations, the claimant can establish that his private law rights have been infringed. However, damages are not available purely for the infringement of a public law right (*R v Knowsley MBC, ex p Maguire* (1992) 142 NLJ 1375).

Summary

In this chapter you have considered the procedure and remedies in a judicial review claim, and how they affect whether a claim is successful. You have considered in particular the following:

- The decision must relate to a public law issue.
- The decision-maker must be a public law body to be amenable to judicial review.
- Claimants must have 'sufficient interest' to have the standing to bring claims.
    - Claimants who are directly affected by a decision have little difficulty in showing this.
    - Pressure groups need to show they have a genuine interest in the proceedings and are not 'busy-bodies'.
- Claimants should apply for permission for judicial review promptly, without undue delay and within three months of the date of the decisions affecting them. A claimant who waits until the end of the three months before lodging a claim runs the risk of undue delay. Courts have the discretion to extend the time limit of three months where good reasons exist.
- Ouster clauses sometimes purport to preclude challenges to the decisions of a decision-maker.
    - The courts have found ways of circumventing legislative attempts to exclude their judicial review jurisdiction and have held that complete ouster clauses will not protect decisions that were never valid ('nullities').
    - The courts are willing to uphold partial ouster clauses that do not attempt to exclude judicial review, but merely shorten the time limit for bringing claims.
- There are two stages to judicial review claims:
    - The permission stage.
    - Full hearing.
- The following remedies are available:
    - Prerogative remedies: quashing (including suspended and prospective orders), mandatory and prohibitory orders.
    - Non-prerogative remedies: declarations, injunctions and damages.

Figure 6.3 Judicial review - summary

1. Can the claimant ('C') make a claim for judicial review?

- Does C's claim raise *public* law issues?
  Is D amenable to judicial review (apply the *ex p Datafin* test)?
  - If Convention rights are engaged, is D a 'public authority' (**HRA, s 6**)?
- Does C have 'sufficient interest' to make a claim (**SCA, s 31(3)**)?
  - If Convention rights are engaged, is C a 'victim' (**HRA, s 7**)?
- Is C within the time limit under **s 31(6)/CPR Pt 54** or any other specific statutory time limit applicable?
- Is court's judicial review jurisdiction affected by 'ouster' provisions/ statutory right of appeal?

↓

2. If so, what are C's likely grounds of challenge?

Apply (where relevant) Lord Diplock's grounds in *CCSU*:

ILLEGALITY
- Acting without legal authority?
- Wrongful delegation?
- Fettering of discretion?
- Purpose(s)?
- Relevant/irrelevant considerations?
- Error of law/error of fact?

IRRATIONALITY
Is the decision challenged 'so unreasonable' that no reasonable decision-maker would have come to it (*Wednesbury*) or 'outrageous in its defiance of logic' (*CCSU*)?

PROCEDURAL IMPROPRIETY
- Procedural (un)fairness
  – fair hearing?
  – bias?
- Procedural *ultra vires*?

Breach of Convention rights. Where these rights are qualified, consider whether:
- right engaged?
- interference prescribed by law?
- legitimate aim?
- proportionate?

↓

3. Procedure

CPR Pt 54
Stage 1 – Permission
Stage 2 – Hearing

↓

4. Appropriate remedy for C?

Discretionary (**SCA, s 31(6)**)

Public law remedies
- Quashing order?
- Mandatory order?
- [Prohibiting order]?

Private law remedies
- Declaration?
- Injunction?
- Damages **SCA, s 31(4)** – only if 'private' law wrong
- Breach of Convention rights – damages under **HRA, s 8**

7 Public Order Law

Learning outcomes

When you have completed this chapter, you should be able to:

- understand and apply the powers of the police to control processions and assemblies under the Public Order Act 1986;
- identify when a breach of the peace occurs;
- analyse the powers of the police to deal with a breach of the peace in the context of processions and assemblies.

7.1 Approach of the law of England and Wales to public order

Historically, protection of individual rights and freedoms under the UK constitution was based on the principle of residual or 'negative' freedom developed at common law, ie that citizens are free to do as they wish unless the law clearly states that such conduct is prohibited. Nonetheless, English judges have traditionally acknowledged that a 'right' to protest exists. For example, in *Hubbard v Pitt* [1976] 1 QB 142, Lord Denning affirmed:

> the right to demonstrate and the right to protest on matters of public concern. These are rights which it is in the public interest that individuals should possess; and, indeed, that they should exercise without impediment so long as no wrongful act is done. It is often the only means by which grievances can be brought to the knowledge of those in authority, at any rate with such impact as to gain remedy.

Although the concept of residual freedoms remains an important principle, as you have seen, the Human Rights Act (HRA) 1998 has had a considerable impact in this area.

The key provisions of the European Convention on Human Rights (ECHR) in the context of public order are Article 10 – freedom of expression – and especially Article 11 – freedom of assembly and association.

The following activity will remind you of some of the important aspects of Article 11 – this time in the context of public order law.

ACTIVITY 1 Article 11

Please re-read Article 11 of the ECHR (see **3.6.1**) and consider the following questions:

1. Which limitations on the right of peaceful assembly under Article 11 do you think are relevant in the following cases? Are any other Convention rights relevant?
   (a) A group of anti-hunt protesters holds a demonstration on farmland, without the permission of the farmer who owns the land. The police remove them at the farmer's request.
   (b) A right-wing group is holding a meeting. There is opposition from a group of their political opponents who are shouting abuse. The police halt the meeting on the basis that violence is about to occur.

   (c) A right-wing group is holding a meeting. There is opposition from a group of their political opponents who are shouting abuse. The police arrest some of those disrupting the meeting.

2. Do you think the police should be able to choose whether to halt the meeting as in (b), or arrest those disrupting it as in (c)?

COMMENT

1. (a) Freedom of assembly can be limited under the Convention 'for the protection of the rights ... of others'. As the demonstration is on private land, without the permission of the owner, the assembly infringes property rights.
   (b) Freedom of assembly can be limited under the Convention 'for the prevention of disorder or crime'. The police are halting the assembly in order to prevent violence.
   (c) Arguably the police are acting to prevent free expression by those opposing the meeting. They could also be said to be interfering with their freedom to assemble (which is closely related to freedom of expression). In either case, they are acting to prevent disorder or crime. They are also interfering with the personal liberty of the opponents by arresting them.
2. You may think that the police should above all maintain public order and that the law should allow them some latitude in their method of achieving this. They are interfering with Convention rights whichever choice they make.

   Alternatively, you may think that the police should act to protect a peaceful, non-provocative exercise of the right of assembly by acting against those who are trying to disrupt a meeting.

   Do you think the Convention points either way?

   Article 11 does create a positive right to freedom of assembly, and this might suggest that the police should protect those trying to hold a lawful meeting. The ECtHR has said that the state may infringe freedom of assembly if it does not take positive measures to protect the exercise of the right (*Plattform 'Ärzte für das Leben' v Austria* (1991) 13 EHRR 204).

   However, this does not require the state to ensure that there is a right of assembly on private land (such as shopping malls), unless this has the effect of preventing any effective exercise of the right to freedom of expression (for example, where there is nowhere else to meet) (*Appleby v United Kingdom* (2003) 37 EHRR 38).

This chapter focuses very much on the Public Order Act (POA) 1986. This is because, although there are other statutes which provide for particular public order offences and powers, such as the Public Order Act 2023 (which, amongst other things, introduces offences relating to locking on and tunnelling), the POA 1986 gives the police general powers in relation to demonstrations. Prior to its enactment in 1986, there were numerous statutory and common law offences concerning public order. Following a period of public disorder that included inner-city riots in 1981 and the miners' strike of 1984–85, which involved violent clashes between miners and the police, the POA 1986 was introduced in reaction to the perceived need to give the police greater powers and to clarify the law.

The basic approach of the law of England and Wales is that processions and meetings are prima facie lawful unless they amount to crimes or torts. As processions are regarded as a reasonable use of a public highway, they are lawful unless disorder or violence breaks out, in which case the possibility arises that the participants may be charged with a public order or other criminal offence. If property is damaged, the participants could in theory face a tort action as well as criminal proceedings.

Protest marches through the streets of a town or city will normally be legal as long as they keep moving. However, if the marchers stop and hold an assembly or meeting, the position alters. For example, meetings on a public highway may amount to wilful obstruction of a highway contrary to s 137 of the Highways Act 1980, which makes it an offence for a person, without lawful authority or excuse, in any way to wilfully obstruct the free passage along a highway. However, in examining 'lawful excuse', courts need to decide if an activity causing an obstruction is itself lawful and whether it is reasonable. In the case of protests, they must take into consideration Articles 10 and 11 of the ECHR, and protesters have sometimes been acquitted where the courts considered that the protesters acted reasonably. See also the discussion at **7.3.4** below.

As processions and meetings are prima facie lawful, the police usually need specific powers if they are to control them. The POA 1986 gives them significant powers to deal with potential disruption to society and threats of violence. These powers have been amended by the Police, Crime, Sentencing and Courts Act 2022, which has inserted new powers relating to noise disruption and one-person protests into the 1986 Act.

This chapter concentrates on preventative measures – the power to impose conditions on or ban public processions and public meetings. Additionally, the POA 1986 created a number of public order offences to replace the mainly common law offences that had existed. These offences range from riot (s 1), with a maximum sentence of 12 years' imprisonment, to threatening, abusive or insulting behaviour (s 5), with a fine of £1,000 as a maximum sentence. The offences in ss 1–4 are outside the scope of this textbook – you studied s 5 in **Chapter 3**. As well as having statutory powers, the police also retain common law powers to prevent breaches of the peace. These sometimes supplement the statutory powers.

7.2 Processions

7.2.1 Advance notice

Section 11(1) of the POA 1986 requires any person organising a 'public procession' for any of the purposes in s 11(1)(a), (b) and (c) to give the police at least six clear days' written notice of the date, time and route of the proposed procession. The purposes set out in these sub-sections are:

(a) to demonstrate support for or opposition to the views or actions of any person or body of persons;

(b) to publicise a cause or campaign; or

(c) to mark or commemorate an event.

Football supporters on their way to watching a match or schoolchildren being led from their school to a local library are therefore outside the notice requirements.

Section 16 defines 'public procession' as 'a procession in a public place' and defines 'public place' as any highway or any other place that the public may lawfully access on payment or otherwise. Public place therefore includes not only places such as public squares, parks and beaches but also privately owned places, such as football grounds and theatres, that the public can access on purchasing a ticket. Accordingly, the definition of public procession would, for example, cover a march into a theatre to protest about a play being performed there.

The POA 1986 does not define a 'procession', but in *Flockhart v Robinson* [1950] 2 KB 498, Lord Goddard stated that 'A procession is not a mere body of persons: it is a body, of persons moving along a route.'

Section 11(4) requires the organisers to deliver the notice to a police station in the police area where the procession will start.

The purpose of the notice provisions is to enable the police to plan and give directions to avoid public disorder or other disruption.

7.2.1.1 Qualifications and exemptions

Not all processions are caught by the requirement to give notice. It does not apply to funeral processions nor to customary or commonly held processions in a given police area (s 11(2)), as in the latter case the police should be aware that it is a regular occurrence. Thus it would not be necessary to give notice of an annual Remembrance Day or Diwali parade.

Kay v Commissioner of Police of the Metropolis [2008] UKHL 69 is a significant case on this topic. It concerned mass cycle rides ('Critical Mass') that had taken place in central London on the last Friday of each month since 1994 for 12 years without any central organisation or any route being pre-planned. The police required the cyclists to give notice under s 11, and one of the cyclists challenged this requirement by way of judicial review. The House of Lords held that Critical Mass was 'commonly or customarily' held even though it did not follow a predetermined route but varied on each occasion. It was therefore exempt from the notice requirement.

There is also an exception for occasions when it is not reasonably practicable to give notice. This would cover an impromptu reaction to some news such as the sudden announcement of a factory closure or unexpected military action by a government.

7.2.1.2 Offences

There are two offences under s 11. The organisers are guilty of the first offence if they do not give the required notice (s 11(7)(a)). They are guilty of the second offence if the processions differ from what the notice specified (s 11(7)(b)). It is a defence to the first offence if the organiser did not know, and did not have any reason to suspect, that s 11 had not been complied with (s 11(8)). It is a defence to the second offence if the departure from the details

Figure 7.1 Advance notice

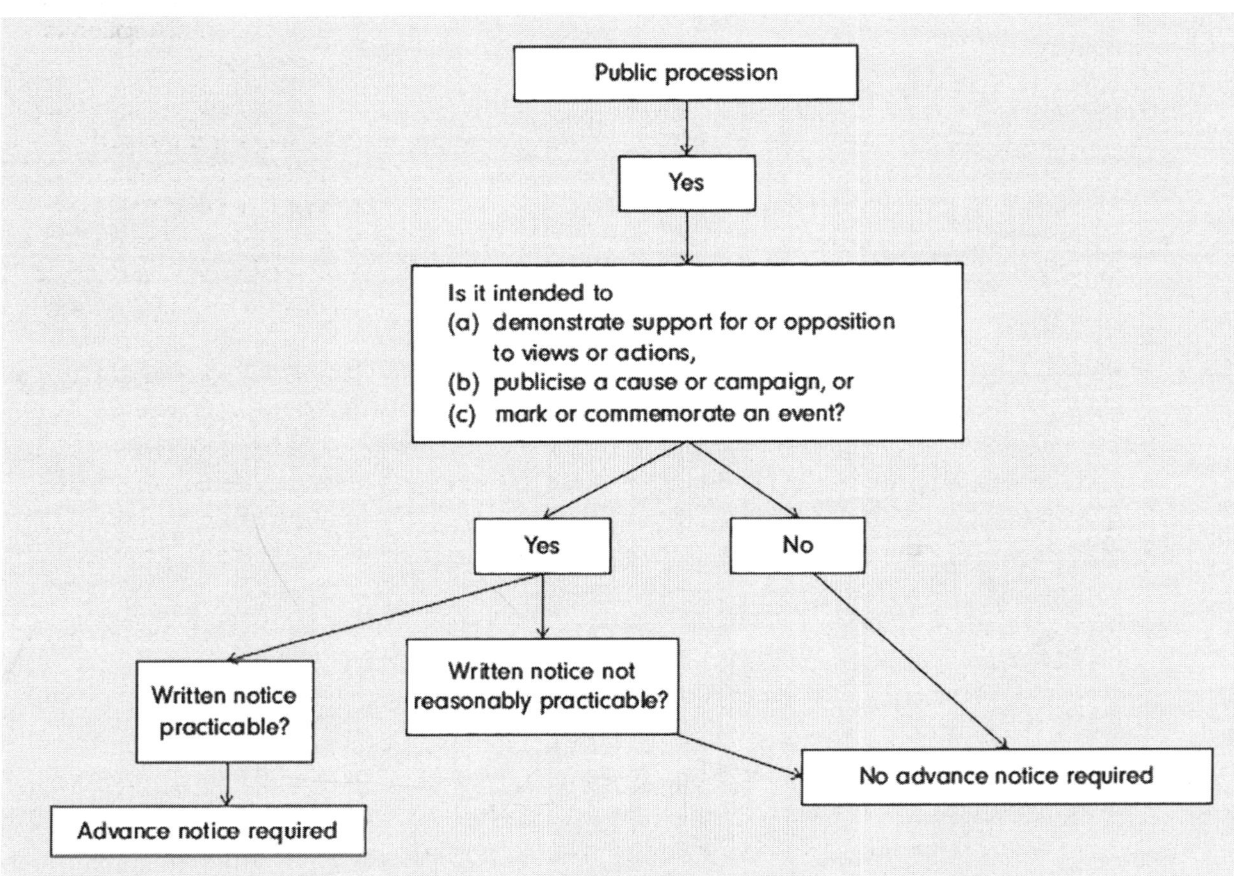

in the notice arose from circumstances beyond the organiser's control or from something done with the agreement of the police or by their direction (s 11(9)). In both cases the burden of proof is on the defendant on the balance of probabilities to prove that the defence exists.

Failure to provide notice results in the organisers committing an offence, but does not render the protest/procession unlawful. Only the organisers commit an offence. It does not make participation in such a procession a criminal offence. The procession itself is lawful.

7.2.2 Imposing conditions on public processions

Under s 12 of the POA 1986, the police have powers to impose conditions upon public processions, provided that a senior police officer reasonably believes that:

- the march will result in serious public disorder, serious damage to property, or serious disruption to the life of the community (s 12(1)(a)); or
- the noise generated by persons taking part in the procession may result in serious disruption to the activities of an organisation which are carried out in the vicinity of the procession or it may have a significant relevant impact on persons in the vicinity of the procession (s 12(1)(aa) – inserted by the Police, Crime, Sentencing and Courts Act 2022); or
- the purpose of the organisers is to intimidate others with a view to compelling them not to do something that they have a right to do, or to do something that they have a right not to do (s 12(1)(b)).

We will now consider some of these criteria in more detail.

7.2.2.1 Serious disruption to the life of the community

The Police, Crime, Sentencing and Courts Act 2022 inserted into the POA 1986 a new s 12(2A) which gave some examples of what would amount to serious disruption to the life of the community. These included where the procession may result in a significant delay to the delivery of a time-sensitive product to consumers of that product or prolonged disruption to any essential goods or services such as the supply of food or health services.

The Public Order Act 1986 (Serious Disruption to the Life of the Community) Regulations 2023 amended s 12(2A) so that serious disruption means disruption that is 'more than minor' and added further examples. Examples given were where the procession may result in the prevention of, or a hindrance that is more than minor to, the carrying out of day-to-day activities (including in particular the making of a journey); the prevention of, or a delay that is more than minor to, the delivery of a time-sensitive product to consumers of that product, or the prevention of, or a disruption that is more than minor to, access to any essential goods or any essential service such as the supply of food or health services.

Under the 2023 Regulations, when considering whether a public procession in England and Wales may result in serious disruption to the life of the community, the senior police officer must take into account all relevant disruption, which includes not only disruption caused by the procession itself but also any other disruption, such as normal traffic congestion. In addition, the senior police officer may take into account any relevant cumulative disruption which may result from the procession itself or other public procession or assembly in the same area.

Additionally, the 2023 Regulations define the term 'community' to mean any group of persons affected by the procession or assembly and not only people who live or work in the vicinity of a given procession or assembly.

The aim of the 2023 Regulations was to assist the policing of protests, such as those carried out by Insulate Britain and Just Stop Oil, by enabling the police to intervene in a wider range of circumstances. However, these Regulations proved controversial, not least because they had been introduced into Parliament as a late amendment to the Public Order Act 2023 but had failed to pass. The Home Secretary then brought in the powers by way of delegated legislation. They were challenged by way of judicial review in the case of *R (on the application of The National Council for Civil Liberties) v Secretary of State for the Home*

Department (Public Law Project intervening) [2025] EWCA Civ 571. The Court of Appeal held that, as a matter of ordinary language, the word 'serious' cannot reasonably encompass anything that is merely 'more than minor'. The Regulations were thus beyond the scope of the enabling power and ultra vires. The Court of Appeal judgment did not quash the Regulations, however, and at the time of writing, they are still in effect.

7.2.2.2 Impact of noise

Cases in which the noise generated may result in serious disruption to the activities of an organisation include where persons connected with that organisation cannot carry out those activities for a prolonged period of time (s 12(2C)).

'Relevant impact' on people in the vicinity means that the noise may result in intimidation or harassment of people of reasonable firmness or may cause such people to suffer alarm or distress (s 12(2D)). In deciding this, the senior police officer must take into account the likely number of people who would be affected and the likely duration and intensity of that impact upon them (s 12(2E)).

7.2.2.3 Intimidation

Intimidation in s 12(1)(b) means more than being a nuisance or causing discomfort, as the reference in the sub-section to 'compelling' suggests. In *Police v Reid* [1987] Crim LR 702, anti-apartheid demonstrators outside South Africa House, where a reception was being held, shouted at guests as they arrived. The demonstrators raised their arms and waved their fingers at the guests as they arrived, chanting 'Apartheid murderers, get out of Britain' and 'You are a dying breed'. The Chief Inspector in charge decided that this was intimidatory and sought to impose a condition on the demonstrators requiring them to move away, relying on s 14(1) of the POA 1986 (see **7.3.2** below). (Although the case concerned s 14, the court's analysis of intimidation is equally applicable to s 12.) The defendant ignored the condition and was arrested and charged with failing to comply with it. The court held that the condition was *ultra vires* as the Chief Inspector had applied the wrong test. He defined intimidation as 'putting people in fear or discomfort' and had thereby incorrectly equated intimidation with discomfort. The demonstrators would have needed an intention to compel the guests not to go into the reception for their activities to amount to intimidation.

7.2.2.4 Conditions

The conditions that the senior police officer may impose are those that appear to be necessary to prevent such disorder, damage, disruption or intimidation. This includes conditions prescribing the route or prohibiting the march from entering a particular public place.

7.2.2.5 Senior police officer

Under s 12(2), the identity of the 'senior police officer' with the power to impose conditions depends on the circumstances. For conditions imposed during the procession, it is the most senior police officer present at the scene (s 12(2)(a)) and they may be given verbally. For conditions imposed in advance, it is the chief officer of police – the Chief Constable of the relevant police force or the Commissioner of Police of the Metropolis or for the City of London (s 12(2)(b)). When given before the event, they must be provided in writing. Additionally, the chief officer of police must provide sufficient reasons so that, first, the demonstrators can understand why the conditions have been imposed and, secondly, a court can assess whether the belief that the procession may result in the consequences listed above (serious disruption etc) is reasonable (*R (Brehony) v Chief Constable of Greater Manchester Police* [2005] EWHC 640 (Admin) – a case on s 14 below applied by analogy to s 12).

When imposing conditions, the police also need to consider the impact of Article 11 of the ECHR. Any conditions they impose must be proportionate.

7.2.3 Offences under s 12

Section 12 of the POA 1986 creates the offences of:

- organising or taking part in a public procession and failing to comply with a condition imposed under s 12(1) where they knew or ought to know that the condition has been imposed (s 12(4) and (5)); and
- inciting a participant in a public procession to commit an offence under s 12(5) (s 12(6)).

Organisers and participants have a defence if they can show that their failure to comply with the conditions was due to circumstances beyond their control, for example that an organiser had become too ill to change the route or that a participant was unwillingly swept along by the crowd. The burden of proof is on the defendant to prove the defence on the balance of probabilities. It is also a defence to prove that the conditions are invalid, as in *Police v Reid*.

Can a person convicted of an offence under s 12 of the POA 1986 argue that such a conviction would be disproportionate? In *Re Abortion Services (Safe Access Zones) (Northern Ireland) Bill* [2022] UKSC 32, the Supreme Court stated that for certain protest-related offences, the ingredients of the offence strike the proportionality balance. These offences included the offences under s 14 of the POA 1986 and would apply by analogy to offences under s 12. This meant that, provided the condition imposed is lawful (ie the officer holds the necessary belief and has reasonable grounds to do so), the court does not have to check that a conviction would be proportionate on the facts of each individual case.

7.2.4 The power to prohibit processions

Section 13(1) of the POA 1986 provides that a chief officer of police can apply for a prohibition order in respect of public processions if they reasonably believe, because of particular circumstances existing in any locality, that the powers in s 12 are insufficient to prevent a risk of serious public disorder (s 13(1)).

The chief officer of police applies to the local authority, which then makes an order with the Home Secretary's consent. Local authorities have no power of their own to seek a ban; the initiative must come from the police.

In London the procedure is different, as s 13(1) does not apply to London. The Commissioner of Police for the City of London or the Commissioner of Police of the Metropolis makes the order for the same reasons as apply outside London, with the Home Secretary's consent s 13(4)).

The order can be for any period not exceeding three months. The order may ban all processions or processions of a particular class, such as political marches. However, there is no power to ban a specific individual procession. The order must be in writing or recorded in writing as soon as practicable after being made (s 13(6)).

It is possible to challenge a ban by way of judicial review, as occurred in *Kent v Metropolitan Police Commissioner* (1981) *The Times*, 15 May. The case concerned equivalent provisions in the Public Order Act 1936 but its reasoning is likely to apply to the POA 1986. Monsignor Bruce Kent, as General Secretary of the Campaign for Nuclear Disarmament (CND), challenged an order banning all processions in the metropolitan district (covering an area of 786 square miles) for 28 days, other than traditional May Day celebrations and those of a religious character. He argued that the order was *ultra vires* because it applied to all processions over a large area and was far too wide in its scope. The Metropolitan Police Commissioner adduced evidence of serious public disorder largely due to National Front and anti-National Front demonstrations. He stated that all processions, however peaceful in intent, were potential targets for extremists.

The Court of Appeal upheld the banning order. The claimant had failed to show that the Metropolitan Police Commissioner had no reasonable grounds for making the banning order, although one Lord Justice did think the reasons were 'meagre'. This shows that the courts are reluctant to quash what are essentially operational decisions. The decision in this case had been taken in a context where there had been significant outbreaks of violence in various parts of London. The Court of Appeal suggested that CND should have applied to the Police Commissioner for a relaxation of the order, which is possible under s 13(5).

The power to prohibit processions has not been used frequently. The overwhelming majority of bans have been imposed in relation to proposed marches by the National Front and more recently by the English Defence League.

7.2.5 Offences under s 13

Offences under s 13 of the POA 1986 are very similar to those that s 12 creates:

- organising or taking part in a public procession knowing that it is prohibited under s 13 (s 13(7) and (8));
- inciting a participant to take part in a public procession that is prohibited under s 13 (s 13(9)).

The following activity will help you check your understanding of s 13.

ACTIVITY 2 POA 1986, s 13

A far-right group is planning a march in the town centre. Previous marches have resulted in significant damage to shops and other premises in the town centre. The chief officer of police reasonably believes that their powers to give directions under s 12 of the POA 1986 are insufficient to prevent a risk of serious damage to property arising from this march. Can the chief officer of police obtain an order banning the far-right march?

COMMENT

There are two reasons why the chief officer of police would not be able to ban the march:

1. There is no power to ban marches on the basis of serious damage to property. The only reason that marches can be banned is where the chief officer of police reasonably believes that their powers to impose conditions under s 12 are insufficient to prevent a risk of serious *public disorder.*
2. There is no power to ban a specific individual procession, so the chief officer of police will not be able to obtain an order banning the far-right march alone. The order may ban all processions or processions of a particular class, such as political marches.

7.3 Meetings

Before the POA 1986, there were no statutory powers to control the holding of public meetings as opposed to processions. Including the power to control meetings in the POA 1986 was a response to concerns that static protests could cause public order problems. The Government was particularly anxious about the impact of mass picketing in industrial disputes such as the miners' strike of 1984–85, although picketing is also covered in trade union legislation.

7.3.1 Meetings: permission sometimes required

Whilst the general rule is that there is no requirement to obtain permission to hold a meeting, it would be wrong to assume that it is possible to hold a meeting in any public space such as a public square or park. Local or private Acts of Parliament or byelaws may lay down a requirement for permission. For example, the Trafalgar Square Byelaws 2012 require anyone wanting to use Trafalgar Square for a meeting to obtain permission from the Greater London Authority. Similarly, the Royal Parks and Other Open Spaces Regulations 1997 make it necessary to seek permission to use a Royal Park such as Hyde Park.

A meeting on private land obviously requires the permission of the owner, otherwise the owner can claim damages for trespass or apply to the courts for an injunction. The police could help to eject any trespassers at the request of the owner, for example if there is a breach of the peace, but they have no independent powers unless there is a breach of the peace or crimes such as criminal damage are being committed.

The general rule remains, though, that the police have no power to ban assemblies, as the power to impose conditions was regarded as being sufficient. The Criminal Justice and Public Order Act 1994 has, however, granted a power to ban 'trespassory assemblies' on limited grounds (see **7.3.5** below).

7.3.2 Imposing conditions on public assemblies

Under s 14 of the POA 1986, a senior police officer can impose conditions on any public assembly if they reasonably believe that it may result in serious public disorder, serious damage to property or serious disruption to the life of the community; or that the noise generated by persons taking part in the assembly may result in serious disruption to the activities of an organisation which are carried out in the vicinity of the assembly or it may have a significant relevant impact on persons in the vicinity of the assembly; or that the purpose of the organisers is the intimidation of others. These are the same criteria that are employed in s 12 for imposing conditions on processions. However, there is no requirement for the organisers of a public assembly to give advance notice.

A public assembly is an assembly comprising two or more persons in a public place that is wholly or partly open to the air (POA 1986, s 16, as amended by the Anti-social Behaviour Act 2003, which reduced the number required from 20 to two). This is a very wide definition. For example, it would include a crowd listening to a brass band playing in a park bandstand or gathered together in the garden of a pub, as well as those attending a political meeting. Unlike for processions, the purpose of the assembly is irrelevant.

The case of *R (on the application of Baroness Jones and others) and others v Commissioner of Police of the Metropolis* [2020] 3 All ER 509 arose from the 'autumn uprising' protest organised by Extinction Rebellion (XRAU). The plan was that a number of protests would be held in different places between 14 and 19 October 2019. The police issued an order stating that 'any assembly linked to the Extinction Rebellion 'Autumn Uprising' ... must now cease their protest within London' by 9pm on 14 October.

The court held that a public assembly in s 14 must be in a location to which the public or any section of the public has access, which is wholly or partly open to the air, and which can be fairly described as a scene. Separate gatherings, separated both in time and by many miles, even if coordinated under the umbrella of one body, are not one public assembly. The XRAU protest intended to be held from 14 to 19 October 2019 was not a public assembly. Therefore, there was no power to impose such a condition.

The conditions that the senior police officer may impose are those which appear to the senior officer as necessary to prevent such disorder, damage, disruption, impact or intimidation. The definition of senior police officer is the same as for s 12.

Under both s 12 and s 14, the police may impose any condition that appears necessary (subject to their reasonableness and proportionality). In both cases any conditions that the police impose in advance must be in writing and give adequate reasons, whilst conditions imposed during a procession or assembly may be given verbally.

Whilst there is no power under s 14 to ban public assemblies, the police may be able in effect to order participants to disperse. The chief officer of police on the scene may impose conditions limiting the duration of the meeting, so, if necessary, the police could impose a condition limiting the maximum duration to five minutes from giving the notice of the condition. However, any condition imposing a maximum duration must be proportionate.

7.3.3 Offences under s 14

Similar offences exist under s 14 of the POA 1986 to those under s 12:

- organising or taking part in a public assembly and failing to comply with a condition imposed under s 14(1) where they knew or ought to know the condition has been imposed (s 14(4) and (5));
- inciting a participant in a public procession to commit an offence under s 14(5) (s 14(6)).

Organisers and participants have a defence if they can show that their failure to comply with the conditions was due to circumstances beyond their control. The burden of proof is on the defendant to establish the defence.

It is also a defence to prove that the conditions are invalid, as in *Police v Reid*. Although an assembly can consist of as few as two people, until the amendments made in 2022 to the POA 1986, it was considered doubtful whether an assembly of two people could cause serious public disorder or serious disruption to the life of the community. Where the police impose conditions on a very small gathering, they might find it problematic to argue that those conditions were proportionate. However, the power introduced in 2022 to impose conditions on protests based on the noise they create may make it easier for the police to impose conditions on small assemblies.

R (Brehony) v Chief Constable of Greater Manchester (above) provides an interesting example of the application of the principle of proportionality. Saturday demonstrations had been taking place regularly for four years outside Marks & Spencer in the centre of Manchester, protesting against the company's support for the Israeli Government and also calling for a boycott of Marks & Spencer's stores. A counter-demonstration in support of Israel had also been taking place outside the same store for some months. In November 2004, the Chief Constable issued a notice under s 14 requiring the demonstration to move to the nearby Peace Gardens over the Christmas shopping period (29 November to 3 January) due to the serious disruption that would otherwise occur when the number of visitors to the city centre would treble.

The judge refused the organiser's judicial review application because the conditions were not unreasonable and were proportionate. The test for proportionality was whether the Chief Constable's legitimate objective of preventing serious disruption could have been achieved by means that interfered less with the claimant's rights. Given the limited and temporary nature of the restrictions, they could not.

7.3.4 One-person protests

Section 14ZA (inserted by the Police, Crime, Sentencing and Courts Act 2022) allows the police to impose conditions on a one-person protest where the senior police officer reasonably believes that the noise generated by the person carrying out the protest may result in serious disruption to the activities of an organisation which are carried out in the vicinity of the protest, or it may have a significant relevant impact on persons in the vicinity of the protest. A one-person protest is defined as a protest which is carried out by one person in a public place (s 14ZA(4)). The police may impose such conditions as appear necessary to prevent such disruption or impact (subject to reasonableness and proportionality). The same factors relating to impact of the noise apply as in ss 12 and 14 (see **7.2.2**).

As for ss 12 and 14, any conditions that the police impose in advance must be in writing and give adequate reasons, whilst conditions imposed during a procession or assembly may be given verbally. The definition of senior police officer is the same as for s 12 (and s 14).

These powers were used by the police as soon as they came into force when they seized the amplifiers of Steve Bray, the anti-Brexit protestor known for his loud protests outside the House of Commons.

A person is guilty of an offence under s 14ZA(10) if they organise or carry out a one-person protest and fail to comply with a condition imposed under s 14ZA(2) where they knew or ought to have known the condition had been imposed.

7.3.5 Trespassory assemblies

It was not until the enactment of the Criminal Justice and Public Order Act (CJPOA) 1994 that the police were given the power to apply for meetings to be banned. The CJPOA 1994 added s 14A to the POA 1986, which introduced the power to ban trespassory assemblies, defined in s 14A(1) as 'an assembly ... to be held ... at a place or on land to which the public has no right of access or only a limited right of access'.

According to s 14A(9), 'assembly means an assembly of 20 or more persons', and land means 'land in the open air'. These definitions are narrower than those applying to the s 14 power to impose conditions in the following ways:

- Under s 14, an assembly need only comprise two people, whilst under s 14A at least 20 people are required.
- The section 14A power only applies to land entirely in the open air, whilst s 14 land applies to land that is just partly in the open air.
- The section 14A power applies only to land to which the public has no or only a limited right of access. Accordingly, the s 14A power (unlike the s 14 power) does not cover assemblies on common land to which the public has an unlimited right of access.

The criteria for banning a trespassory assembly are also narrower than those for imposing conditions. The chief officer of police must reasonably believe that it is intended to hold a trespassory assembly:

- without the permission of the occupier or outside the terms of any permission or right of access; and
- which may result in serious disruption to the life of the community or significant damage to the land, building or monument which is of historical, archaeological or scientific importance.

The chief officer may then apply to the local authority for an order prohibiting for a specified period the holding of all trespassory assemblies in the district or part of it. There are, however, strict time and geographical limits on the scope of the order. It must not last for more than four days and must not apply to an area greater than that represented by a circle of five miles' radius from a specified centre. The local authority must also obtain the Home Secretary's consent for the making of such an order.

In London, the Police Commissioner for the Metropolis or the Commissioner of the City of London Police may make such an order with the consent of the Secretary of State.

The POA 1986 as amended by the CJPOA 1994 creates the offences of:

- organising or taking part in an assembly knowing it to be prohibited (s 14B(1) and (2));
- incitement to organise or participate in an assembly if the person knows it is prohibited (s 14B(3)).

It is important to note, though, that a notice prohibiting trespassory assemblies does not constitute an absolute ban on all assemblies on that land. Such a notice only prohibits assemblies to the extent that those taking part in it are trespassing on the land. This point has been particularly pertinent in relation to public roads, ie highways, as an assembly on a highway is only trespassory if the participants go outside their right of access. *DPP v Jones* [1999] 2 AC 240 is a leading case on this. Salisbury District Council had made an order prohibiting certain trespassory assemblies within a radius of four miles from Stonehenge. Two protesters were arrested while participating in a peaceful, non-obstructive demonstration of 21 people on a highway near Stonehenge. The High Court held that the magistrates had correctly convicted them under s 14B(2), holding that the public's right to use the highway was restricted to passing and repassing and any activities ancillary or incidental to that right, and that a public assembly was not incidental to the right of passage.

The Lords ruled by a 3:2 majority that the defendants had not committed an offence. A public highway was a public place that the public might enjoy for any reasonable purpose, provided the activity in question did not involve a public or private nuisance and did not unreasonably obstruct the highway. Accordingly, the power to ban trespassory assemblies is not as far-reaching as it might seem at first sight.

Additionally, s 14C gives a constable in uniform who reasonably believes that a person is on their way to a trespassory assembly the power to stop that person and direct them not to proceed in the direction of the assembly. It is an offence to ignore such a direction.

7.4 The common law: breach of the peace

The police also have common law powers to prevent a breach of the peace. The police can use these powers in many contexts, and their use to control assemblies remains relevant despite the extensive statutory powers granted by the POA 1986.

The authoritative definition of breach of the peace is that set out by the Court of Appeal in *R v Howell* [1982] QB 416: 'there is a breach of the peace whenever harm is actually done or likely to be done to a person or in his presence to his property or a person is in fear of being so harmed through an assault, an affray, a riot, unlawful assembly or other disturbance.'

7.4.1 Police powers

A breach of the peace is not a criminal offence but triggers various police powers to take action to prevent the breach. At common law, the police have a power of arrest, not only if a breach of the peace has occurred, but also to prevent one from occurring. They also have powers to take steps falling short of arrest, such as requiring people breaching the peace or threatening to do so to move away. Likewise, the police can attend and disperse a gathering if they reasonably fear a breach of the peace. Section 17(6) of the Police and Criminal Evidence Act 1984 preserves the common law powers of entry without a warrant to prevent a breach of the peace.

The case of *Duncan v Jones* [1936] 1 KB 218 shows how the police can use their common law powers to prevent a public meeting. The appellant was about to address a meeting of about 30 people taking place in a road to protest against the Incitement to Disaffection Bill. There was evidence that previous meetings the appellant had addressed at that location had led to disturbances. A police officer ordered the appellant not to hold the meeting, but she persisted in trying to hold it and obstructed the police officer when he tried to stop her doing so. No breach of the peace actually occurred, but the Divisional Court upheld the appellant's conviction of wilfully obstructing the officer in the execution of their duty. The fact that the officer reasonably apprehended a breach of the peace justified the finding that the officer was acting in the execution of their duty. The police had the power to prevent a demonstration on a public highway where there was any fear of a breach of the peace.

As we have just seen, the police do not need to wait until actual violence occurs before they exercise such powers and can take preventative action to prevent gatherings that could result in a breach of the peace. However, the circumstances in which they can take preventative action against demonstrators have proved contentious, as demonstrated by the case of *Moss v McLachlin* [1985] IRLR 76.

During the miners' strike of 1984–85, the police stopped a convoy of up to 80 striking miners at a junction on the M1 about 1.5 and 5 miles from four collieries at which miners were still working. The striking miners were intending to picket those collieries. The police feared a breach of the peace as violent confrontations were likely to take place if the striking miners continued to their destination. Accordingly, to prevent a breach of the peace, the police instructed the miners not to proceed towards the collieries. Some of the miners tried to push past the police cordon, and they were arrested and subsequently convicted by magistrates of obstructing a police officer in the execution of their duty.

On appeal, the Divisional Court upheld the convictions. There had been numerous violent confrontations during the course of the strike and so the police had acted lawfully. The police had a duty to prevent a reasonably apprehended breach of the peace. The possibility of a breach of the peace in close proximity both in place and time was real and immediate and not remote.

7.4.2 Impact of Articles 10 and 11 ECHR

However, under the impact of the HRA 1998 and Articles 10 and 11 of the ECHR, the approach of the courts appears to have shifted. In *R (Laporte) v Chief Constable of Gloucester* [2006] UKHL 55 a group of about 120 anti-Iraq War campaigners were travelling to a demonstration outside RAF Fairford when their coaches were stopped by the police who then escorted them the 90 miles back to London without permitting breaks for relief or refreshment. The claimant argued that her Article 10 right to freedom of expression and Article 11 right to freedom of peaceful assembly had been violated. The Court of Appeal held that it was lawful for the police to prevent demonstrators joining the demonstration if they reasonably apprehended a breach of the peace, stating that the requirement that the breach should be 'imminent' in a strict sense did not apply to actions short of arrest. On further appeal, the House of Lords held that:

(1) The police were purporting to use powers to prevent a reasonably apprehended breach of the peace. However, these powers are only available when a breach is 'imminent'. On the facts, the police did not believe that a breach of the peace was imminent.

(2) The House of Lords rejected the distinction made by the Court of Appeal between powers of arrest and other powers to prevent a breach of the peace (eg the power to disperse a meeting). In all cases the breach of the peace must be 'imminent'.

Although the House of Lords distinguished *Laporte* from *Moss v McLachlan*, the reasoning in *Laporte* very much relies on the ECHR principle of proportionality. Even if intervention had been permissible, the police would have been unable to show that their actions had constituted a proportionate restriction of Convention rights. Their intervention had been premature. As extensive precautions had been put in place at RAF Fairford to handle the protests, it had been unreasonable to assume that the protesters on the coaches would have become involved in violent protest upon arrival. The police could have taken less drastic action such as allowing everyone to continue to the airbase and arresting anyone who subsequently acted, or threatened to act, violently. The police's conduct was indiscriminate, failing to distinguish between the majority of protesters who had peaceful intent and the small minority who actually threatened violence.

However, the decision of the ECtHR in *Austin & Others v The United Kingdom* (2012) 55 EHRR 14 (see **2.5.2.3**) shows that the police can in limited circumstances take drastic action to prevent a breach of the peace, even if it adversely impacts innocent bystanders. The ECtHR ruled in favour of the UK, stating that the police measures were the least intrusive possible on the facts and there was no obvious point at which the restriction on movement turned into a deprivation of liberty.

The common law powers relating to breach of the peace do give the police considerable discretion in relation to demonstrations and assemblies. However, case law does show that the police need to show that their conduct is a proportionate response to the situation they are facing to ensure that they do not violate Convention rights.

Summary

- In this chapter, you have looked at police powers to control public processions and public assemblies.
- Under s 11 of the POA 1986, organisers of a public procession must, subject to certain exceptions, give the police six clear days' advance notice of their plans.
- Under s 12 of the POA 1986, the police have the power to impose conditions on public processions if necessary to prevent serious adverse consequences to the community or intimidation. The police can impose conditions in advance of the procession or during it.
- Under s 13 of the POA 1986, the chief officer of police may apply to the local authority to prohibit a public procession if necessary to prevent serious public disorder. The local authority must obtain the Home Secretary's consent to make the order. The procedure in London is slightly different.
- Under s 14 of the POA 1986, the police have the power to impose conditions on public assemblies if necessary to prevent serious adverse consequences to the community or intimidation. The police can impose conditions in advance of the assembly or during it.
- Under s 14ZA of the POA 1986, the police have the power to impose conditions on noisy one-person protests.
- Under s 14A of the POA 1986, the chief officer of police may apply to the local authority to prohibit a trespassory assembly to prevent serious disruption to the life of the community or significant damage to land, buildings or monuments of particular importance. The prohibition can only last for a maximum of four days and can only cover an area represented by a circle with a radius of no more than five miles from a specified centre.

Index

Note: Page numbers in **bold** and *italics* denote tables and figures, respectively.

Q

R

S

T

U

V

W